Margaret Simpson

Ostsee

(Under Russian adm.)

Danzig
(Gdansk)

OS

Stettin
(Szczecin)

MMERN

Part of Germany until 1945
(Now under Polish adm.)

P O L E N

Warschau

Oder

Neiße

Breslau (Wroclaw)

Weichsel

(Vistula)

S C H L E S I E N

Elbe

Prag

Krakau

D

RUßLAND

T S C H E C H O - S L O V A K E I

Donau

Wien

EICH

Graz

DIE DEUTSCHEN LÄNDER
------- Ländergrenzen
I   SCHLESWIG - HOLSTEIN
II   HAMBURG
III BREMEN
IV   NIEDERSACHSEN
V   NORDRHEIN - WESTFALEN
VI   HESSEN
VII RHEINLAND - PFALZ
VIII SAARLAND
IX   BADEN - WÜRTTEMBERG
X   BAYERN

V. Gray - 58

D1241379

Dieter Cunz, Ph.D., University of Frankfurt am Main, Germany, is Chairman of the Department of German at The Ohio State University, a post he assumed in 1957. Previously he was Professor of German at the University of Maryland. Dr. Cunz is the author of several books, including *Ulrich Zwingli* and *The Maryland Germans*.

Ulrich A. Groenke, Ph.D., University of Göttingen, is Associate Professor, Department of German, at The Ohio State University. He formerly lectured and held the position of Assistant Supervisor of Language Instruction, European Division, at the University of Maryland.

Curtis C. D. Vail (1903–1957) taught German at Hunter College, Columbia University, and the University of Buffalo, and was Professor of Germanic Languages and Literature at the University of Washington at the time of his death. He was a former President of the American Association of Teachers of German and Editor of its publication *The German Quarterly*.

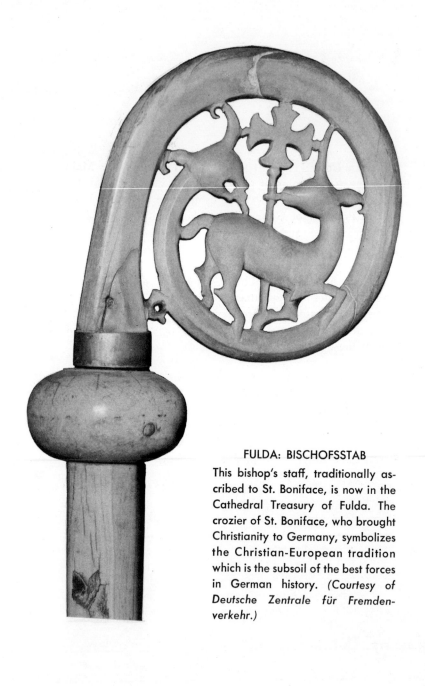

FULDA: BISCHOFSSTAB

This bishop's staff, traditionally ascribed to St. Boniface, is now in the Cathedral Treasury of Fulda. The crozier of St. Boniface, who brought Christianity to Germany, symbolizes the Christian-European tradition which is the subsoil of the best forces in German history. (Courtesy of Deutsche Zentrale für Fremdenverkehr.)

GERMAN
FOR
BEGINNERS

DIETER CUNZ
The Ohio State University

ULRICH A. GROENKE
The Ohio State University

CURTIS C. D. VAIL
Late of the University of Washington

Second Edition

THE RONALD PRESS COMPANY · NEW YORK

Copyright © 1965, 1958, by
THE RONALD PRESS COMPANY

All Rights Reserved

No part of this book may be reproduced
in any form without permission in writing
from the publisher.

7

VR-VR

Library of Congress Catalog Card Number: 65-12746

PRINTED IN THE UNITED STATES OF AMERICA

PREFACE

German for Beginners in this Edition is a college grammar of the descriptive-prescriptive type—thus, a "traditional" textbook. What singles it out from the wider category of traditional textbooks is the realism and the rigor of its description of grammar and the absence of standard clichés. The prescriptions, i.e., the rules, have also been set up and delimited more carefully. Thus the grammatical concepts have been defined with greater precision. We have endeavored throughout the text to take due consideration of the normal "naïve native speaker" of English and have adhered to the principle of the contrastive presentation of German vs. English. At the same time we have had in mind the inexperience of the graduate teaching assistant, who nowadays so often is entrusted with instruction on the elementary level. The "old hand" in the teaching profession therefore may occasionally find principles worded and explicated in this text that may appear rather a matter of course to him. May he then, too, remember his young colleagues, who will appreciate guidance that the experienced teacher does not need. On the other hand, the experienced teacher may welcome the linguistic realism of some definitions that have replaced certain traditional schoolmaster rules.

The Translation Exercises as well as the Grammatical Exercises are also thoroughly revised to reflect actual spoken or written usage. They avoid practicing of "abstract" grammar and insistence on false symmetry of structure where symmetry does not exist in linguistic reality.

In the Reading Selections we tried to use the active vocabulary as much as possible. These writings deal with everyday life and they employ primarily everyday vocabulary. A student who masters the active vocabulary and who has heard the tape recording of the Reading Section two or three times should be able to participate in a simple conversation about the little story which is told in the beginning of each lesson.

The Supplementary Readings *(Lesestücke)* were written with the intent to give the beginner, even in a grammar book, a glimpse into some of the facets of German folklore, history, geography, and culture. They present a slightly more difficult syntactic structure and should thus prepare the student for the mastery of future reading materials.

While writing a basically traditional textbook, we were by no means unaware of the great strides that language instruction has made in recent years. *German for Beginners,* Second Edition, is accompanied by all the supplementary material required by the teacher and the student to facilitate current teaching methods. All these materials are related to and developed from the book.

An extensive set of pattern drills—nowadays an indispensable teaching aid in the traditional and structural approach as well—has been prepared. The drills are recorded on tape and completely written up in an *Instructor's Supplement,* which also contains a drill syllabus and brief instructions on the effective use of the material. There are sixty-three drills, developed around the twenty-one lessons in the book. Each drill employs only that vocabulary the student has already learned in the lessons. Throughout the drills there are appropriate pauses for student repetition and response.

In addition we have taped the readings in the textbook, which are related to the questions, and when used in conjunction with them can form a basis for oral-aural instruction. The material consists of the twenty-one Reading Selections that begin each lesson and the twenty-one *Lesestücke* that conclude the lesson. It also includes two stories by the Brothers Grimm and the *Lieder und Gedichte* from the Appendix.

The authors admit unabashedly and without any feelings of guilt that they want to teach some basic grammar. The more intelligent student often resents the monotony of repeating again and again structures and patterns; he wants explanations. Classroom drills, if overdone, wear out teachers and students. The authors have tried to overcome this difficulty by relegating the drill primarily to the laboratory, where the student can do it alone, within a frame of programmed learning. In this way the book attempts to combine the best features of the traditional method with the most fruitful experiences gained by the new method, with the hope of avoiding the pitfalls of either.

Many of our friends and colleagues have written to us after the publication of the first edition to offer suggestions for a revision of the book. We have gratefully accepted this help. We would like to express our thanks in particular to Professor Wolfgang Fleischhauer and Professor Paul Gottwald of The Ohio State University, Professor Werner Neuse of Middlebury College, Professor Karl-Heinz Planitz of Wabash College, and Professor Annemarie Sauerlander of the University of Washington for their constructive criticism. And we are especially indebted to Professor Eleanor Webster Bulatkin and Professor Oskar Seidlin, both of The Ohio State University, for their unfailing willingness to give us help and advice.

Dieter Cunz
Ulrich A. Groenke

January, 1965

CONTENTS

Appendix

GERMAN
FOR
BEGINNERS

INTRODUCTION

THE GERMAN LETTERS
AND THEIR PRONUNCIATION

In German as in other languages, the letters of the alphabet cannot be taken as exact signs for the sounds of the language. Correct pronunciation can only be learned through oral practcice from your instructor or in the language laboratory.

Where English "parallels" are given below, it must be understood that they are only approximations.

I. German Vowels

It must be noted that German differs from English in that a single vowel sign in German always indicates a single vowel, never a "gliding" vowel or diphthong. German vowels may be long or short.

Long vowels are represented in writing

1. by double letter, e.g., **Haar, See, Boot;**
2. by adding a "silent" *h,* e.g., **Bahn, Stuhl, ihn;**
3. by single letter, when a single consonant and another vowel follows, e.g., **Gabe, geben, oben.**

German vowels are short when unaccented or followed by two consonants (not counting inflectional endings).

3

In many one-syllable words, however, German writing does not indicate whether the vowel is long or short, e.g., **Hut, der, den** (long); **hat, das, in** (short).

When a German verb has a long vowel in the infinitive, the long vowel is retained in the various inflected forms, e.g., **fragen, frage, fragst, fragt** (all of which have a long vowel). There are only a very few exceptions to this rule.

A. Single Vowels

long a   is similar to *a* in *father* (but the vowel is held longer than in English): **Bahn, sagen, Haar, fragen.**

short a   is similar to the vowel in *but*, e.g., **Mann, Stadt, kann.**

long e   is similar to *a* in *gate* (but cf. our introductory note on non-gliding vowels): **Regen, gehen, legen, See.**

short e   is like *e* in *met:* **Bett, retten, Ecke, setzen.** (Note that final or unaccented *e* is like *a* in comma, or *e* in *taken,* e.g., in the second syllable in **komme, Lampe, sagen, Regen.**)

long i   is like *i* in *machine:* **Lied, ihn, Silo.** (In most words, long **i** is spelled **ie** in German: **liegen, Marie, viel, die.**)

short i   is like *i* in *hit:* **mit, Mitte, finden, hinter.**

long o   is similar to *o* in *joke:* **so, Boot, holen, wohnen.**

short o   is similar to *o* in *hot* (in the British pronunciation): **kosten, Sommer, Wort, kommen.**

long u   is similar to *oo* in *shoot:* **du, gut, Hut, Blume.**

short u   is like *u* in *put:* **Mutter, Butter, Suppe, und.**

B. Umlaut

The letters **ä, ö, ü** denote modifications—called *umlaut*—of **a, o, u** respectively.

long ä   is similar to *a* in *share:* **Schläge, sähe, Mädchen, Väter.**

short ä   is like *e* in *met* (i.e., like German **short e**): **Städte, Männer, hält, Hände.**

The pronunciation of **ö** and **ü** cannot be described briefly in a satisfactory way. It must be learned through oral practice from the instructor or in the laboratory.

long ö   **schön, mögen, höflich, Söhne**
short ö   **Götter, öffnen, können, gösse**
long ü   **über, grün, Tür, Süden**
short ü   **Mütter, Hütte, fünf, müssen**

The letter **y** is pronounced as **ü.** It occurs in words of foreign origin, e.g., **Lyrik, typisch, Physik.**

C. Diphthongs

au   is similar to *ou* in *house:* **Haus, auf, laut, kaufen.**
ei   is similar to *i* in *bike:* **ein, mein, Fleisch, Rhein.**
ai, ay, and **ey** are pronounced like **ei.** These combinations are rare and confined to some proper names, e.g., **Main, Bayern, Meyer.**

eu
äu } are similar to *oi* in *oil:* **heute, Europa, läuft, Häuser.**

II. German Consonants

If the letter represents a consonant which is represented by the same letter in English, no remark or comment is made.

b   **Boot, Baum, aber;** in final position pronounced like **p,** e.g., **Grab, gab, lieb.**
d   **dann, du, oder;** in final position pronounced like **t,** e.g., **Rad, Wand, rund.**
f   **fallen, Fenster, rufen, auf.**
g   is always like *g* in *good:* **gut, geben, sagen;** in final position pronounced like **k,** e.g., **lag, bog, Steg.** The ending **–ig** is pronounced like **–ich,** e.g., **König, fleissig.** (Note that there is no consonant in German like the one in English *germ, gender, ginger.*)

h   **haben, Herr, Haus, behalten, abholen.** (Note, however, item 2 of the list on page 3.)

k   **kalt, Kaiser, Haken, Musik.**

ck   is like *ck* in English; cf. **dick** and *thick*.

l   is notably different (phonetically) from its English counterpart, but will be perceived by English speakers as a variant of their own *l*. Conversely, German speakers perceive English *l* as a variant of their **l**. Correct pronunciation can be learned only from your instructor or in the language laboratory.

m   **mein, Mutter, Dame, kam.**

n   **nun, nehmen, Söhne.**

p   **Park, Oper, April, Pumpernickel.**

q   is always combined with **u: qu.** It is a cluster, pronounced like *kv*, e.g., **Quelle, Qualität, Quantität.**

r   What was said about **l** applies also to **r.** Correct pronunciation can therefore be learned only from your instructor or in the language laboratory.

s   before a vowel is like English *z* in *zeal,* e.g., **sie, so, Hase, gewesen.** In other positions it is like English *s* in *yes,* e.g., **es, Haus, uns, best.**

ss   is like English *ss* in *miss,* e.g., **Klasse, essen, müssen.**

ß   this symbol appears only in print; in writing (except in Gothic script) it is usually replaced by **ss.** It stands for **double–s** and is used at the end of a word or a syllable, or to indicate a long preceding vowel: **Fluß** (but **Flüsse**), **Rußland; Fuß, Füße, Straße.**

t   **Teil, tun, beten, Hut.**

v   is equal to German and English *f;* cf. **Vater** and *father,* **vier** and *four,* **vergessen** and *forget.*

w   is like English *v* in *village;* e.g., **was, Wasser, Winter.** (Note that there is no German consonant like the one in English *what, water, winter.*)

x   is a cluster, *ks,* like *x* in English *fix:* **Axt, Max.** This letter, however, is rare in German. More common is the form **chs** (see below).

z
tz } is a cluster like *ts* in *hearts, hats, cuts:* **z** is written after **l, r, n** and diphthongs, **tz** after single vowels; e.g., **Pelz, kurz, ganz, Weizen, Katze, sitzen**; **z** is frequent in the beginning of words, e.g., **Zahl, zehn, Zimmer, zu, zwei**. (Cf. the rare English example *tsetse fly*.)

Orthographic particulars, clusters, etc.

c was omitted in the list above because it occurs only in foreign words, where it is pronounced like **k** as in **Café** (before **a, o, u**), or like **ts** as in **Cäsar** (before **e, i, y, ä**).

The letter **c** is combined with other signs to represent consonants for which the Latin alphabet has no signs.

ch has no equivalent in English. Correct pronunciation must be learned through oral practice from the instructor or in the laboratory. (Note that there are two different qualities of **ch**, depending upon the preceding vowel, e.g., **Dach, hoch, Buch;** *and* **mich, echt, reich.**)

sch is like *sh* in *ship:* **Schiff, schon, geschchen, waschen.** (Note that in German **sch** can precede consonants which in English are never preceded by *sh*, e.g., **schlafen, schmecken, schnell, schwer.**)

chs is like *x;* cf. **sechs** and *six*.

sp at the beginning of the word or a syllable is pronounced like *shp*, e.g., **spät, sprechen, spielen.**

st at the beginning of the word or a syllable is pronounced like *sht*, e.g., **Stadt, stehen, Straße.**

ng always denotes a single nasal as in English *singer* (never a nasal plus *g* as in *finger*): **singen, bringen, Finger.**

nk always denotes a nasal plus *k*, just as in English; cf. **Bank** and *bank*, **trinken** and *drinking*.

gn pronounce both letters, e.g., **Gnade.**
kn pronounce both letters, e.g., **Knie, Knabe.**
pf pronounce both letters, e.g., **Pfund, pflanzen, Pfennig.**
ps pronounce both letters, e.g., **Psychologie, Pseudonym.**
ph is like **f**: **Philosophie, Physik.**
dt is just like **tt**; **Stadt** sounds like **statt.**
th is like **t**: **Theater, Thema, Goethe.**

(Note that there are no consonants in German like the ones in English *think, thin; this, then.*)

III. The Glottal Stop

English tends to carry over a final consonant from one word to the initial vowel of the next word, e.g., to pronounce *roses are* as *rozizar,* i.e., all run together. In German the glottal stop, or glottal catch, prevents this.

For example, if you say *a apple* very clearly and distinctly, you will notice that your breath comes forth explosively just before each *a;* that is the glottal stop. Try this on the following examples: **ein Apfel, der Apfel, das Essen, erinnern.**

English also palatalizes between vowels, e.g., we often pronounce **the Alps** in such a way that the result is *the yalps.* In German, the glottal stop prevents running vowels together, e.g., **beobachten, beachten, eine Ehre.**

IV. Capitalization

All German nouns, or words used as nouns, are capitalized: **das Zimmer, die Schule, der Alte** (*the old man*).

German adjectives (when not used as nouns or part of an official title) are regularly spelled without a capital, e.g., **die deutsche Sprache.** [Names of places plus **–er** are, however, capitalized, e.g., **die Schweizer Landschaft,** *the Swiss landscape,* or **Münchener Bier,** *Munich beer.*]

The polite personal pronoun **Sie** and the adjective **Ihr** are always capitalized. [In correspondence, all German words for *you* and *your* are capitalized.]

V. Syllabification and Vowel Length

A single consonant goes with the following syllable; and a vowel at the end of a syllable is long: **schla-fen, re-den, lo-ben, Ha-fen.**

Of more than one consonant, only the last one usually goes with the following syllable, and the preceding vowel is short.

Our rule for vowel length, after syllabification, is this: If the syllable ends in a vowel, the vowel is long (**Me-ter, Schu-le, Stra-ße, Bo-den**); if the syllable ends in a consonant, the vowel is short (**Mes-ser, Mut-ter, Klas-se, Som-mer**).

Compounds are broken down into their components: **Schul-zeit, Frei-heit, Blei-stift.**

VI. Accent

In general, the accent is on the first, or root syllable of German words and stays there: **Mäd'chen, Win'ter, Schu'le, stell'en, stell'te, gestellt'.**

The prefixes **be–, ge–, emp–, ent–, er–, ver–, zer–** are never accented.

Compound nouns are regularly accented more heavily on the first element, e.g., **Son''nenschein'**, *sun''shi'ne*.

Foreign words are usually accented on the last syllable: **Student', interessant', Philosoph', Kultur', Natur'.**

VII. Punctuation

A comma is always used: 1) to separate main clauses from each other, if each is complete (having a verb and subject of its own); 2) to separate main clauses from subordinate clauses; 3) before an infinitive phrase when it has modifiers.

ARTICLES AND CASES
PRESENT OF HABEN AND SEIN
PREDICATE ADJECTIVES

I. Reading Selection

Mein Freund Herbert und ich sind Studenten aus Amerika.
Aber wir sind jetzt nicht in Amerika, denn wir wohnen jetzt
in Deutschland. Wir haben ein Zimmer bei einer deutschen
Familie. Das Zimmer hat zwei Fenster. In dem Zimmer sind
ein Tisch, ein Sessel, eine Lampe und zwei Betten. Hier
wohnen Herbert und ich. Herbert sitzt auf dem Stuhl und
schreibt die Aufgabe. Er braucht viel Zeit, denn die Aufgabe
ist sehr schwer.

Herbert fragt: „Conrad, schreibst du deine Aufgabe?"
10   Ich sage: „Nein, ich bin krank."

Er sagt: „Du bist nicht krank, du bist faul."

Ich sage: „Ich sehe ein Schulbuch, und ich bin sofort krank.
So ist es."

Er sagt: „Ja, ja, Conrad, die Schule ist nicht gut für deine
Gesundheit."

.   .   .

Herbert und ich haben einen Lehrer. Er lehrt Deutsch. Er ist alt, denn sein Haar ist weiß. Der Lehrer fragt: „Seid ihr fertig? Habt ihr die Aufgabe?" Herbert schreibt die Aufgabe an die Tafel. Der Lehrer sagt: „Herbert, das ist sehr gut. Conrad, wo ist deine Aufgabe?" 20

Aber es klingelt in diesem Augenblick, und der Lehrer sagt: „Du hast Glück. Du schreibst deine Aufgabe morgen an die Tafel."

II. Vocabulary

Starred items (*) are *active vocabulary*, i.e., the student is expected to be able to give the German word in response to its English equivalent, or to use it in sentences independently. The other items are *passive vocabulary*, i.e., the student is expected only to be able to recognize the meaning of such words when he sees or hears them.

aber but, however
***alt** old
***Amerika** (*neut.*) America
 an alongside of, on
 auf upon, on, up
***die Aufgabe** the lesson
 der Augenblick the moment
 aus out of, from
 bei with, at the house of
***das Bett, die Betten** the bed, beds
 brauchen, er braucht (to) need, he needs
***das** that
 deine your (*singular familiar*)
***denn** for, because
***der, die, das** (*definite article*) the
***deutsch, Deutsch** German
***Deutschland** (*neut.*) Germany
 diesem this (*dative* of dieser)
***du** you (*singular familiar*)
***ein, eine, ein** (*indefinite article*) a, an, one
***eins** one

***er** he, it
***es** it
 die Familie the family
 faul lazy
***das Fenster** the window
 fertig ready, done, finished
 fragen, er fragt (to) ask, he asks
***der Freund** the friend
 für for
 die Gesundheit the health
 das Glück luck, good fortune
***gut** good, well
***das Haar** the hair
***haben** (to) have
***hier** here
***ich** I
***ihr** you (*plural familiar*)
***in** in, into
***ja** yes
 jetzt now
 klingeln, es klingelt (to) ring, it (the bell) rings
***krank** sick, ill

die **Lampe** the lamp
*__lehren, er lehrt__ (to) teach, he teaches
*__der Lehrer__ the teacher
 mein my
*__morgen__ tomorrow
*__nein__ no
*__nicht__ not
*__sagen, ich sage__ (to) say, I say
*__schreiben, du schreibst, er schreibt__ (to) write, you write, he writes
 das **Schulbuch** the school book
*__die Schule__ the school
*__schwer__ difficult; heavy, hard
 sehen, ich sehe (to) see, I see
*__sehr__ very
*__sein__ (to) be
 sein his
*__der Sessel__ the armchair, easy chair
*__sie__ they, she, it
*__Sie__ you (*formal form, singular or plural*)

*__sitzen, er sitzt__ (to) sit, he sits
*__so__ so, thus, this way
*__sofort__ at once, immediately
*__der Student, die Studenten__ the student, students
*__der Stuhl__ the chair
*__die Tafel__ the blackboard
*__der Tisch__ the table
*__und__ and
*__viel__ much, a lot (of)
*__wann__ when
*__was__ what
*__weiß__ white
*__wer__ who
*__wie__ how
*__wir__ we
*__wo__ where
*__wohnen__ (to) live
 die **Zeit** the time
*__das Zimmer__ the room
 zwei two

Idiom

er hat Glück he is lucky

III. Grammar

A. The Articles

German, like English, has a definite and an indefinite article, which precede the noun. German nouns, however, are distributed among the three gender categories: masculine, feminine, and neuter. Accordingly, the definite article, which English expresses with one word *the,* has three forms in German: **der** for the masculine, **die** for the feminine, **das** for the neuter gender. The corresponding forms for the indefinite article, expressed in English as *a* or *an,* are: **ein, eine, ein.**

With the exception of nouns denoting persons, the gender cannot be determined in a logical way. To be sure, **der Mann** (*the man*) is masculine, **die Frau** (*the woman*) is feminine; but **der Tisch** (*the table*) is masculine, **die Tafel** (*the blackboard*) is feminine, **das Fenster** (*the window*) is neuter.

The gender of each noun must be memorized by the student. This is done conveniently by memorizing each noun together with its corresponding definite article.

B. The Cases

In English, the function of the noun is indicated by its position in the sentence. In German, it is indicated mainly by the form of the article preceding the noun. These forms are called cases: 1) the nominative, 2) the genitive, 3) the dative, 4) the accusative.

The nominative case

The nominative is the case of the subject of the sentence. The subject is

the one who is, e.g.,	*the man* is old
	der Mann ist alt
the one who has, e.g.,	*the man* has a house
	der Mann hat ein Haus
the one who does, e.g.,	*the man* buys a house
	der Mann kauft ein Haus

The accusative case

The accusative is the case of the direct object—therefore called in English the "objective case." The object is the counterpart of the one who does or the one who has; for example:

The man buys *a chair*
Der Mann kauft **einen Stuhl**
The man has *a friend*
Der Mann hat **einen Freund**

(Note that the counterpart of the one who is, is *not* an object, but the so-called predicate noun, which appears in the nominative. See Subsection D.)

The dative case

The dative denotes the one for whom (or against whom) the action is performed, e.g., I give *the man* the book ich gebe **dem Mann** das Buch. In our example, *the man* **dem Mann** is the so-called indirect object—the beneficiary of the action, the one who receives the direct object. In English, this idea can be expressed by a prepositional phrase: I give the book *to the man.* This cannot be done in German.

The genitive case

The genitive conveys a relation of "possession" or "belonging to" between two nouns or a pronoun and a noun (for this reason the case is called the *possessive* in English). For example:

> The house *of my father* = the house which my father possesses
> The roof *of the house* = the roof which belongs to the house
> A student *of this university* = a student who is part of (belongs to) this university
> The price *of the book* = the price which "goes with" the book

You will notice that in English the idea of "belonging to" is expressed by the preposition *of* between the two nouns. However, when referring to a human being, the genitive can also be expressed in English by placing the "owner" in front of the other noun and adding an *'s:* the book of the teacher = the teacher's book. This can also be done in German: des Lehrers Buch. Preferable, however, is the arrangement **das Buch des Lehrers,** where, as can be seen, the two nouns are placed in the same order as in the English construction with *of:*

> the book *of the teacher*
> das Buch **des Lehrers**

Note that a construction with a preposition like the one in English may not be substituted for the construction above in German. ("Das Buch von dem Lehrer" is substandard German.)

You will find below a table showing the declension of one noun of each gender in the singular with both the definite and the indefinite articles. Note that all nouns in German are capitalized. It is helpful to remember that, in the feminine and neuter, the accusative for articles and nouns is always identical with its nominative. Study especially the articles in this lesson.

The forms below are arranged in this sequence: nominative, genitive, dative, accusative, which is the conventional arrangement. You will find nominal paradigms * arranged in this way throughout the book.

NOUNS WITH DEFINITE ARTICLE IN THE SINGULAR

	Masc.	Fem.	Neut.
Nom.	der Freund	die Aufgabe	das Fenster
Gen.	des Freundes†	der Aufgabe	des Fensters†
Dat.	dem Freund(e)†	der Aufgabe	dem Fenster
Acc.	den Freund	die Aufgabe	das Fenster

NOUNS WITH INDEFINITE ARTICLE IN THE SINGULAR

Nom.	ein Lehrer	eine Tafel	ein Bett
Gen.	eines Lehrers†	einer Tafel	eines Bettes†
Dat.	einem Lehrer	einer Tafel	einem Bett(e)
Acc.	einen Lehrer	eine Tafel	ein Bett

Note that **ein** has no ending in the singular nominative masculine, or in the singular nominative and accusative neuter. Also note that in the forms marked with a dagger (†) not only the article but the noun itself changes; this will be explained in the next lesson.

C. haben and sein in the Present Tense

The most basic verbs in English and German are (*to*) *be* **sein** and (*to*) *have* **haben.** Here is the present tense conjugation:

---

* A paradigm is an example of a word (noun, verb, adjective) in its various inflections (declension and conjugation). The paradigms **Freund** and **Lehrer** show the conventional arrangement that will be used throughout this book.

PRESENT TENSE

SINGULAR

1. ich habe	I have	ich bin	I am
2. du hast	you have	du bist	you are
3. er / sie / es } hat	he / she / it } has	er / sie / es } ist	he / she / it } is

PLURAL

1. wir haben	we have	wir sind	we are
2. ihr habt	you have	ihr seid	you are
3. sie (Sie) } haben	they (you) } have	sie (Sie) } sind	they (you) } are

Note that, for the word *you* (the person addressed), German has three different forms: **du, ihr, Sie.**

The pronoun **du** is the singular and the pronoun **ihr** the plural of the so-called "familiar form" of address. In general, we can say that the familiar form is used among members of the family, in talking to people whom we call by their first names, and in addressing youngsters through their lower teens.

In all other instances, the so-called "polite form" of address, **Sie** (always capitalized), is used. It is both singular and plural, i.e., applicable no matter whether one person or two or more persons are being addressed. The verb form that goes with the pronoun **Sie** is the third person plural. Thus: **Herr und Frau Schmidt, sind Sie krank?** *Mr. and Mrs. Schmidt, are you sick?*

D. The Cases after **haben** and **sein**

After **haben**: Accusative

Der Schüler	hat	einen Bleistift
SUBJECT		OBJECT
(the one who has)		*(what he has)*

After **sein**: Nominative

Der Lehrer	ist	ein Mann
SUBJECT		PREDICATE NOUN
(the one who is)		*(what he is)*

IV. Grammatical Exercises

A. Fill in the missing form of **haben** or **sein**:

1. Ich _____ krank. 2. _____ ihr fertig? 3. Ich _____ die Aufgabe.
4. Wir _____ Studenten. 5. Wir _____ ein Zimmer bei einer
deutschen Familie. 6. _____ Sie faul? 7. Das _____ sehr gut.
8. _____ du deine Aufgabe? 9. _____ ihr die Aufgabe? 10. Du
_____ nicht alt. 11. Der Lehrer _____ weißes Haar. 12. Sie _____
ein Schulbuch.

B. Supply the proper form of the definite article:

1. Was sagt _____ Lehrer? 2. Ist das _____ Schule? 3. Wo ist
_____ Stuhl? 4. _____ Student schreibt _____ Aufgabe an _____
Tafel. 5. Wo wohnt _____ Freund? 6. _____ Stuhl und _____
Tisch sind alt. 7. _____ Haar ist nicht schwer. 8. _____ Zimmer
hat zwei Fenster. 9. _____ Bett ist weiß. 10. Das ist _____ Sessel.

C. Supply the proper form of the indefinite article:

1. Conrad ist _____ Student. 2. Wir haben _____ Lampe. 3. Das
ist _____ Sessel. 4. Er hat _____ Freund. 5. Das Zimmer hat
_____ Fenster. 6. _____ Student schreibt die Aufgabe an die
Tafel. 7. Sie haben _____ Lehrer. 8. Sie hat _____ Schulbuch.

V. Translation Exercise

1. I am not sick. 2. Where is the school? 3. Are you a student?
4. The hair is white. 5. The chair and the table are old. 6. German is not very difficult. 7. They have a bed. 8. We are in
Germany. 9. Have you (*three forms*) the lesson? 10. The teacher
teaches German. 11. They are students. 12. We have a room.
13. It has a window. 14. He sits here. 15. He writes the lesson.
16. Is he old? 17. The teacher is old. 18. Herbert has a lesson.
19. Is the table heavy? 20. You write very much.

VI. Fragen

(Always answer in complete sentences!)
1. Was sind Herbert und Conrad? 2. Sind Conrad und Herbert in Amerika? 3. Wo wohnen sie? 4. Ist Herbert krank? 5. Was lehrt der Lehrer? 6. Wie ist sein Haar? 7. Was schreibt Herbert an die Tafel? 8. Was sagt der Lehrer? 9. Wann schreibt Conrad die Aufgabe an die Tafel?

VII. Lesestück

Vier Tage, zweihundert Dollar, dreitausend Meilen

Amerika ist ein Kontinent. Deutschland ist ein Land. Zwischen Amerika und Deutschland liegt der Atlantische Ozean. Er ist 3 000 (dreitausend) Meilen breit. Im Jahre 1620 (sechzehnhundertzwanzig) fuhr ein Schiff, die Mayflower, über den Atlantischen Ozean. Die Reise dauerte 9 (neun) Wochen. Ein großes, modernes Schiff in unserer Zeit macht die Reise in 4 (vier) oder 5 (fünf) Tagen, ein Flugzeug in 7 (sieben) Stunden. Amerika und Deutschland sind getrennt durch 3 000 (dreitausend) Meilen Entfernung, 4 (vier) Tage Fahrzeit und 200
10 (zweihundert) Dollar Fahrpreis in der Touristenklasse.

Viele Schiffe fahren von Europa nach Amerika über den Atlantischen Ozean. Die meisten Schiffe landen in New York. New York ist die größte Stadt und der größte Hafen auf dem amerikanischen Kontinent. Die Schiffe fahren dann wieder zurück nach Europa, d.h. nach England, Deutschland, Frankreich, Holland, Italien oder Schweden. Sie landen in Southampton, Hamburg, Le Havre, Genua oder Göteborg.

Die Reise über den Atlantischen Ozean ist im Sommer oft sehr schön. Das Wasser ist dann glatt, ruhig und blau. Im
20 Winter ist der Ozean oft sehr bewegt, unruhig und grau. Doch ein modernes Schiff fährt ruhig und sicher durch den größten Sturm.

VIII. Wörterverzeichnis

The vocabulary of the Reading Selections was chosen primarily for everyday use of the language, for conversational purposes. Our main idea in including Supplementary Readings (*Lesestücke*) was to present certain material and to familiarize you—on a modest scale—with the folklore, the geographical background, and the cultural history of the country whose language you are beginning to learn. We also hope that they will help you to acquire a certain efficiency in reading a simple German text.

Words with an asterisk, given in the Reading Selections of previous lessons, are of course not repeated here. Even some new words are not listed, such as "England, Holland, Rotterdam, Hamburg," etc. We have used such words as "Pastor, Tradition, Uniform, Symbol, Theater, Museum" without translating them in the supplementary vocabularies. We even did not list words which are not completely identical, but so close that everyone will know their meanings at first sight, such as "Manuskript, Charakter, Oktober, Medizin."

amerikanisch American
der Atlantische Ozean the Atlantic
    Ocean
auf on
bewegt rough
blau blue
breit wide
dann then
d.h. abbr. for das heißt i.e., that is
dauerte lasted
doch however, but, yet
durch through, by
die Entfernung the distance
fahren; fährt; fuhr (to) go; goes;
    went
der Fahrpreis the fare
die Fahrzeit the travel time
das Flugzeug the airplane
Frankreich France

getrennt separated
glatt smooth
grau gray
groß; der größte big; the biggest
der Hafen the harbor
heute today
Italien Italy
im Jahre in the year
der Kontinent the continent
das Land the land, country
landen (to) land
liegt lies
macht makes
die Meilen the miles
die meisten the most, most of
modern modern
nach to
oder or
oft often

die **Reise** the trip
ruhig calm, quiet
das **Schiff** the ship
schön nice, beautiful
Schweden Sweden
sicher safe
im **Sommer** in the summer
die **Stadt** the city
die **Stunde** the hour
der **Sturm** the storm
der **Tag** the day
die **Touristenklasse** the tourist class

über over, across
unruhig restless
unser our
viele many
von from'
das **Wasser** the water
wieder again
im **Winter** in the winter
die **Woche** the week
die **Zeit** the time
zurück back
zwischen between

AUFGABE ZWEI

DECLENSION OF SINGULAR NOUNS
DATIVE PREPOSITIONS

I. Reading Selection

Das Fenster des Zimmers ist offen. Die Luft kommt durch das Fenster in das Zimmer. Der Lehrer sagt: „Die Farbe des Bleistifts ist rot." Mein Freund Herbert sagt: „Die Farbe des Buches ist grün." Der Lehrer fragt: „Haben wir auch die Farbe weiß in dem Zimmer?" „Ja", sagt Herbert, „das Heft ist weiß, die Wand und die Kreide sind weiß."

Der Lehrer fragt: „Haben wir auch die Farbe schwarz in dem Zimmer?" Ich sage sofort: „Ja, die Tafel ist schwarz, mein Haar ist schwarz, die Schuhe sind schwarz." Der Lehrer lacht und sagt: „Auch dein Gewissen ist schwarz, denn du hast deine 10 Aufgabe nicht in dem Heft."

Der Lehrer sagt: „Wir üben jetzt den Genitiv: Conrads Aufgabe ist schwer. Das Glück des Schülers ist groß. Die Geduld des Lehrers ist sehr groß."

Herbert sagt: „Ich übe den Dativ: Ich bin in dem Zimmer. Ich zeige dem Freund das Buch. Ich schreibe der Mutter den Brief. Ich schreibe mit dem Bleistift."

„Gut", sagt der Lehrer, „Conrad, schreibst du jetzt einen Satz mit dem Accusativ an die Tafel?"

20   „Nein", sage ich, „es ist zu schwer, und ich bin zu dumm."

„Ja", sagt der Lehrer, „Mark Twain schreibt: I would rather decline a good drink than decline a German noun."

II. Vocabulary

*auch also
*aus from, out of
*bei near, with, at the place of
*der Bleistift the pencil
*der Brief the letter
*das Buch the book
*dumm stupid, dumb
*durch through
*die Farbe the color
*fragen to ask
  die Geduld the patience
  das Gewissen the conscience
*groß big, large, great
*grün green
*das Heft the notebook
*jetzt now
*kommen, er kommt (to) come, he comes
*die Kreide the chalk
*lachen, er lacht (to) laugh, he laughs
*die Luft the air
*mein my
*mit with

die Mutter the mother
*nach to (*with names of countries and cities*), toward; after
*offen open
*rot red
*der Satz the sentence
*der Schuh, die Schuhe the shoe, shoes
*der Schüler the pupil
*schwarz black
*seit (*preposition*) since
*üben; er übt (to) practice; he practices
*von of, from
*die Wand the wall
*warum why
  werden, ich werde (to) get, become; I get, I become
*zeigen, ich zeige, er zeigt (to) show, I show, he shows
*zu too
*zu (*preposition*) to
*zwei two

III. Grammar

A. The Noun in the Singular

By now you have learned the forms of the definite and the indefinite articles in the singular. For this lesson you should refer back to Section III,B of Lesson I. Read it with care, and then study the reading selection of this lesson to see how the cases of the nouns are used.

We saw in Lesson I that the articles had a variety of forms to indicate the different cases of the noun: four for the masculine, two for the feminine, and three for the neuter.

The noun is less complicated. A few rules describe its changes and may prove helpful to you: 1) There is no change in the singular of any feminine noun; thus, once we know the word **Frau,** we know that only this form will be used throughout the singular. 2) All neuter and most masculine nouns form their genitive by adding –s, e.g., **Fensters** and **Lehrers** (see the table in Lesson I). However, if the masculine or neuter noun is a monosyllable (e.g., **Freund** or **Bett**), we add –es to form its genitive singular (e.g., **Freundes, Bettes**). 3) These monosyllabic nouns may take an –e in the dative singular (e.g., **Manne, Bette, Tische, Satze**), but since in present-day German use of the dative ending is becoming more and more infrequent, the student should not try to imitate it. 4) Proper names normally add –s for the genitive singular, e.g., **Conrads, Herberts, Maries.**

A few nouns, almost all of them masculine, do not follow the above pattern, but in all cases except the nominative add –n or –en. Most of these nouns end in an –e in the nominative (in which case only –n is added), or they are words (mostly of foreign origin) accented on the last syllable. For example: **der Junge, des Jungen, dem Jungen, den Jungen,** or **der Student, des Studenten, dem Studenten, den Studenten.**

B. Prepositions

There are four different groups of prepositions. The feature that distinguishes these four groups is the fact that they are followed by different cases of the noun or pronoun. So that your memory will not be unduly burdened, we shall introduce these groups one at a time. The first group follows on the next page.

Prepositions with the dative

We have already encountered all those prepositions which are always followed by the dative case. They are: **aus, von, seit, bei, mit, nach, zu.** *gegenüber*

IV. Grammatical Exercises

A. Fill in the proper endings where needed:

1. Was ist d____ Farbe d____ Luft? 2. D____ Haar d____ Lehrer____ ist weiß. 3. D____ Farbe d____ Kreide und d____ Wand ist auch weiß. 4. D____ Farbe ein____ (*of one*) Tafel ist schwarz. 5. D____ Aufgabe d____ Schüler____ ist schwer. 6. D____ Fenster ein____ (*of one*) Zimmer____ ist offen. 7. D____ Farbe d____ Bleistift____ ist grün. 8. D____ Farbe d____ Buch____ ist rot. 9. Was ist d____ Farbe d____ Fenster____? 10. Ist Conrad____ Zimmer groß?

B. Fill in the proper endings where needed:

1. Wir haben ein____ Lehrer. 2. Ich habe ein____ Zimmer. 3. D____ Student schreibt d____ Aufgabe. 4. Ich sehe d____ Schulbuch. 5. Hast du d____ Aufgabe? 6. Schreibt er d____ Satz? 7. Ich zeige d____ Bleistift. 8. Hat d____ Schüler ein____ Heft? 9. Er hat ein____ gute Mutter. 10. Schreibst du ein____ Brief?

C. Fill in the proper endings:

1. D____ Schüler schreibt d____ Freund ein____ Brief. 2. Er kommt aus d____ Zimmer. 3. Sie geht (*goes*) zu d____ Schule. 4. Wir haben d____ Kreide von d____ Student____. 5. Schreiben Sie mit d____ Bleistift? 6. Er sitzt mit d____ Buch an d____ Tisch. 7. Er zeigt d____ Lehrer d____ Heft.

D. Re-do sentences 2, 4, 5 and 6 of Exercise C using the indefinite article instead of the definite article, wherever it makes sense.

V. Translation Exercise

1. I have the book. 2. He practices the sentence. 3. Who has the pencil? 4. The color of the book is black. 5. The color of the wall is green. 6. Herbert's book is open. 7. I show the lesson to the teacher. 8. You write a letter to a friend. 9. Conrad shows the student a sentence from (*aus*) the book. 10. Who writes with the pencil? 11. Is the lesson from the book? 12. Herbert comes from America with a friend.

Re-do sentences 1, 2, 3, 7, 9, 10 and 11, replacing the definite article with the indefinite article wherever it makes sense.

VI. Fragen

1. Wie ist das Fenster des Zimmers? 2. Was kommt durch das Fenster? 3. Wie ist die Farbe des Buches? 4. Wie ist das Heft? 5. Was fragt der Lehrer? 6. Warum ist Conrads Gewissen schwarz? 7. Wie ist die Geduld des Lehrers? 8. Warum schreibt Conrad den Satz nicht? 9. Ist Herbert ein Schüler?

VII. Lesestück

Amerika und Deutschland

Ein Mann in Deutschland sagt: „Ich habe ein amerikanisches Auto." Er meint damit, er hat ein Auto aus den Vereinigten Staaten, einen Ford, einen Pontiac oder einen Chrysler. Ein anderer Mann sagt: „Die Amerikaner haben zu viel Geld." Er sagt „Die Amerikaner" und er meint „Die Leute aus den Vereinigten Staaten." Für viele Leute in Europa sind die Worte Amerika und Vereinigte Staaten fast Synonyme.

Ein Mann in Amerika sagt: „Ich war im Sommer in Deutschland." Finden wir auf der Karte von Europa ein Land mit dem Namen Deutschland? Nein. Es gibt heute zwei deutsche Staaten, 10 aber keiner heißt Deutschland. Der eine Staat im Westen heißt

„Bundesrepublik Deutschland", der andere im Osten „Deutsche Demokratische Republik." Von 1871 (achtzehnhunderteinundsiebzig) bis 1945 (neunzehnhundertfünfundvierzig) hieß das Land im Herzen Europas „Deutsches Reich." In den tausend Jahren vor 1806 (achtzehnhundertsechs) war Deutschland ein Teil des „Heiligen Römischen Reiches."

Für die Bundesrepublik Deutschland gebrauchen wir heute oft den Namen Westdeutschland. In Amerika gibt es 50 (fünf-
20 zig) „Vereinigte Staaten." In Westdeutschland gibt es 10 (zehn) Länder. Sie heißen Schleswig-Holstein, Niedersachsen, Nordrhein-Westfalen, Hessen, Rheinland-Pfalz, Baden-Württemberg, Bayern, Saarland, Hamburg und Bremen. Hamburg und Bremen sind Stadtstaaten.

Die Verfassung der Bundesrepublik Deutschland hat viele Ähnlichkeiten mit der amerikanischen Verfassung. Es gibt aber auch Verschiedenheiten. An der Spitze der amerikanischen Regierung steht ein Mann, der Präsident. An der Spitze der deutschen Bundesrepublik stehen zwei Männer, der Bundes-
30 präsident und der Bundeskanzler. Der eine repräsentiert, der andere regiert.

VIII. Wörterverzeichnis

aber but
Ähnlichkeiten similarities
der Amerikaner the American, **die
   Amerikaner** the Americans
amerikanisch American
der andere the other
bis until
der Bundeskanzler the Federal
   Chancellor
der Bundespräsident the Federal
   President
die Bundesrepublik Deutschland
   the Federal Republic of Ger
   many
damit by that

**die Deutsche Demokratische Re
   publik** the German Democratic
   Republic
das Deutsche Reich the German
   Empire
der eine the one
Europa Europe
fast almost
finden wir? do we find?
für for
gebrauchen (to) use
das Geld the money
es gibt there is, there are
das Heilige Römische Reich the
   Holy Roman Empire

heißt, hieß; sie heißen is called; was called; they are called
das Herz the heart
heute today
auf der Karte on the map
keiner none, neither
das Land; die Länder the land, country; the lands, countries. (Technical constitutional term for *"The States"* of the Federal Republic of Germany)
die Leute the people
der Mann; die Männer the man; the men
meint means
der Name the name
der Osten the east
der Präsident the president
regiert rules
die Regierung the government
repräsentiert represents

im Sommer in the summer
an der Spitze at the head
die Staaten the states
die Stadtstaaten the city states
steht stands
Synonyme synonyms
tausend Jahre a thousand years
der Teil the part
die Vereinigten Staaten the United States
die Verfassung the constitution
die Verschiedenheiten the differences
viele many
vor before
war was
Westdeutschland West Germany
der Westen the west
wie like
das Wort the word

PRESENT TENSE CONJUGATION
ACCUSATIVE PREPOSITIONS

I. Reading Selection

Herbert und ich wohnen in dem Hause der Familie Löwenzahn. Wir wohnen und essen mit der Familie. Es wird jetzt spät, und ich werde hungrig. Ich gehe in die Küche und frage Frau Löwenzahn: „Essen wir bald?"

Sie sagt: „Wir essen in einer halben Stunde. Warum bist du so hungrig?"

Ich antworte: „Die Arbeit in der Schule macht mich so hungrig. Wir arbeiten zu viel."

„Nein", sagt Frau Löwenzahn, „du wächst zu schnell. Du
10 wirst zu groß."

Ich gehe nun in das Wohnzimmer. Hier sitzt Herr Löwenzahn. Er sitzt in einem Sessel und liest die Zeitung. Er trägt eine Brille auf der Nase, denn er sieht nicht gut. Er hört auch nicht gut. Wir sprechen, aber er versteht uns nicht immer.

Herbert spricht zu Herrn Löwenzahn: „Was lesen Sie in der Zeitung?"

Herr Löwenzahn sieht durch die Brille und fragt: „Was sagst du?"

Ich sage zu Herbert: „Warum sprichst du nicht lauter?"

28

Herbert sagt noch einmal sehr laut: „Was lesen Sie in der 20 Zeitung?"

Herr Löwenzahn antwortet: „Ich lese den Wetterbericht. Er sagt für morgen: sonnig, warm und trocken. Das ist gut für den Garten."

Frau Löwenzahn kommt in das Wohnzimmer und sagt: „Conrad, holst du Blumen für mich aus dem Garten? Ich brauche Blumen für das Eßzimmer."

Ich sage: „Blumen? Vielleicht Löwenzahn? Oder Löwenmaul?"

Sie lächelt und sagt: „Nein, nein, wir haben Tulpen und 30 Vergißmeinnicht im Garten. Wir haben genug Löwen im Haus, nicht wahr, Papa?"

Herr Löwenzahn fragt: „Möwen? Möwen? Sagst du, wir haben Möwen im Haus?"

II. Vocabulary

*aber but, however
*antworten (to) answer, reply
*die Arbeit the work
*arbeiten (to) work
*auf on, upon
*bald soon
*die Blume, die Blumen the flower, flowers
*brauchen (to) need
die Brille the glasses
*drei three
einmal once, one time
*essen (i) (to) eat
*das Eßzimmer the dining room
*die Familie the family
*die Frau the woman, Mrs.
*für for
*der Garten the garden
*gegen against, towards
*gehen (to) go, walk
genug enough
halb half

*das Haus the house
der Herr the gentleman, Mr., sir
holen (to) get, fetch
*hören (to) hear, listen
hungrig hungry
ihn (accusative) him
im = in dem
*immer always
*die Küche the kitchen
*lächeln (to) smile
*laufen (äu) (to) run
laut, lauter loud, louder
*lesen (ie) (to) read
der Löwe the lion
das Löwenmaul the snapdragon
der Löwenzahn the dandelion
*machen (to) make, do
mich (accusative) me
die Möwe, die Möwen the sea gull, sea gulls
die Nase the nose
*nun now

*ohne without
schnell quick, fast
*sehen (ie) (to) see, look
sonnig sunny
*spät late
*sprechen (i) (to) speak
*die Stunde the hour
*tragen (ä) (to) carry; wear
trocken dry
die Tulpe, die Tulpen the tulip, tulips
*um around
uns (*dative* or *accusative*) us

das Vergißmeinnicht the forget-me-not
verstehen (to) understand
vielleicht perhaps
vom = von dem
*wachsen (ä) (to) grow
wahr true
*warm warm
*werden (i) (to) get, become
der Wetterbericht the weather report
*das Wohnzimmer the living room
*die Zeitung the newspaper

Idioms

*in einer halben Stunde in half an hour
*nicht wahr is used at the end of questions and means literally "isn't it true?" In each of the following questions, nicht wahr would translate the italicized portion: We live with the Löwenzahns, *don't we?* We are going to school, *aren't we?* He does study, *doesn't he?* etc.
noch einmal again, once more

III. Grammar

A. The Present Tense of Verbs

"Present tense" means much the same in English as it does in German. In English, however, distinctions are made in describing an action, which are unknown in German. These distinctions are called "verbal aspects." In this respect English is more complicated than German. Compare:

I *come*	ich **komme**
I *am coming*	ich **komme**
I *do* (not) *come*	ich **komme** (nicht)
do you *come?*	**kommst** du?
are you *coming?*	**kommst** du?

Remember: German has neither a progressive form (*I am coming*) nor an emphatic form (*I do come*). Do not try to imitate in German those English patterns which German does not use. When translating from German into English, choose the English pattern which is appropriate in the context:

> Herbert **kommt** gerade jetzt aus der Schule
> Herbert *is coming* from school just now
>   (and not: Herbert comes from school just now).

The form of the verb you will find in all dictionaries or vocabularies is called the *infinitive*. In German, the infinitive always ends in **–en** or **–n.** When we remove the infinitive ending **–en** or **–n,** we have left the stem, which is the part we work with.

The vast majority of German verbs form the present tense by adding to the stem the endings shown below in boldface type:

	Singular			Plural	
1. ich komme	*I come*		wir kommen	*we come*	
2. du kommst	*you come*		ihr kommt	*you come*	
3. er sie } kommt es	he she } *comes* it		sie (Sie) } kommen	they (you) } *come*	

Note that the infinitive is always identical with the first and third person plural forms (except for the verb **sein,** which is irregular).

There are a few minor deviations from the normal form in the present tense:

' 1) Most verbs whose stem ends in **–t** or **–d** add the vowel **e** between the stem and the endings **–st** and **–t,** for instance: **du arbeitest, er arbeitet, ihr arbeitet.**

2) With verbs whose stem ends in an **s**-sound (**s, ss, z, tz**) the **s** of the second person singular ending **–st** is not indicated in writing, e.g., **du ißt, du sitzt** (instead of "du sitzst").

3) There is a group of verbs which change the stem vowel in the second and third person singular. The vowels affected are:

a changing to **ä**
au changing to **äu**
e (short) changing to **i** (short)
e (long) changing to **ie, i** (long)

In the Vocabularies, this change of vowel is given in parentheses following the infinitive, e.g., <u>wachsen</u> (ä), laufen (äu), essen (i), or <u>lesen</u> (ie). The following table shows the present tense conjugation of four verbs with vowel changes.

	tragen	laufen	sprechen	sehen
1.	ich trage	laufe	spreche	sehe
2.	**du trägst**	**läufst**	**sprichst**	**siehst**
3.	er **sie** } **trägt** es	**läuft**	**spricht**	**sieht**
1.	wir tragen	laufen	sprechen	sehen
2.	ihr tragt	lauft	sprecht	seht
3.	sie (Sie) } tragen	laufen	sprechen	sehen

One very important verb of this group, **werden,** (*to*) *get* or *become,* is slightly irregular in the singular present tense:

ich werde	wir werden
du wirst	ihr werdet
er sie } **wird** es	sie (Sie) } werden

Remember: Verb forms indicating tense, person, and number are called *finite.* Infinitives and past participles are not finite verbs since they have neither person (first, second, third) nor number (singular or plural).

B. The Personal Pronouns **er, sie, es**

Since nouns have no grammatical gender in English, the one pronoun *it* is used to refer to such things as inanimate objects, abstract ideas, etc. In German, the idea *it* must be expressed by **er, sie,** or **es,** depending upon the grammatical gender of the noun for the thing referred to:

ENGLISH	GERMAN
the table: it	**der Tisch:** er
the color: it	**die Farbe:** sie
the house: it	**das Haus:** es

C. Word Order

The finite verb is the second unit in a German declarative or negative sentence. A German declarative or negative sentence may start with any other unit (for instance: adverb, direct object, indirect object), but the finite verb must be the second grammatical unit. Examples: Ich **schreibe** dem Lehrer jetzt einen Brief. Jetzt **schreibe** ich dem Lehrer einen Brief. Dem Lehrer **schreibe** ich jetzt einen Brief. Einen Brief **schreibe** ich jetzt dem Lehrer.

D. Position of **nicht** in Main Clauses and Questions

1) **Nicht** generally follows the object:

   Er ißt die Suppe nicht *He does not eat the soup.*

2) It follows time expressions:

   Er kommt morgen nicht *He is not coming tomorrow.*

3) It precedes all other expressions:

   Sie ist nicht in der Küche *She is not in the kitchen.*
   Sie ist jetzt nicht in der Küche *She is not in the kitchen now.*
   Er ist nicht der Lehrer *He is not the teacher.*

4) It never precedes the finite verb:

   Die Suppe ißt er nicht *He does not eat the soup.*
   Morgen kommt er nicht *He is not coming tomorrow.*
   In der Küche ist sie nicht *She is not in the kitchen.*
   Der Lehrer ist er nicht *He is not the teacher.*

5) The position of **nicht** does not change in questions:

   Ißt er die Suppe nicht? *Doesn't he eat the soup?*
   Kommt er morgen nicht? *Isn't he coming tomorrow?*
   Ist sie nicht in der Küche? *Isn't she in the kitchen?*
   Ist er nicht der Lehrer? *Isn't he the teacher?*

E. Prepositions with the Accusative

Prepositions which are always followed by the accusative case are: **durch, für, gegen, ohne, um.** (Note that **in,** which we use in this lesson, takes the dative, unless it means *into,* when it takes the accusative; for example: ich wohne **in dem Haus**; ich gehe **in das Haus.** The complete list of prepositions which may take either the accusative or the dative will be given in the next lesson.)

IV. Grammatical Exercises

A. Fill in the proper verb endings:

1. Ich komm_____ in das Haus. 2. Du schreib_____ an die Tafel. 3. Der Lehrer lach_____. 4. Herbert und ich lern_____ die Aufgabe. 5. Geh_____ ihr in die Küche? 6. Die Studenten wohn_____ bei der Familie Löwenzahn. 7. Herr Löwenzahn hör_____ nicht gut.

B. Fill in the proper form of the verb given in the infinitive:

1. (Werden)_____ du hungrig? 2. Warum (tragen)_____ Herr Löwenzahn eine Brille? 3. (Tragen)_____ du auch eine Brille? 4. Herbert (wachsen)_____ zu schnell. 5. Er (essen)_____ zu viel. 6. (Arbeiten)_____ er auch zu viel? 7. Der Schüler (lesen) _____ in der Zeitung. 8. Herbert (gehen)_____ in die Küche. 9. Frau Löwenzahn (kommen)_____ aus der Küche. 10. Conrad (sprechen)_____ nicht laut. 11. (Sprechen)_____ du lauter? 12. Was (lesen)_____ du in der Schule? 13. Das Wetter (werden) _____ schlecht (*bad*). 14. Du (wachsen)_____ auch zu schnell. 15. Er (laufen)_____ in die Schule.

C. Re-do sentences 1, 2, 3, 4 of IV,A, and sentences 7, 8, 9, 13, 15 of IV,B, beginning each sentence with *Jetzt.*

V. Translation Exercise

1. Herbert is growing, isn't he? 2. You are speaking (*three forms*) to Mrs. Löwenzahn. 3. What is she reading in the newspaper? 4. He is running into the garden. 5. Do you see (*three forms*) my notebook? 6. Herbert asks: are you working very

hard? 7. Conrad eats too much. 8. He goes into the kitchen, for he is getting hungry. 9. The teacher teaches without a book. 10. She needs flowers from the garden for the table. 11. What are you carrying from the dining room? 12. The teacher does not see well.

VI. Fragen

1. Wo wohnen Herbert und Conrad? 2. Warum wird Conrad jetzt hungrig? 3. Was fragt er Frau Löwenzahn? 4. Arbeitet er zu viel? 5. Wer sitzt in dem Sessel? 6. Was macht Herr Löwenzahn? 7. Was trägt er auf der Nase? 8. Versteht er Herberts Frage? 9. Wie wird das Wetter morgen? 10. Was holt Conrad aus dem Garten? 11. Wo braucht Frau Löwenzahn Blumen?

VII. Lesestück

Zwei deutsche Humoristen

In Amerika lachen die Leute über die Geschichten von Mark Twain. Auch die Deutschen haben Humoristen, z.B. Wilhelm Busch und Fritz Reuter. Wilhelm Busch schrieb seine Geschichten in Versen. Sehr berühmt wurde seine Geschichte von Max und Moritz. Max und Moritz, zwei Schuljungen, begehen viele böse Streiche. Sie töten die Hühner einer alten Frau. Sie ärgern einen alten Schneider und lassen ihn in einen Bach fallen. Schließlich bekommen sie die Strafe für ihre bösen Streiche. Max und Moritz wurden später auch in Amerika berühmt unter dem Namen Katzenjammerkids.   10

Fritz Reuter schrieb seine Geschichten in dem Dialekt der norddeutschen Ebene. Dieser norddeutsche Dialekt heißt „Plattdeutsch." Wir lernen in der Schule „Hochdeutsch." Alle Bücher und Zeitungen gebrauchen Hochdeutsch. Die Leute außerhalb der norddeutschen Ebene können Fritz Reuters Plattdeutsch kaum verstehen.

Hier erzählen wir eine Geschichte von Fritz Reuter, aber wir erzählen sie auf Hochdeutsch.

20 Fritz Reuter kommt an einem Sonntag in ein kleines norddeutsches Dorf und geht in die Kirche. Nach der Predigt geht er zu dem Pastor und sagt: „Es war eine schöne Predigt, aber ich habe zu Hause ein Buch, und in dem Buch steht diese Predigt, Wort für Wort."

Der Pastor wird rot und sagt: „Es war meine Predigt. Ich habe sie geschrieben. Könnten Sie mir das Buch schicken?"

„Ich schicke es Ihnen morgen", sagt Fritz Reuter.

Am nächsten Tag bekam der Pastor mit der Post ein Wörterbuch.

VIII. Wörterverzeichnis

ärgern (to) annoy
außerhalb outside of
der Bach the brook, creek
begehen (to) do, commit
bekommen; bekam (to) receive, get; received, got
berühmt famous
böse bad
die Bücher the books
die Deutschen the Germans
der Dialekt the dialect
dieser, diese this
das Dorf the village
die Ebene the plain
erzählen (to) tell
fallen (to) fall
flach level
gebrauchen (to) use
die Geschichte; die Geschichten the story; stories
geschrieben written
zu Hause at home
heißt is called
Hochdeutsch High German
die Hühner the chickens

der Humorist; Humoristen the humorist; humorists
ihn him
Ihnen to you
kaum hardly
die Kirche the church
klein small
können; könnten Sie? can; could you?
lassen (to) let
lernen (to) learn
die Leute the people
mir to me
am nächsten Tag the next day
der Name the name
norddeutsch North-German
mit der Post by mail
die Predigt the sermon
sagte said
schicken (to) send
schließlich finally
der Schneider the tailor
schön beautiful
schrieb wrote
die Schuljungen the schoolboys

seine his
der Sonntag Sunday
später later
steht is, stands
die Strafe the punishment
die Streiche (*plu.*) the tricks, pranks
töten (to) kill
unter under
in Versen in verse

verstehen (to) understand
viele many
von of, by
war was
das Wort the word
das Wörterbuch the dictionary
wurde, wurden got, became
z.B. *abbr. for* **zum Beispiel** e.g., for example

AUFGABE VIER

DER-WORDS AND EIN-WORDS
TWO-WAY PREPOSITIONS

I. Reading Selection

Frau Löwenzahn ruft aus ihrer Küche: „Euer Essen ist fertig."

Jetzt gehen wir in unser Eßzimmer. Wir sitzen an unserem Tisch und warten auf Frau Löwenzahn. Sie trägt die Schüsseln, und Herbert hilft. Dann falten wir alle die Hände und beten

> Danket dem Herrn, denn er ist freundlich
> und seine Güte währet ewiglich.[1]

Auf dem Tisch steht mein Teller. Neben meinem Teller liegen mein Löffel, meine Gabel und mein Messer.

10   Zuerst essen wir unsere Suppe. In der Mitte des Tisches steht ein Teller mit Brot. Das Brot ist sehr dunkel. Man nennt es Pumpernickel.

Frau Löwenzahn sagt: „Dieses Brot ist sehr gut. Es kommt vom Lande. Ich bekomme es jeden Dienstag von einer Bauernfrau."

Herr Löwenzahn fragt: „Sauerkraut?"

[1] Give thanks unto the Lord, for He is gracious, and His mercy endures forever.

38

„Bauernfrau", ruft Frau Löwenzahn laut.

Mein Freund Herbert fragt: „Was essen wir heute?"

Frau Löwenzahn antwortet: „Heute essen wir Schweinebraten, Kartoffeln, Sauerkraut und Tomatensalat." 20

Herr Löwenzahn schüttelt den Kopf und sagt zu seiner Frau:
„Ich verstehe wieder Sauerkraut."

Frau Löwenzahn sagt: „Richtig. Wir essen Sauerkraut. Die
Deutschen essen immer Sauerkraut, so denkt ihr in Amerika,
nicht wahr, Conrad?"

Ich sage: „Auch viele Amerikaner essen Sauerkraut."

Nach dem Essen trägt jeder seinen Teller und die Schüsseln
in die Küche, und dann gehen wir in unser Zimmer. Jetzt ist es
sehr ruhig im Haus, denn Herr Löwenzahn schläft. Jeden Nachmittag schläft er auf seinem Sofa. Sein Kopf liegt auf einem 30
Kissen. Auf diesem Kissen lesen wir ein Sprichwort:

> Ein gutes Gewissen
> Ist ein sanftes Ruhekissen.[2]

II. Vocabulary

*alle (*plural*) all
*der Amerikaner, die Amerikaner
 the American, Americans
*an at, to
 die Bauernfrau the peasant woman
 bekommen (to) get, receive
*beten (to) pray
 das Brot the bread
*dann then
*dein your
 denken (to) think
*die Deutschen the Germans
 der Dienstag Tuesday
*dieser this; *plu.* these
 dunkel dark
*das Essen the meal, food
*euer your
 falten (to) fold

fertig ready
 die Gabel the fork
*die Hand, die Hände the hand,
 hands
*helfen (i) (to) help (takes the
 dative in German)
*heute today
*hinter behind
*ihr her, their
*Ihr your
 im = in dem
*jeder each, every
*die Kartoffel, die Kartoffeln the
 potato, potatoes
*kein (*adj.*) no, not any
 das Kissen the pillow
*der Kopf the head
*das Land the country, land

[2] A good conscience is a soft pillow.

*liegen (to) lie, be situated
der Löffel the spoon
man (*indefinite pronoun*) one
*mancher many a
das Messer the knife
die Mitte the middle
*der Nachmittag the afternoon
*neben alongside of, by
nennen (to) call, name
der Pumpernickel pumpernickel
richtig correct, right
*rufen (to) call, shout
ruhig quiet, calm
das Sauerkraut sauerkraut
*schlafen (ä) (to) sleep
die Schüssel, die Schüsseln the
platter, dish
schütteln (to) shake
der Schweinebraten the pork
roast

*sein his, its
das Sofa the sofa
*solcher such (a)
das Sprichwort the proverb
*stehen (to) stand, be
die Suppe the soup
*der Teller the plate
der Tomatensalat the tomato salad
*über over, above
*unser our
*unter under, beneath
*viele many
*vier four
*vor in front of, before
*warten auf (*with acc.*) (to) wait
for
*welcher which, what
*wieder again
zuerst first, at first
*zwischen between

Idioms

*jeden Nachmittag every afternoon ꞈ
*vom Lande from the country

III. Grammar

A. der–Words in the Singular

We have already learned the declension of the definite article in the singular in all three genders (Lesson I, Section III,B). The following is a list of words which belong to the same group: **dieser, jeder, mancher, solcher, welcher**; and **jener** (*that*) which is very rarely used in present-day speech. All these words are called **der-words** because they are declined like the definite articles **der, die, das**:

	MASCULINE	FEMININE	NEUTER
Nom.	dieser Mann	diese Frau	dieses Buch
Gen.	dieses Mannes	dieser Frau	dieses Buches
Dat.	diesem Mann(e)	dieser Frau	diesem Buch(e)
Acc.	diesen Mann	diese Frau	dieses Buch

	MASCULINE	FEMININE	NEUTER
NOM.	jeder Schüler	jede Schule	jedes Haus
GEN.	jedes Schülers	jeder Schule	jedes Hauses
DAT.	jedem Schüler	jeder Schule	jedem Haus(e)
ACC.	jeden Schüler	jede Schule	jedes Haus

B. ein–Words in the Singular $poss$ $adj.$

In Section III,B of Lesson I we also learned the declension of
ein in the singular. The group of ein-words is as follows: ein,
kein, and the possessive adjectives (which are mein, dein, sein,
ihr, sein; unser, euer, ihr, and Ihr). They are declined exactly
like ein, except that unser and euer may drop an e before an
ending (e.g., unserem, unsrem, and unserm are equally correct;
eure and unsre are frequently used in place of the longer forms
euere and unsere).

Do not be confused because the stems of ihr, unser, euer, and
Ihr happen to end in –(e)r; they are still ein-words and therefore take no ending in the following three cases: a) *the nominative masculine*, b) *the nominative neuter*, c) *the accusative
neuter*.

The following endings in boldface type are added to all ein-
words:

	MASCULINE	FEMININE	NEUTER
NOM.	mein Kopf	meine Hand	mein Haus
GEN.	meines Kopfes	meiner Hand	meines Hauses
DAT.	meinem Kopf	meiner Hand	meinem Haus(e)
ACC.	meinen Kopf	meine Hand	mein Haus
NOM.	unser Lehrer	ihre Küche	Ihr Zimmer
GEN.	unseres Lehrers	ihrer Küche	Ihres Zimmers
DAT.	unserem Lehrer	ihrer Küche	Ihrem Zimmer
ACC.	unseren Lehrer	ihre Küche	Ihr Zimmer

Each possessive adjective corresponds to a personal pronoun;
it will be helpful to remember the following sequence:

Ich habe **mein** Buch	**wir** haben **unser** Buch
du hast **dein** Buch	**ihr** habt **euer** Buch
er hat **sein** Buch ⎫	**sie** haben **ihr** Buch
sie hat **ihr** Buch ⎬	(**Sie** haben **Ihr** Buch)
es hat **sein** Buch ⎭	

(Logically, of course, numerous combinations are possible: e.g., ich habe sein Buch, sie hat unser Buch, wir haben ihr Buch, etc.)

The possessive adjective **dein** corresponds only to the personal pronoun **du**; **euer** only to **ihr**; and **Ihr** only to **Sie.**

German prefers to use the definite article (instead of the possessive adjective, as in English) to refer to persons or items of one's private sphere, such as members of one's family, parts of one's body, or clothing. Examples: Er fragt **den** Vater. Herr Löwenzahn hat eine Brille auf **der** Nase. Er schüttelt **den** Kopf.

C. The "Negative Article" kein

The negative article **kein** corresponds to English *no* in statements like

> **kein Fenster ist offen**   *no window is open*
> **in diesem Haus ist keine Küche**   *in this house (there) is no kitchen.*

kein must also be used where English expresses negation by *not . . . a,* for example:

> **ich habe kein Buch**   *I do not have a book.*

Note that *not . . . a* can be replaced here by *not . . . any.* This can be used as a checking device for correct negation in German; for example:

> I do not have the pencil (cannot be replaced by *not . . . any*):
> **Ich habe den Bleistift nicht**
> I do not have a pencil (= I do not have any pencil):
> **Ich habe keinen Bleistift.**

D. Verb First Position

You learned in the preceding lesson that the verb is the second grammatical unit in a German declarative or negative sentence. The verb is placed first, however, in questions; e.g., **Lernen Sie Deutsch? Gehst du in den Garten? Wächst er zu schnell?**

If the question is introduced by an interrogative, it is placed in front of the question, so the verb now appears in the second position, e.g., Warum **lernen** Sie Deutsch? Wann **gehst** du in den Garten? Warum **wächst** er zu schnell?

The verb is also placed first in the imperative. (The imperative will be treated extensively in Lesson VIII.)

It should be noted that **ja** and **nein,** interjections, or calling someone by name, do not count in determining word order, e.g., Ja, ich **lerne** Deutsch. Nein, er **wächst** nicht zu schnell. O, was **mache** ich nun? Conrad, **gehst** du in den Garten? The verb is in the same position it would have occupied if we had not used the words **ja, nein, O,** or **Conrad.**

E. Two-Way Prepositions

There are some "two-way prepositions" which require either the accusative or the dative. They are: **an, auf, hinter, in, neben, über, unter, vor, zwischen.** They take the *accusative* to indicate *motion or direction toward or into* the place. They take the *dative* to indicate *position or location or action within* the place. Examples:

Herbert geht in **den** Garten. (*Acc.,* motion *into* the place)
Herbert ist in **dem** Garten. (*Dat.,* location *in* the place)
Herbert arbeitet in **dem** Garten. (*Dat.,* action *within* the place)

Note: Action within the place may very well be motion. Important is the difference between motion *toward* and motion *within:*

Herbert geht in **den** Garten *vs.*
Herbert geht in **dem** Garten herum (= *around*)

The above prepositions do not always indicate local relations: **über,** for example, can mean *concerning, about,* and then requires the accusative; **unter** can mean *among,* and then requires the dative. These idiomatic usages must be memorized.

Especially important are such verbal idioms as:

warten auf (*acc.*)	(to) wait for
wohnen bei (*dat.*)	(to) live with
schreiben an (*acc.*)	(to) write on *or* to
sprechen über (*acc.*)	(to) speak about
sitzen an (*dat.*)	(to) sit at
sitzen auf (*dat.*)	(to) sit on

You will be introduced to idioms of this type in practically every chapter.

IV. Grammatical Exercises

A. Supply the proper endings where needed:

1. D____ Buch dies____ Schüler____ liegt auf mein____ Tisch. 2. Jed____ Frau arbeitet in ihr____ Küche. 3. Welch____ Buch holt Conrad aus sein____ Zimmer? 4. Herr Löwenzahn geht nicht in sein____ Küche. 5. Jetzt trägt er sein____ Zeitung in unser____ Wohnzimmer. 6. Dann liest er eine halbe Stunde in sein____ Zeitung. 7. Jeden Nachmittag schläft er auf dies____ Sofa. 8. Er kommt in unser____ Eßzimmer ohne sein____ Teller. 9. Hinter unser____ Haus liegt ein____ Garten. 10. Wir gehen hinter euer____ Haus. 11. Ich gehe an dies____ Tisch. 12. Ich sitze an dies____ Tisch. 13. Neben unser____ Eßzimmer ist unser____ Wohnzimmer. 14. Über mein____ Tisch ist ein____ Lampe. 15. Steht ihr____ Freund vor Ihr____ Haus? 16. Zwischen mein____ Messer und mein____ Gabel steht mein____ Teller.

B. Practice the **ein-word** endings:

1. Mein____ Bleistift ist rot. 2. Die Farbe unser____ Hauses ist weiß. 3. Sein____ Buch liegt auf ihr____ Tisch. 4. Unser____ Lampe ist grün. 5. Die Farbe euer____ Lampe ist auch grün. 6. Liegt Ihr____ Buch neben Ihr____ Zeitung? 7. Ich sehe mein____ Lampe. 8. Dein____ Buch ist schwarz. 9. Die Farbe sein____ Buches ist nicht schwarz. 10. Ihr____ Heft liegt auf unser____ Buch. 11. Euer____ Buch ist groß.

C. Re-do some sentences of Exercise B using **dieser** in place of the **ein-words.**

D. Supply the proper endings, when needed, and translate into proper English:

1. D____ Schüler hat kein____ Bleistift und kein____ Buch. 2. Habt ihr kein____ Kreide? 3. Ich habe kein____ Tisch in mein____ Zimmer. 4. Sie spricht kein____ Deutsch. 5. Sie haben kein____ Garten hinter ihr____ Haus.

V. Translation Exercise

1. Is Mrs. Löwenzahn calling from her kitchen? 2. Do you go into your room? 3. I go to my table. 4. We are sitting at our table. 5. Now they are in their dining room. 6. This table stands in the middle (*in der Mitte*) of this room. 7. We have no easy chair in our room. 8. Our dining room is situated between our living room and our kitchen. 9. They have no garden in front of their house. 10. What does Mr. Löwenzahn say to his wife? 11. What does he do every afternoon after the meal? 12. He carries his plate into the kitchen. 13. Is Mrs. Löwenzahn in our kitchen? 14. The teacher doesn't have any chalk. 15. The pupil is helping his friend.

VI. Fragen

1. Was ruft Frau Löwenzahn? 2. Wohin (*where to*) gehen wir dann? 3. Was macht Herbert? 4. Was machen wir alle vor dem Essen? 5. Was steht auf dem Tisch? 6. Was liegt neben meinem Teller? 7. Was essen wir zuerst? 8. Wie ist das Brot? 9. Wie nennt man dieses Brot? 10. Warum spricht Frau Löwenzahn so laut? 11. Was essen wir heute? 12. Was denken viele Amerikaner? 13. Wohin gehen die Studenten nach dem Essen? 14. Was macht Herr Löwenzahn jeden Nachmittag? 15. Wo schläft er?

VII. Lesestück

Grenzen und Nachbarn

Deutschland liegt im Herzen Europas. Es hat nur im Norden und Süden natürliche Grenzen, im Norden die See und im Süden ein Gebirge. Der Nachbar im Norden ist Dänemark. Deutschland und Dänemark haben fast immer in Frieden gelebt; nur einmal, im Jahr 1864 (achtzehnhundertvierundsechzig), waren sie in einem Krieg. Im Norden von Deutschland sind die Nordsee, ein Teil des Atlantischen Ozeans, und die Ostsee. Nordsee und Ostsee sind durch den Nord-Ostsee-Kanal verbunden. Der Kanal beginnt bei der Stadt Kiel, so sprechen wir auf englisch 10 oft vom Kiel Kanal.

Die Nachbarn im Süden sind die Schweiz und Österreich. Beide Länder waren früher ein Teil des Deutschen Reiches. In Österreich und im größten Teil der Schweiz sprechen die Leute deutsch. Es gab nie einen Krieg zwischen Deutschland und der Schweiz, aber es gab im Jahre 1866 (achtzehnhundertsechsundsechzig) einen Krieg zwischen den norddeutschen Staaten und Österreich. Nach dem Krieg wurde Österreich ein selbständiger Staat.

Die Nachbarn Deutschlands im Westen sind die Niederlande, 20 Belgien, Luxemburg und Frankreich. Die Grenze im Westen hat oft gewechselt. Wir lesen in der deutschen Geschichte von vielen Kriegen wegen dieser Grenze. Frankreich und Deutschland haben viele Kriege geführt. Elsaß-Lothringen und das Saarland waren manchmal in deutschen, manchmal in französischen Händen, und die größte Stadt im Elsaß hieß manchmal Straßburg, manchmal Strasbourg.

Die Nachbarn im Osten sind Polen und die Tschecho-Slowakei. Hier war keine natürliche Grenze, kein Gebirge, kein Ozean. Die Grenze im Osten war noch problematischer als die 30 Grenze im Westen. Polen und Deutschland, Rußland und Deutschland haben Kriege geführt wegen des Landes an der

Oder und Weichsel. Noch in unserer Zeit ist das Problem der deutschen Grenze im Osten eins der größten Probleme der europäischen Politik.

VIII. Wörterverzeichnis

als than
der Atlantische Ozean the Atlantic Ocean
auf englisch in English
beginnen (to) start, begin
bei near
beide both
Belgien Belgium
Dänemark Denmark
das Deutsche Reich the German Empire
einmal once
Elsaß-Lothringen Alsace-Lorraine
Europa Europe
europäisch European
fast almost
Frankreich France
französisch French
der Friede the peace; **in Frieden** in peace
es gab there was
das Gebirge the mountain range
geführt lead, conducted; **Kriege geführt** waged wars
gelebt lived
die Geschichte history
gewechselt changed
die Grenze; Grenzen the boundary; boundaries
der größte the greatest
das Herz the heart
hieß was called
das Jahr the year
der Kanal the canal
der Krieg the war
die Leute the people
manchmal sometimes
der Nachbar the neighbor

natürlich natural
nie never
die Niederlande Holland
noch still
norddeutsch North-German
der Norden the north
die Nordsee the North Sea
nur only
die Oder the Oder (River)
oft often
der Osten the east
Österreich Austria
die Ostsee the Baltic Sea
Polen Poland
die Politik politics
das Problem; Probleme the problem; problems
problematischer more problematic
Rußland Russia
das Saarland the Saarland (*before 1957 the "Saar District"*)
die Schweiz Switzerland
die See the sea
selbständig independent
der Staat the state
die Stadt the city
der Süden the south
der Teil the part
die Tschecho-Slowakei Czechoslovakia
verbunden connected
war, waren was, were
wegen on account of
die Weichsel the Vistula (River)
weil because
der Westen the west
wurde became
die Zeit the time

PERSONAL PRONOUNS
WORD ORDER

I. Reading Selection

Herbert und ich haben eine Verabredung mit zwei Mädchen auf dem Tennisplatz. Der Tennisplatz liegt auf einem Berg über der Stadt. Neben unserm Tennisplatz ist ein Wald. *(daneben)*

Um drei Uhr sind wir am Tennisplatz. Die Mädchen sind noch nicht da. Wir warten auf sie. Mädchen kommen immer zu spät.

Hinter dem Tennisplatz steht ein Häuschen. Darin verkauft ein Mann Limonade, Coca Cola, Schokolade und Zigaretten. Wir gehen zu dem Häuschen und sprechen mit dem Mann.

10 „Eine Limonade für mich", sage ich zu ihm. Er gibt mir eine Flasche Limonade mit einem Glas. Ich nehme das Glas und trinke daraus. *(aus dem Glas)*

„Ein Coca Cola für mich", sagt Herbert. Der Mann gibt ihm die Flasche. Sie ist noch nicht offen.

Plötzlich sagt Herbert: „Ich habe kein Geld bei mir."

Sofort nimmt der Mann seine Flasche zurück und sagt: „Ohne Geld keine Flasche."

Ich nehme mein Geld aus der Tasche und sage: „Ich habe Geld. Ich zahle für ihn und mich."

48

Ich gebe dem Mann eine Mark. Damit zahle ich für uns 20
beide. Der Mann gibt mir zehn Pfennig zurück. Ich gebe sie ihm
zurück. „Das ist ein Trinkgeld für Sie", sage ich.

Jetzt sehen wir auf dem Weg zwischen dem Wald und dem
Tennisplatz die Mädchen. Wir treffen sie vor dem Tennisplatz.

Monika gibt Herbert und mir die Hand und sagt: „Es tut
mir leid, wir kommen zu spät, und wir haben keine Entschuldigung. Sie kennen meine Freundin Vera Sütterlin noch nicht.
Vera und ich spielen heute Tennis gegen Sie."

Sie sagt zu ihrer Freundin: „Vera, dies sind meine Freunde
Herbert Craig und Conrad Hofer aus den Vereinigten Staaten. 30
Sie leben ein Jahr in Deutschland und lernen Deutsch. Ich
hoffe, wir schlagen sie im Tennis."

Ich sage: „Sie hoffen zu viel. Unser Tennis ist nicht so
schlecht wie unser Deutsch."

II. Vocabulary

beide both
*der **Berg** the mountain
*da there, here
die **Entschuldigung** the excuse
*die **Flasche** the bottle
*die **Freundin** the friend (*female*),
   girl friend
*fünf five
*geben (i) (to) give
*das **Geld** the money
*das **Glas** the glass
das **Häuschen** the little house
*hoffen auf (*acc.*) (to) hope for
das **Jahr** the year
kennen (to) be acquainted with,
   know
*leben (to) live
die **Limonade** the lemonade
*das **Mädchen, die Mädchen** the
   girl, girls
*der **Mann** the man, husband

*die **Mark** the mark (*German coin*
   = *25 cents*)
*nehmen (**nimmst, nimmt**) (to)
   take
*der **Pfennig** the pfennig (*100
   pfennig make one mark*)
*plötzlich suddenly
schlagen (ä) (to) beat, hit, strike
schlecht bad
die **Schokolade** the chocolate
spielen (to) play
die **Stadt** the city
*die **Tasche** the pocket
*der **Tennisplatz** the tennis court
*treffen (i) (to) meet
*trinken (to) drink
das **Trinkgeld** the tip
*tun (to) do
die **Uhr** the clock
die **Verabredung** the appointment,
   date

*die Vereinigten Staaten the United States
*verkaufen (to) sell
*der Wald the forest, woods
*der Weg the road, way

*zahlen (to) pay
zehn ten
die Zigarette, die Zigaretten the cigarette, cigarettes
*zurück back

Idioms

*er gibt mir die Hand he shakes hands with me
*es tut mir leid I am sorry

*noch nicht not yet
*so . . . wie as . . . as
*um drei Uhr at three o'clock

III. Grammar

A. Declension of Personal Pronouns

The personal pronouns, like the nouns, appear in the four different cases, but the genitive of the pronouns is so rarely used that we will not bother with it. The dative and accusative, however, are used frequently.

SINGULAR

	1st	2nd	Masc.	Fem.	Neut.
			3rd		
NOM.	ich	du	er	sie	es
DAT.	mir	dir	ihm	ihr	(ihm)
ACC.	mich	dich	ihn	sie	es

PLURAL

	1st	2nd	3rd	(polite)
NOM.	wir	ihr	sie	(Sie)
DAT.	uns	euch	ihnen	(Ihnen)
ACC.	uns	euch	sie	(Sie)

Remember (and look up again Lesson III, Section III,B): the personal pronoun of the third person singular (in English *it* when referring to an inanimate object) must show in German the gender of the noun to which it refers. Examples: **Der Bleistift** ist grün = **er** ist grün; er nimmt **meinen Bleistift** = er nimmt **ihn**; **die Blume** ist rot = **sie** ist rot; ich sehe **die Blume** =

ich sehe **sie**; das **Buch** ist schwarz = **es** ist schwarz; sie liest **das Buch** = sie liest **es.**

B. da– Combinations

English makes very little use of such combinations as *therewith, therefrom, thereto, thereby, therein,* etc., as substitutes for *with it, from it, to it, by it, in it,* etc.

German uses such combinations frequently. *When a pronoun in conjunction with a preposition refers to a thing (but not a person), German is apt to use a* da– **combination** *instead of the personal pronoun.* Such possibilities include **dabei, damit, danach, davon, dazu; dadurch, dafür, dagegen; dahinter, daneben, davor, dazwischen.** If the preposition begins with a vowel, the form **dar–** precedes (cf. English *therein*): **darin, daran, darauf, daraus, darüber, darunter, darum.**

Translating from German to English, we can work with the equation: **German da + preposition = English preposition + it (or them).** From English to German, of course, the equation can simply be reversed.

C. Prepositional Contraction's

We have already seen that **in dem** can be contracted to **im,** or **von dem** to **vom.** Such contractions are frequent. The most common ones are: **am** (an dem), **ans** (an das), **aufs** (auf das), **im** (in dem), **ins** (in das), **beim** (bei dem), **vom** (von dem), **zum** (zu dem), and **zur** (zu der).

D. Word Order

1. No separation of subject and verb by adverb

In a simple declarative sentence, the adverb never occurs between subject and verb. *He suddenly takes the money:* **er nimmt plötzlich** das Geld. *He also sells his house:* **er verkauft auch** sein Haus.

2. Position of direct and indirect objects

In German, the indirect object precedes the direct object, unless the latter is a personal pronoun. Some examples: Ich gebe **dem Mann das Buch.** Ich gebe **ihm das Buch.** *But:* Ich gebe **es dem Mann.** Ich gebe **es ihm.**

3. Time before place

In German, time expressions precede place expressions. Note the following examples: Wir sind **um drei Uhr auf dem Tennis-platz.** Sie gehen **morgen in die Schule.** Er ißt **heute in der Küche.**

If an expression of manner (answering the question *how?*) joins expressions of time and place, it will occur between time and place. Examples: Er schläft heute **sehr gut** auf seinem Sofa. Sie schreibt jetzt **mit der Kreide** an die Tafel.

E. dies and das

In English and German, *this* = **dies** and *that* = **das** can be the subject of a sentence:

This	is	my book		*That*	is	my book
Dies	ist	mein Buch	*or*	**Das**	ist	mein Buch
(Subj.)		(Pred. Noun)				

Note that **dies** as the subject has *no ending.* Remember, however, that it has an ending when it is a part of a unit. Compare:

Dies	ist	mein Buch	*with*	**Dieses** Buch	ist interessant
(Subj.)		(Pred. Noun)		(Subj.)	

Even when the predicate noun is a plural, **dies** or **das** serves as the subject:

> *These are* the students from America
> **Dies sind** die Studenten aus Amerika

IV. Grammatical Exercises

A. Rearrange the German sentences in III, D 3 above, beginning each sentence with the expression of time.

B. Supply the proper pronouns where needed and translate into proper English:

1. Die Studenten sind aus den Vereinigten Staaten; _____ lernen Deutsch. 2. Das Zimmer ist groß; _____ hat drei Fenster. 3. Dieser Stuhl ist sehr alt; verkaufen Sie _____? 4. Die Amerikaner kommen jetzt aus dem Haus; sehen Sie _____? 5. Hier ist ein Brief von deinem Lehrer. Was schreibt er _____? 6. Der Tennisplatz ist sehr schön (*beautiful*); _____ liegt auf einem Berg. 7. Die Flasche kostet eine Mark; _____ ist offen. 8. Die Frau zahlt dem Mann eine Mark; dann gibt _____ _____ eine Flasche Coca Cola. 9. Vor dem Wald steht ein Häuschen. Siehst du _____? 10. Der Schüler trifft seinen Lehrer und gibt _____ die Hand.

C. Supply the proper form of the personal pronoun for the English:

1. Der Mann gibt *me* eine Mark. 2. Ist diese Flasche für *you* (*use three forms*)? 3. Dieses Mädchen gibt *you* (*use three forms*) die Hand. 4. Kommt ihr mit *us*? 5. Sie sehen *us*. 6. Herr Löwenzahn ruft *me*.

D. Replace the prepositional phrases with a **da– combination**:

1. Die Studenten sind in ihrem Zimmer. 2. Herbert sitzt auf seinem Stuhl. 3. Die Schule ist nicht gut für seine Gesundheit. 4. Ich schreibe die Aufgabe an die Tafel. 5. Ich schreibe mit einem Bleistift. 6. Er lebt von seinem Geld. 7. Vor dem Haus ist kein Garten. 8. Mein Buch liegt neben der Lampe. 9. Was sagen Sie zu diesem Buch? 10. Ein Häuschen liegt hinter dem Tennisplatz. 11. Nach der Schule essen wir. 12. Der Tennisplatz liegt über der Stadt. 13. Die Stadt liegt unter dem Berg.

E. Replace all nouns in boldface with personal pronouns:

1. Ich schreibe **meiner Mutter** einen Brief. 2. Wir wohnen bei **einer deutschen Familie**. 3. Wir warten auf **Frau Löwenzahn**. 4. Sie bekommt **das Brot** von **einer Bauernfrau**. 5. Was sagt **Herr Löwenzahn** zu seiner Frau? 6. **Die Studenten** haben eine Verabredung mit **zwei Mädchen**. 7. **Die Flasche Coca Cola** ist

für **meinen Freund.** 8. Wir spielen gegen **die Mädchen.** 9.
Herbert steht neben **dem Mädchen.** 10. **Herbert und Conrad**
stehen zwischen **den beiden Mädchen.**

V. Translation Exercise

1. I am waiting for money; I am waiting for it. 2. I am
waiting for my friend; I am waiting for him. 3. The man in the
house takes my mark and gives me five pfennig back. 4. We hope
they do not come too late. 5. Is this your book? 6. He doesn't
pay for the bottle, for he doesn't have any money. 7. Who is running into the house? Is that your friend? 8. These are Americans;
they live with my family. 9. My friend (*fem.*) writes me a letter,
and I write her also one (*einen*). 10. The girls shake hands with
him. 11. Every afternoon at four o'clock he waits on this road
for his girl friend. 12. This is his house; his garden is behind it.

VI. Fragen

1. Wo treffen die Studenten die Mädchen? 2. Wo liegt der
Tennisplatz? 3. Was liegt daneben? 4. Was steht dahinter? 5.
Was bekomme ich von dem Mann? 6. Was kostet sie? 7. Was
gebe ich dem Mann? 8. Wer kommt mit Monika zum Tennisplatz? 9. Warum kommen die Mädchen zu spät? 10. Wie ist
das Tennis der Studenten aus Amerika?

VII. Lesestück

Hauptstädte

Jedes Land hat eine Hauptstadt. Die Hauptstadt der Vereinigten Staaten ist Washington. Auch die 50 (fünfzig) amerikanischen Staaten haben Hauptstädte. Oft ist es die größte Stadt
im Staat, wie Boston in Massachusetts oder Richmond in Virginia,
oft ist es eine kleine Stadt, wie Annapolis in Maryland oder
Dover in Delaware.

Courtesy of German Tourist Information Office, Chicago

Das neue Rathaus in Stuttgart

Deutschland hatte viele Jahrhunderte keine Hauptstadt. Der
König hatte Burgen. Er wohnte zwei oder drei Monate auf einer
Burg, dann auf einer anderen und so weiter. In Frankfurt wurden
10 die deutschen Könige gewählt, in Aachen wurden sie gekrönt,
aber weder Frankfurt noch Aachen waren Hauptstädte wie Paris
in Frankreich oder London in England. Die deutschen Staaten
hatten Hauptstädte: München war die Hauptstadt von Bayern,
Stuttgart die Hauptstadt von Württemberg, Dresden die Hauptstadt von Sachsen. Im Jahre 1871 (achtzehnhunderteinundsiebzig) hatte das Deutsche Reich zum ersten Mal eine Hauptstadt:
Berlin. Berlin war die deutsche Hauptstadt von 1871 bis zum
Ende des zweiten Weltkriegs.

Heute ist die Hauptstadt von Westdeutschland die Stadt Bonn
20 am Rhein. Früher war es eine kleine Universitätsstadt, aber seit
1949 (neunzehnhundertneunundvierzig) wächst die Stadt sehr
schnell. Bonn ist der Sitz des Bundespräsidenten, des Bundes-
kanzlers und des Bundestags. Auf dem Haus des Bundestags sieht
man die schwarz-rot-goldene Fahne der Bundesrepublik.

Auch jedes deutsche Land hat eine Hauptstadt. Es ist nicht
immer die größte Stadt des Landes. Frankfurt ist die größte
Stadt im Lande Hessen, aber die Hauptstadt ist Wiesbaden.
Sehr oft ist die größte Stadt auch die Hauptstadt: München in
Bayern, Hannover in Niedersachsen, Kiel in Schleswig-Holstein.
30 Die Hauptstadt von Nordrhein-Westfalen ist Düsseldorf. „Dorf"
ist das deutsche Wort für *village,* aber Düsseldorf ist kein Dorf,
es ist eine große Stadt mit mehr als 700 000 (siebenhundert-
tausend) Einwohnern.

VIII. Wörterverzeichnis

eine andere another
Bayern Bavaria
der Bundeskanzler the Federal
Chancellor
der Bundespräsident the Federal
President

die Bundesrepublik the Federal
Republic
der Bundestag the Federal Legislature
die Burg; Burgen the castle; castles
das Dorf the village

der **Einwohner** the inhabitant
bis zum Ende until the end
die **Fahne** the flag
Frankreich France
früher formerly, earlier
gekrönt crowned
gewählt chosen, elected
der **größte** the largest
hatte, hatten had
die **Hauptstadt; Hauptstädte** the capital; capitals
Hessen Hesse
im Jahre in the year
das **Jahrhundert** the century
klein little
der **König** the king
das **Mal** time; **zum ersten Mal** for the first time
mehr als more than
der **Monat** the month
München Munich
Niedersachsen Lower Saxony

Nordrhein-Westfalen North Rhine-Westphalia
oft often
am Rhein on the Rhine
Sachsen Saxony
der **Sitz** the seat
der **Staat** the state
die **Stadt** the city
und so weiter; usw. and so on; etc.
die **Universitätsstadt** the university city
viele Jahrhunderte for many centuries
von of; from
war, waren was, were
weder . . . noch neither . . . nor
der **Weltkrieg** the World War
wohnte lived
das **Wort** the word
wurden were
Württemberg Wurttemberg
der **zweite** the second

AUFGABE SECHS

PLURALS

I. Reading Selection

Frau Löwenzahn sagt: „Ich gehe heute in die Stadt. Conrad, kommst du mit mir?"

Ich antworte: „Gern. Wohin gehen Sie in der Stadt?"

Sie sagt: „Ich gehe in ein Warenhaus. Ich kaufe ein Geschenk für den Geburtstag meines Mannes."

Wir fahren mit der Straßenbahn in die Stadt. Auf den Straßen sind viele Leute, Straßenbahnen und Autos.

„Wo ist das Warenhaus?" frage ich.

„Es liegt hinter dem Marktplatz", antwortet Frau Löwenzahn,
10 „zwischen der Kirche und dem Park."

Auf den Tischen im Warenhaus liegen viele Dinge. Hier auf diesem Tisch liegen Kleider für Frauen. Zwei Frauen vor dem Tisch haben einen Streit.

„Dies ist mein Kleid", sagt die eine.

„Nein, es ist mein Kleid", sagt die andere. „Ich kaufe es."

Ein Verkäufer kommt und sagt: „Keinen Streit, meine Damen. Wir haben zwei Kleider in diesen Farben und mit diesem Kragen."

Beide Frauen werden still.

20 „Was sagen Sie?" ruft die eine, „zwei Kleider in diesen

58

Farben und mit diesem Kragen? Dann kaufe ich dieses Kleid nicht."

„Ich auch nicht", sagt die andere und geht schnell weg.

„Auf welchem Stock haben Sie Schreibtischlampen?" fragt Frau Löwenzahn eine Verkäuferin.

„In der Abteilung für Möbel", antwortet die Verkäuferin. „Stock Nummer sechs."

In der Abteilung für Möbel stehen viele Tische, Schreibtische, Stühle, Sessel und Lampen. An den Wänden stehen Bücherbretter ohne Bücher. 30

Wir kaufen eine Schreibtischlampe für Herrn Löwenzahn. Sie ist gelb, sehr schön und kostet vierzig Mark zwanzig.

Ich kaufe zwei Hemden für mich und eine Krawatte für Herrn Löwenzahn. Dann fahren wir mit der Straßenbahn zurück.

II. Vocabulary

die **Abteilung** the department
*das **Auto** the auto, car
das **Bücherbrett** the bookshelf, bookcase
*die **Dame** the lady
*das **Ding** the thing
die **eine, die andere** the one, the other
fahren (ä) mit (to) ride, travel, go by or with
*der **Geburtstag** the birthday
*gelb yellow
gern(e) gladly, I'd like to
*das **Geschenk** the present
*das **Hemd** the shirt
*kaufen (to) buy
*die **Kirche** the church
*das **Kleid** the dress
*kosten (to) cost
der **Kragen** the collar
die **Krawatte** the necktie

*die **Lampe** the lamp
*die **Leute** (*plu.*) people
*manche some (*plu.*)
der **Marktplatz** the market place
die **Möbel** the furniture
*die **Nummer** the number
*der **Park** the park
*schnell quick, fast
schön beautiful, nice
der **Schreibtisch** the desk
die **Schreibtischlampe** the desk lamp
*sechs six
*die **Stadt** the city
*still still, quiet
der **Stock**, *plu.:* die **Stockwerke** the floor, story
*die **Straße** the street
*die **Straßenbahn** the trolley, street car
der **Streit** the quarrel

*der Verkäufer the salesman, seller, vendor
*die Verkäuferin the salesgirl, seller, vendor
vierzig forty

das Warenhaus the department store
*weg away, off
*wohin where (to)
*zwanzig twenty

Idioms

*ich auch nicht nor I either, neither I
*in der Stadt in the city, in town, downtown
*in die Stadt to the city, to town, downtown
*in die Schule to school; in die Kirche to church
*mit der Straßenbahn by streetcar; *mit dem Auto by car (means of transportation: by = mit)
*was für ein (plu. was für) what kind of

III. Grammar

A. Nominative Plurals of Nouns

In English, the plural of nouns ends in –s. But there are some exceptions, such as *children, men, feet, geese*, etc., which are residual forms of an ancient system. These English exceptions are just the rule in German.

The plural markers of German nouns are endings and/or umlaut of the stem vowel. There are four categories of plural forms in German:

1) no ending, usually umlaut;
2) ending –e, usually umlaut;
3) ending –er, always umlaut:
4) ending –(e)n, never umlaut.

Remember that umlaut means a change from **a** to **ä**, **o** to **ö**, **u** to **ü**, and **au** to **äu**.

Group 1: no ending, usually umlaut

This group comprises masculine and neuter nouns whose stems end in –el, –en, –er, all diminutives (they can be identified by the endings –chen, –lein), and two isolated feminine nouns **Mutter** and **Tochter** (*mother, daughter*).

Our active vocabulary assigned up to this chapter contains the following nouns belonging to group 1:

MASCULINE		NEUTER		
der Sessel	: die Sessel	das Fenster	:	die Fenster
der Garten	: die Gärten	das Mädchen	:	die Mädchen
der Amerikaner	: die Amerikaner	das Zimmer	:	die Zimmer
der Lehrer	: die Lehrer			
der Schüler	: die Schüler			
der Teller	: die Teller			
der Verkäufer	: die Verkäufer			

Group 2: ending –e, usually umlaut

The majority of the masculine nouns belong to this group. There are relatively few feminine and neuter nouns in group 2. Our active vocabulary up to this lesson contains the following:

MASCULINE

der Berg	:	die Berge
der Bleistift	:	die Bleistifte
der Brief	:	die Briefe
der Freund	:	die Freunde
der Geburtstag	:	die Geburtstage
der Kopf	:	die Köpfe
der Nachmittag	:	die Nachmittage
der Park	:	die Parke
der Satz	:	die Sätze
der Schuh	:	die Schuhe
der Stuhl	:	die Stühle
der Tisch	:	die Tische
der Weg	:	die Wege

FEMININE		NEUTER		
die Hand	: die Hände	das Ding	:	die Dinge
die Luft	: die Lüfte	das Geschenk	:	die Geschenke
die Stadt	: die Städte	das Haar	:	die Haare
die Wand	: die Wände	das Heft	:	die Hefte

Group 3: ending –er, always umlaut

The majority of the neuter nouns belongs to this group. There are only a very few masculine nouns and no feminine nouns in group 3.

Our active vocabulary up to this lesson contains the following:

MASCULINE			NEUTER		
der Mann	:	die Männer	das Buch	:	die Bücher
der Wald	:	die Wälder	das Glas	:	die Gläser
			das Haus	:	die Häuser
			das Kleid	:	die Kleider
			das Land	:	die Länder

Group 4: ending –(e)n, never umlaut

This group comprises nouns whose stems end in –e. With the exception of a very few masculines, they are all feminine. Our active vocabulary up to this lesson contains:

die Aufgabe	:	die Aufgaben	die Küche	:	die Küchen
die Blume	:	die Blumen	die Lampe	:	die Lampen
die Dame	:	die Damen	die Schule	:	die Schulen
die Familie	:	die Familien	die Straße	:	die Straßen
die Farbe	:	die Farben	die Stunde	:	die Stunden
die Flasche	:	die Flaschen	die Tasche	:	die Taschen
die Kirche	:	die Kirchen			

To the same group belong the feminine nouns with the suffix –in. The suffix must be written –inn– before the plural ending –en.

die Freundin	:	die Freundinnen
die Verkäuferin	:	die Verkäuferinnen
die Lehrerin	:	die Lehrerinnen
die Schülerin	:	die Schülerinnen

This group also comprises feminine nouns whose stem ends in –el or –er. Their plural ending is simply –n.

die Kartoffel	:	die Kartoffeln
die Tafel	:	die Tafeln
die Nummer	:	die Nummern

Other feminine nouns in this group (again taken from our active vocabulary) are:

die Arbeit	:	die Arbeiten
die Frau	:	die Frauen
die Straßenbahn	:	die Straßenbahnen
die Zeitung	:	die Zeitungen

Masculine nouns of foreign origin (stem ending in **–ent** or **–or**) also belong to group 4:

der Studént	:	die Studénten
der Proféssor	:	die Professóren
der Dóktor	:	die Doktóren
der Aútor	:	die Autóren

We have in our active vocabulary only two neuters of group 4, **das Bett** and **das Hemd**; their plurals are **die Betten** and **die Hemden**. One frequently used neuter is very irregular in the singular: Nom. **das Herz** (*the heart*), Gen. **des Herzens**, Dat. **dem Herzen**, Acc. **das Herz**; its plural is **die Herzen**.

Many masculines of this group, especially those ending in **–e**, or accented on the last syllable, form all cases other than the nominative by adding **–n** or **–en**; for example, **der Student** is, in every case other than the nominative singular, **Studenten**; **der Knabe** (*boy*) other than in the nominative singular is always **Knaben**. To call attention to nouns having this characteristic, in future vocabularies the genitive singular form will be given in addition to the nominative case.

Another irregular noun belonging to group 4 is **der Herr** (*the gentleman*): Nom. **der Herr**, Gen. **des Herrn**, Dat. **dem Herrn**, Acc. **den Herrn**; all plural forms are **Herren**.

B. Plural Formations of Compound Nouns

In a noun compound in German, the gender and the plural form is determined by the last element of the compound. Therefore it is **das** Schul**buch**; *plural* **die** Schul**bücher**. The gender of the first element (feminine) and its plural form (**–n**) do not affect the gender and plural form of the compound.

C. Plural Declension of Nouns, der–Words, and ein–Words

As in the singular, there are four cases in the plural, but there is no differentiation of genders. Below we use the plural of **der—die—das** with one noun, of **dieser** with another, and of **mein** with a third to show the proper endings for the articles, and the **der-** and **ein-**words. (As a sample of the **ein-**words we take the possessive adjective **mein,** *since the indefinite article has, as in English, no plural.* The plural of **ein Buch** [*a book*] is **Bücher** [*books*].)

PLURAL

Nom.	die Fenster	diese Tische	meine Taschen
Gen.	der Fenster	dieser Tische	meiner Taschen
Dat.	den Fenstern	diesen Tischen	meinen Taschen
Acc.	die Fenster	diese Tische	meine Taschen

Notice and remember: *the dative plural of nearly every German noun ends in* **–n.** If the nominative plural does not already show **–n,** it has to be added in the dative.

D. Infrequent –s Plurals

A very few nouns of foreign origin form **–s** plurals, e.g., **die Autos, die Radios, die Restaurants.** Family names likewise form **–s** plurals: **die Löwenzahns, die Meyers,** etc. Such nouns do not add **–n** to the dative plural. Remember: Do not mistake the **–s** of the masculine and neuter genitive singular for a plural sign!

E. Some Idiomatic Irregularities

With expressions of weight and measure, the singular is used where logically the plural would be expected. Thus, **DM 5,20** is **fünf Mark zwanzig,** or **DM 0,20** is **zwanzig Pfennig.** (German regularly uses a comma as a decimal mark.) This corresponds to the English "he is six *foot* two."

IV. Grammatical Exercises

A. Put the following sentences into the plural:

1. Der Student schreibt seine Aufgabe. 2. In dem Zimmer ist ein Tisch, ein Sessel und eine Lampe. 3. Ich schlafe in diesem

Bett. 4. Du siehst durch das Fenster. 5. Der Amerikaner ist jetzt in Deutschland und wohnt bei dieser Familie. 6. Ihre Freundin ist eine Verkäuferin in einem Warenhaus. 7. Der Stuhl ist nicht grün. 8. Mein Schuh ist auch nicht grün. 9. Ich sitze an einem Tisch und schreibe die Aufgabe in mein Heft. 10. Ich schreibe sie auch in mein Buch und an die Tafel. 11. Du schreibst den Brief mit deinem Bleistift. 12. Die Dame trägt eine Blume. 13. Der Freund gibt mir dieses Geschenk. 14. Trinkt das Mädchen Coca Cola aus der Flasche oder aus einem Glas? 15. In diesem Park ist ein Weg.

B. Put the following sentences into the singular:

1. Die Freundinnen tragen die Kleider in ihre Häuser. 2. Die Blumen wachsen in den Wäldern. 3. Die Frauen haben Stühle in ihren Küchen. 4. Sie haben keine Teller für die Kartoffeln. 5. Sprechen die Mädchen mit den Verkäuferinnen? 6. Die Männer lesen die Zeitungen. 7. Ihr fahrt mit zwei Autos. 8. Sie geben uns Geschenke zu unsern Geburtstagen. 9. Die Farbe der Wände ist gelb. 10. Treffen die Studenten die Mädchen vor den Schulen oder auf den Straßen?

V. Translation Exercise

1. Mr. Löwenzahn speaks about (*über*) his autos. 2. They sleep every afternoon in their beds. 3. The friends are going downtown now. 4. The ladies ride on the street cars. 5. The salesladies show us clothes. 6. What kind of man is Mr. Löwenzahn? 7. They cost five marks twenty. 8. The students go to school with their books. 9. Their pencils only cost twenty pfennigs. 10. They have tables, chairs, and easy chairs in their rooms. 11. Some people in the cities of Germany go to the forests every afternoon. 12. How many rooms are in your school? 13. Mrs. Löwenzahn is buying presents for her husband's birthday. 14. Many churches are in these cities. 15. Where is he going (to)? 16. Now he is going away. 17. He is travelling to Berlin by car.

18. What kind of easy chair does she have for Mr. Löwenzahn?
19. What kind of lamp do you have in your room? 20. What kind
of books does he read?

VI. Fragen

1. Wohin geht Frau Löwenzahn heute? 2. Wer geht mit ihr?
3. Wie fahren sie in die Stadt? 4. Wo liegt das Warenhaus?
5. Wer ist auf den Straßen? 6. Warum geht Frau Löwenzahn in
das Warenhaus? 7. Was liegt auf den Tischen des Warenhauses?
8. Was verkaufen die Verkäufer in einem Warenhaus? 9. Was für
Möbel stehen in der Abteilung? 10. Was kaufen sie für Herrn
Löwenzahn? 11. Wie ist diese Lampe? 12. Was kostet sie? 13.
Was kauft Conrad? 14. Was für eine Krawatte ist das? 15. Wie
fahren Frau Löwenzahn und Conrad zurück?

VII. Lesestück

Berlin

Berlin war nicht nur viele Jahre die deutsche Hauptstadt, es
war auch seit Jahrhunderten die Hauptstadt von Preußen. In
der Mitte des 17. (siebzehnten) Jahrhunderts war Berlin eine
kleine Stadt mit nur 8 000 (achttausend) Menschen. Berlin ist
groß geworden als Hauptstadt von Preußen. Die Könige von
Preußen, die Hohenzollern, hatten hier ihr Schloß. Der berühm-
teste der Hohenzollernkönige, Friedrich der Große, hatte Berlin
nicht gern. Er baute ein neues Schloß, das Schloß Sanssouci,
außerhalb von Berlin.

10   Im 18. (achtzehnten) und 19. (neunzehnten) Jahrhundert
wuchs die Stadt mehr und mehr, aber erst nach der Gründung
des Deutschen Reiches wurde sie eine Millionenstadt. Seit 1930
(neunzehnhundertdreißig) leben zwischen drei und vier Millionen Menschen in Berlin. Es war nicht nur die Hauptstadt
des Deutschen Reiches und die Hauptstadt von Preußen, es war

Courtesy of German Information Center, New York

Berlin: Das Brandenburger Tor und die Mauer

auch eine der größten Industrie- und Handelsstädte des Landes.
Der Fluß, der durch Berlin fließt, die Spree, ist nur sehr klein,
aber durch Kanäle ist die Stadt mit zwei großen Flüssen (Elbe
und Oder) und mit den Industriestädten im Westen verbunden.
20   In den 50 (fünfzig) Jahren vor dem zweiten Weltkrieg wurde
Berlin berühmt durch seine kulturellen Institutionen, seine
Theater, Konzerte, Museen und eine große Universität. In der
Mitte der Stadt läuft von Osten nach Westen eine breite Straße.
Sie heißt „Unter den Linden." An einem Ende der Straße ist
die Universität, die Oper und das Rathaus, am anderen Ende das
berühmte Brandenburger Tor, das Reichstagsgebäude und ein
großer Park.

Nach dem Weltkrieg wurde Berlin von amerikanischen,
britischen, französischen und russischen Soldaten besetzt. Bald
30 war die Stadt in einen Westsektor und einen Ostsektor geteilt.
Dadurch wurde das Leben der Berliner sehr schwierig. Aber
die Berliner sind in Deutschland berühmt durch ihren Witz
und Humor. Sie haben gelernt, das Leben leicht zu nehmen.

VIII. Wörterverzeichnis

amerikanisch American
das andere the other
außerhalb von outside of
baute built
die Berliner the Berliners
berühmt; berühmtest famous; most
   famous
besetzt occupied
das Brandenburger Tor the Brandenburg Gate
breit broad
britisch British
der; in der which; in which
das Deutsche Reich the German
   Empire
das Ende the end
erst only, not until
fließen (to) flow

der Fluß; Flüsse the river; rivers
französisch French
Friedrich der Große Frederick the
   Great
gelernt learned
gern haben (to) like
geteilt divided
ist geworden has become
der größte the largest
die Gründung, –en the founding
die Handelsstadt, ‥e the commercial city
hatte, hatten had
die Hauptstadt, ‥e the capital
es heißt it is called
der Humor the humor
die Industriestadt, ‥e the industrial city

das Jahrhundert, –e the century
seit Jahrhunderten for centuries
der Kanal, ⁻e the canal
klein small
der König, –e the king
kulturell cultural
das Leben the life
leicht nehmen (to) take easy
mehr more
die Menschen the people
die Million, –en the million
die Millionenstadt, ⁻e the city with a million inhabitants
das Museum; Museen the museum
neu new
nur only
der Osten the east
der Ostsektor the East Sector
Preußen Prussia
das Rathaus, ⁻er the city hall

das Reichstagsgebäude the Parliament Building
russisch Russian
das Schloß, Schlösser the castle
schwierig difficult
der Soldat, –en the soldier
die Universität, –en the university
Unter den Linden Under the Lindens
verbunden connected
viele Jahre for many years
von by, of
war, waren was, were
der Weltkrieg the World War
der Westen the west
der Westsektor the West Sector
der Witz the wit
es wuchs it grew
es wurde it became
der zweite the second

PAST TENSE CONJUGATION WEAK AND STRONG VERBS

I. Reading Selection

werden

haben

Gestern hatte Herr Löwenzahn Geburtstag. Er wurde sechzig Jahre alt. Wir machten ihm einen Geburtstagstisch mit vielen Blumen und Geschenken. In der Mitte des Tisches stand die Lampe von Frau Löwenzahn. Darunter lagen Geschenke, eine Krawatte von mir, eine Pfeife von Herbert, eine Armbanduhr von den Löwenzahnkindern, ein paar Flaschen Wein und viele Zigarren. Nach dem Essen kamen ein paar Freunde von Herrn Löwenzahn. Es war an diesem Abend sehr warm im Haus. So blieben wir nicht im Haus, sondern gingen auf den Balkon und
10 in den Garten. Frau Löwenzahn hatte viel Arbeit. Herbert und ich halfen ihr. Wir trugen Stühle und zwei Tische auf den Balkon und stellten viele Gläser auf die Tische. Herr Löwenzahn ging mit seinen Gästen durch den Garten und zeigte ihnen seine Blumen. Er rief aus dem Garten: „Lisette, ist die Erdbeerbowle fertig?" und Frau Löwenzahn antwortete: „Ja, Heinrich, sie ist fertig und wartet auf dich." Nun hatte Herr Löwenzahn plötzlich kein Interesse mehr für Blumen, er nahm zwei seiner Freunde beim Arm und ging zurück zum Haus.

Herr Löwenzahn feierte seinen Geburtstag mit einer Erdbeer-

bowle. Ein paar Stunden vor der Ankunft der Gäste schnitt er 20
zwei Pfund Erdbeeren mit Zucker in eine Glasschüssel und goß
fünf Flaschen Wein darüber. Nach zwei oder drei Stunden war
die Erdbeerbowle fertig. Sie schmeckte sehr gut und machte uns
sehr lustig. Herr Löwenzahn stand auf dem Balkon, hatte ein
Glas in der Hand, den Lampenschirm auf dem Kopf und sang:
„Oh, wie ist es am Rhein so schön!"

Frau Löwenzahn sagte leise etwas zu ihrer Freundin, und
Herr Löwenzahn rief: „Sie fragt: wird dieser Mann heute sechzig
oder sechzehn Jahre alt?"

Frau Löwenzahn sagte: „Heinrich, ich denke, du hörst 30
nicht gut."

Er kam zu ihr, gab ihr einen Kuß und sagte: „Lisette, nach
einer Flasche Wein höre ich wieder gut."

Wir saßen bis spät in der Nacht auf dem Balkon, und Herr
Löwenzahn sang noch oft
„Oh, wie ist es am Rhein so schön!"

II. Vocabulary

NOTE: Plurals of nouns will be indicated thus henceforth: – for
no ending; ⸚ for no ending, but with umlaut; –e for an –e ending; ⸚e
for an –e ending with an umlaut; etc.

If the genitive singular of a masculine noun adds –n or –en, that
will be indicated between the singular and plural forms.

*der Abend, –e the evening
die Ankunft, ⸚e the arrival
*der Arm, –e the arm
die Armbanduhr, –en the wrist
  watch
der Balkon, –e the balcony
*bei by
*bis until
*bleiben (to) remain
die Erdbeerbowle, –n the strawberry punch
die Erdbeere, –n the strawberry
*etwas something, some (*sing.*),
  a small amount of

feiern (to) celebrate
*fertig ready
*der Gast, ⸚e the guest
der Geburtstagstisch, –e the birthday table
*gestern yesterday
*gießen (to) pour
die Glasschüssel, –n the glass bowl
*das Interesse, –n the interest
*das Jahr, –e the year
*das Kind, –er the child
der Kuß, Küsse the kiss
der Lampenschirm, –e the lamp
  shade

*leise soft, quiet
*lustig merry, cheerful
*die Mitte the middle
*die Nacht, ⁓e the night
 oder or
 die Pfeife, –n the pipe
 das Pfund the pound
 der Rhein the Rhine (River)
*schmecken (to) taste (good)
*schneiden (to) cut

*schön beautiful, nice
 sechzehn sixteen
 sechzig sixty
*sieben seven
*singen (to) sing
*sondern but (on the contrary)
*stellen (to) place, put
*der Wein, –e the wine
*die Zigarre, –n the cigar
 der Zucker the sugar

Idioms

*ein paar a couple of, a few
*kein . . . mehr no . . . any more, no . . . any longer, no more, not
. . . any more

III. Grammar

The Past Tense

Like English, German has two types of verbs, which are distinguished by the formation of their past tense. In English they are called regular and irregular verbs. In German, the correponding groups are called *weak,* or *suffix verbs* and *strong,* or *vowel-changing* verbs.

As in the present tense (and in all other tenses), the German past tense has neither a progressive nor an emphatic form. So there is in German no difference between: *I asked, I was asking, I did ask.* (See Lesson III, Section III,A.)

A. The Past Tense of Weak (or Suffix) Verbs

In English, the past tense of this group of verbs is formed by adding –ed (or sometimes –t) to the stem. Thus the past tense of *ask* is *asked.* In German, the suffix –te is added to the stem of such verbs. So the past tense of frag-en is frag-te. This is the basic form for the conjugation in the past tense, and it is called *the second principal part* of the verb (the first principal part being the infinitive form). Below is given the complete conjugation of a weak verb in the past tense. Notice that in the first and third persons singular no ending is added to the second principal part.

1. ich frag-te   ich wart-e-te
2. du frag-test   du wart-e-test

3. er / sie / es } frag-te   er / sie / es } wart-e-te

1. wir frag-ten   wir wart-e-ten
2. ihr frag-tet   ihr wart-e-tet

3. sie (Sie) } frag-ten   sie (Sie) } wart-e-ten

If the stem of a verb ends in a –t or –d, an –e– is inserted between the stem and the suffix –te of the second principal part (see above the forms of **warten**). The verbs **antwort-en, arbeit-en,** and **kost-en,** which you have already learned, belong to this group.

The weak verb **haben** is slightly irregular. Its second principal part is **hat-te** (**du hattest, er hatte,** etc.).

B. The Past Tense of Strong (or Vowel-Changing) Verbs

As in English, to form the past tense of verbs of this group, no ending is added to the stem, but the vowel of the stem itself is changed. Thus, in English, the past tense of *sing* is *sang*. In German, we have the same verb, **singen**; its past tense is **sang.** In English, as in German, the second principal part must be memorized, because there is no way to know how the stem vowel will change. Given below is the complete conjugation of a strong verb in the past tense. Notice: the personal endings of the past tense are identical for both the weak and the strong verbs. Again the first and third persons singular do not have an ending.

1. ich sang   1. wir sangen
2. du sangst   2. ihr sangt

3. er / sie / es } sang   3. sie (Sie) } sangen

The past tense forms of the irregular verb **sein** are:

1. ich war   1. wir waren
2. du warst   2. ihr wart
3. er
   sie } war   3. sie
   es   (Sie) } waren

Werden is slightly irregular. Its past tense forms are:

1. ich wurde   1. wir wurden
2. du wurdest   2. ihr wurdet
3. er
   sie } wurde   3. sie
   es   (Sie) } wurden

    In following vocabularies, the past tense of all strong verbs will be listed for memorization. If, for instance, you find the entry **lesen (ie), las,** you will know: a) it is a strong, or vowel-changing, verb; b) the stem vowel changes from **e** to **a** for the past tense; c) in the second and third persons singular of the present tense, the **e** of the infinitive changes to **ie.** If the principal parts of a verb are not listed in the vocabulary, it is a weak verb.

    So far, you have learned the following strong (or vowel-changing) verbs:

INFINITIVE		PAST TENSE	
bleiben	*remain*	**blieb**	*remained*
essen (i)	*eat*	**aß**	*ate*
fahren (ä)	*ride, travel*	**fuhr**	*rode, traveled*
geben (i)	*give*	**gab**	*gave*
gehen	*go*	**ging**	*went, walked*
gießen	*pour*	**goß**	*poured*
helfen (i)	*help*	**half**	*helped*
kommen	*come*	**kam**	*came*
laufen (äu)	*run*	**lief**	*ran*
lesen (ie)	*read*	**las**	*read*
liegen	*lie*	**lag**	*lay*
nehmen (nimmt)	*take (takes)*	**nahm**	*took*
rufen	*call*	**rief**	*called*
schlafen (ä)	*sleep*	**schlief**	*slept*
schneiden	*cut*	**schnitt**	*cut*
schreiben	*write*	**schrieb**	*wrote*
sehen (ie)	*see, look*	**sah**	*saw, looked*
sein (ist)	*be (is)*	**war**	*was*

INFINITIVE		PAST TENSE	
singen	*sing*	sang	*sang*
sitzen	*sit*	saß	*sat*
sprechen (i)	*speak*	sprach	*spoke*
stehen	*stand*	stand	*stood*
tragen (ä)	*carry, wear*	trug	*carried, wore*
treffen (i)	*meet*	traf	*met*
tun	*do*	tat	*did*
trinken	*drink*	trank	*drank*
wachsen (ä)	*grow*	wuchs	*grew*
werden (wird)	*become (becomes)*	wurde	*became*

C. aber and sondern

German has two words for *but*: **aber** and **sondern**. **Sondern** is used when the English *but* is used with the connotation *on the contrary* and is preceded by a negative. Otherwise use **aber**. Examples: Er saß am Tisch, aber er aß nicht. Er hat einen Bleistift, aber er schreibt nicht damit. Die Tafel ist nicht weiß, sondern schwarz. Wir blieben nicht im Haus, sondern gingen in den Garten. In our first two examples, two conditions co-exist. In our last two examples, one condition is refuted as non-existent.

D. Nouns of Measure

In English, after nouns of measure, we use the preposition *of*, e.g., *a bottle of lemonade, four bottles of wine, two pounds of strawberries*, etc. In German the two nouns are linked without a preposition: **eine Flasche Limonade, vier Flaschen Wein, zwei Pfund Erdbeeren.**

Masculine and neuter nouns of measure do not appear in the plural in such cases, e.g., **zwei Pfund Erdbeeren.** (See Lesson VI, Section III,E.)

IV. Grammatical Exercises

A. Put the infinitive into the proper form of the present tense:

1. Der Mann (bleiben) im Haus. 2. Er (essen) zu viel. 3. Das Mädchen (geben) dem Studenten die Hand. 4. Die Frau

(gehen) in die Stadt. 5. Du (haben) zwei Flaschen Wein. 6.
Conrad (helfen) mir. 7. Du (kommen) zu spät in das Eßzimmer.
8. Was (lesen) ihr in der Zeitung? 9. Was (liegen) auf dem Tisch?
10. Was (sagen) Frau Löwenzahn? 11. Was (antworten) du?
12. Was (kosten) die Lampe? 13. Herr Löwenzahn (nehmen)
zwei Pfund Erdbeeren. 14. Er (schneiden) sie in eine Schüssel.
15. Dann (gießen) er Wein darüber und (trinken) etwas. 16.
Frau Löwenzahn (rufen) sehr laut. 17. Aber Herr Löwenzahn
(schlafen) ruhig. 18. (Sehen) du die Aufgabe? 19. (Schreiben)
du sie in dein Heft? 20. (Sein) ihr mit der Aufgabe fertig?
21. (Sitzen) du in dem Sessel? 22. Oder (stehen) du vor dem
Schreibtisch? 23. Conrad (treffen) das Mädchen am Tennisplatz. 24. Er (sprechen) über dies und das. 25. Der Herr
(tragen) eine Brille. 26. Der Student (wachsen) zu schnell.
27. Es (werden) spät. 28. Er (laufen) in den Garten.

    B. Re-do Exercise A in the past tense.

    C. Add the endings required, if any:

1. Ich aß____ Schweinebraten. 2. Er fuhr____ mit der Straßenbahn. 3. Du sprach____ von einer Flasche Limonade. 4. Wir
nahm____ die Kreide in die Hand. 5. Gestern traf____ sie mich
am Tennisplatz. 6. War____ ihr gestern in der Stadt? 7. Es
lag____ zwischen der Kirche und dem Park. 8. Ging____ sie in
den Garten? 9. Half____ Sie ihr bei der Arbeit?

    D. Place the verbs in Exercise C in the present tense (replac-
ing *gestern* by *heute*).

    E. Insert *aber* or *sondern* as needed:

1. Gestern gingen sie nicht in die Schule, ____ spielten Tennis.
2. Er sah Monika, ____ er sprach nicht mit ihr. 3. Er kam
nicht ins Haus, ____ er ging zurück in den Garten. 4. Dieser
Wein kostet nicht viel, ____ er schmeckt sehr gut. 5. Ihr Tennis
ist nicht gut, ____ auch nicht schlecht. 6. Nein, diese Aufgabe

ist nicht leicht (*easy*), ——— sehr schwer. 7. Sie ist noch nicht alt, ——— sie ist sehr krank.

V. Translation Exercise

1. I went downtown yesterday. 2. The salesman sold me a couple of bottles of wine. 3. This wine is not white, but red. 4. We remained with our guest until late in the night. 5. Suddenly he ran into the house. 6. The church was situated behind the park, wasn't it? 7. We remained in the garden until late in the night. 8. The guests ate and drank something. 9. Mrs. Löwenzahn was waiting for the students on the road before the house. 10. She met them in the garden. 11. They were carrying presents into the garden. 12. What did you do? 13. They gave her something to drink.   14. Yesterday they went downtown on the street car. 15. They stood and talked with a salesman. 16. They saw many things on the tables. 17. They were helping the woman. 18. It cost four marks. 19. It was getting late. 20. They took their books and went into the house. 21. They were sitting at their tables and writing their lessons. 22. They worked very hard and then went to (*zu*) bed.

VI. Fragen

1. Warum kamen gestern viele Freunde zu Herrn Löwenzahn? 2. Wie alt wurde er? 3. Was machten wir für ihn? 4. Was stand in der Mitte des Tisches? 5. Was lag darunter? 6. Wer kam nach dem Essen? 7. Warum gingen sie in den Garten? 8. Was trugen Herbert und Conrad auf den Balkon? 9. Was zeigte Herr Löwenzahn seinen Gästen? 10. Was rief er aus dem Garten? 11. Was antwortete seine Frau? 12. Wie macht man eine Erdbeerbowle? 13. Warum wurden sie alle sehr lustig? 14. Was machte Herr Löwenzahn? 15. Wie alt wurde Herr Löwenzahn an diesem Tag?

VII. Lesestück

Till Eulenspiegel heilt

Till Eulenspiegel lebte vor 600 (sechshundert) Jahren, aber noch heute sprechen die Leute in Deutschland über seine lustigen Streiche.

Er kam einmal nach Nürnberg, ging zum Bürgermeister und sagte: „Ich bin ein großer Arzt, ich heile alle Kranken."

Der Bürgermeister sagte: „Du bist der Mann, den wir in Nürnberg brauchen. Unser Krankenhaus ist nicht groß genug. Wir haben zu viele Kranke und nicht genug Betten."

„In zwei Tagen sind alle Betten in eurem Krankenhaus leer",
10 sagte Eulenspiegel.

„Wenn du die Wahrheit sagst", antwortete der Bürgermeister, „dann zahlen wir dir 100 (hundert) Gulden."

„Gut", sagte Eulenspiegel, „aber ich muß mit jedem Kranken allein sprechen."

Er ging in das Krankenhaus und sagte zu dem ersten Kranken: „Ich kann euch alle heilen, aber ich muß den Kränksten von euch zu Pulver verbrennen, und ihr müßt dann dieses Pulver als Medizin essen. Morgen komme ich zurück und rufe ‚Wer nicht krank ist, komme heraus.' Wer als Letzter kommt, ist der
20 Kränkste, und dann verbrennen wir ihn zu Pulver."

So ging Eulenspiegel von einem Bett zum nächsten und zum nächsten und sprach leise mit jedem Kranken allein.

Am nächsten Tag kam er mit dem Bürgermeister zurück und rief in das Krankenhaus: „Wer nicht krank ist, komme heraus."

Sofort war das Krankenhaus in großer Aufregung. Alle Kranken sprangen aus ihren Betten und liefen weg, denn keiner wollte der Kränkste und Letzte sein.

„Ich habe sie in einer Nacht geheilt", sagte Eulenspiegel zum
30 Bürgermeister. „Alle Betten sind leer, nicht wahr?"

„Du sagtest die Wahrheit, du bist ein großer Arzt", antwortete
der Bürgermeister und gab ihm die 100 (hundert) Gulden.

Nach zwei Tagen kamen alle Kranken zurück. Bald war
wieder in jedem Bett ein Kranker.

„Wo ist Eulenspiegel?" rief der Bürgermeister.

Aber Till Eulenspiegel war nicht mehr da, und er kam nie
wieder nach Nürnberg zurück.

VIII. Wörterverzeichnis

allein alone
als as
der Arzt, ⸚e the physician, doctor
die Aufregung the excitement
der Bürgermeister, – the mayor
den whom
einmal once
der erste the first one
genug enough
der Gulden, – the guilder (coin)
heilen (to) heal, cure
ich kann I can
klein small
komme heraus (imp.) come out!
das Krankenhaus, ⸚er the hospital
der Kränkste the sickest one
leer empty
der letzte the last one
die Medizin, –en the medicine

ich muß I must
ihr müßt you must
der Nächste the next one
nicht mehr no longer
noch still
das Pulver the powder
springen aus; sprang (to) jump
    out of; jumped
der Streich, –e the trick, prank
der Tag, –e the day
über about
verbrennen; verbrannte (to) burn;
    burned
vor sechshundert Jahren six hun-
    dred years ago
die Wahrheit the truth
wenn if
wer whoever
er wollte he wanted to

AUFGABE ACHT

INTERROGATIVES AND IMPERATIVES

in der Zeitung stehen

I. Reading Selection

Auf einer Bank im Park saß ein Mädchen. Sie war jung, hübsch und blond. Herbert und ich saßen auch auf einer Bank. Wir lasen eine Zeitung. Darin war eine Prüfung über deutsche Geschichte.

Ich las eine Frage: „Wodurch wurde Gutenberg berühmt?"

Herbert antwortete: „Durch die Erfindung der Buchdruckerkunst."

Er las: „Wer war Buxtehude?"

Ich antwortete: „Buxtehude war ein Komponist."

10   Er sagte: „Nein, Buxtehude ist eine Stadt an der Elbe, und das Mädchen ist sehr hübsch."

Ich sagte: „Sprich nicht so dumm. Die Frage ist nicht, ‚was ist', sondern ‚wer war'."

Herbert sagte leise: „Sie raucht jetzt eine Zigarette."

Ich sagte: „Wer? Die Stadt an der Elbe? Lies die Fragen und sieh nicht immer nach der Bank. Außerdem ist es nicht richtig: man sagt auf deutsch ‚es raucht eine Zigarette'. M ä d c h e n [1] ist ein Neutrum."

---

[1] German uses letterspacing, i.e., the letters are "spaced out," where we use italic type in English for purposes of emphasis, etc.

Herbert gab mir die Zeitung und sagte: „Nimm sie, ich
meine die Zeitung, und lies." 20

Ich las: „Was warf Luther nach dem Teufel?" *werfen*

„Für wen kämpfte der General Wallenstein?" *wofür*

„Wann lebte der Freiherr vom Stein?"

„Mit wem war Maria Theresia verheiratet?"

Herbert unterbrach: „Sagtest du: verheiratet?—Höre! Ich *heiraten*
habe Angst vor ihr. Gehe zu ihr und sprich zu ihr!"

Ich ging mit der Zeitung zu der Bank und fragte das
Mädchen: „Mit wem war Maria Theresia verheiratet?" *womit*

Sie sagte: „Speak English. I'm from Kansas City."

Ich sagte: „Sprechen Sie deutsch, Fräulein Amerika! Wir 30
verstehen englisch, aber wir sprechen es nicht."

Sie sagte: „Aren't you two Americans?"

Ich antwortete: „Gewiß. Ich bin aus Pennsylvania, und die
Eltern meines Freundes wohnen in Colorado. Wir sind ein Jahr
in Deutschland und sprechen nur deutsch. Wir lernen die
Sprache und üben sie jeden Tag."

Ich glaube, sie verstand kein Wort.

„Lernen Sie nicht Deutsch?" fragte ich sie.

Sie sagte etwas zu mir auf englisch. Es war nichts für Guten-
bergs Buchdruckerkunst. Not fit to print, sagen wir auf englisch. 40

Ich nahm Herbert beim Arm, und wir gingen nach Hause.
Mit der Zeitung. Ohne das Mädchen.

„Was sagte sie?" fragte Herbert.

„Die Übersetzung ist schwer", sagte ich. „Sie sagte: ihr seid
Nüsse."

Herbert war an diesem Abend sehr traurig.

II. Vocabulary

*acht eight
*außerdem besides, moreover
*die Bank, ⸗e the bench
*berühmt famous
*blond blond

die Buchdruckerkunst the art of
  printing
die Elbe the Elbe (River)
*die Eltern (*plu.*) the parents
*englisch English

die **Erfindung, –en** the invention
*die **Frage, –n** the question
*das **Fräulein, –** the girl, Miss., the young lady
der **Freiherr, (–n), –en** the baron
*die **Geschichte, –n** the story; history
*gewiß sure, certain(ly)
*glauben (to) believe
*hübsch pretty, nice
*jung young
kämpfen (to) fight, struggle
der **Komponist, (–en), –en** the composer
*lernen (to) study, learn
*meinen (to) mean, think, remark
das **Neutrum** the neuter
*nichts nothing
die **Nuß, Nüsse** the nut

*die **Prüfung, –en** the test, quiz, examination
*rauchen (to) smoke
*die **Sprache, –n** the language, speech
*der **Tag, –e** the day
der **Teufel, –** the devil
*traurig sad
*über (with *acc.*) about, concerning
*die **Übersetzung, –en** the translation
*unterbrechen (i), unterbrach (to) interrupt
verheiratet married
*werfen (i), warf nach (to) throw at
*die **Zigarette, –n** the cigarette

Idioms

*er hat Angst vor (*dat.*) he is afraid of
*auf deutsch in German
*auf englisch in English
*nach Hause home (always motion toward, e.g., ich gehe *or* komme nach Hause)
*er stellt eine Frage he asks a question

III. Grammar

A. Interrogatives

Questions may be introduced by interrogatives which refer to time, place, direction, reason, etc. In our active vocabulary have occurred: **wann,** *when;* **wo,** *where;* **wohin,** *where (to)*; **warum,** *why;* **wie,** *how;* **wer,** *who;* **was,** *what.*

Examples: Wann gehen wir in die Stadt? Warum wächst Conrad zu schnell? Was lag auf den Tischen des Warenhauses? Wie macht man eine Erdbeerbowle? Wo wohnten die Studenten? Wohin gingen Sie gestern? Wer saß auf der Bank?

Note that English *where* must be translated by **wohin** when the question refers to a direction (*where to*); while **wo** refers only to a location (*in what place*).

In the answer to a **wohin**-question the place appears in the accusative. In the answer to a **wo**-question the place appears in the dative. Examples:

Wohin gehst du?   In **die** Stadt.
Wo wohnst du?   In **der** Stadt.

B. The Interrogative Pronoun **wer**.

The interrogative pronoun **wer** corresponds to English *who*:

Nom.	wer	*who*
Gen.	wessen	*whose*
Dat.	wem	(*to, for*) *whom*
Acc.	wen	*whom*

Examples: Wer war im Garten? Wessen Übersetzung ist das? Wem gab Conrad ein Geschenk? Wen siehst du in der Straßenbahn?

C. **Wo–** Combinations

Before going on, read again what was said in Lesson V, Section III,B about the da– combinations.

When the interrogative **was** (which always refers to an inanimate object or an idea) is used with a preposition, German is apt to use a **wo– combination**. We again have the reversible equation:

English preposition + what = German **wo** + preposition. Such combinations are: **wobei, wodurch, wofür, wohinter, womit, wonach, wovon, wozu**; when the preposition begins with a vowel, the form **wor–** precedes (cf. Eng. *wherein*): **woran, worauf, woraus, worin, worüber, worunter.** Examples:

Worauf wartest du? Womit machte er die Erdbeerbowle? Wovon lebt er? Wodurch wurde er berühmt?

Auf wen wartest du *and* **worauf wartest du? Mit wem fuhr Herbert in die Stadt** *and* **womit fuhr Herbert in die Stadt?**

D. Imperatives

A language may have as many forms of the imperative (for giving commands) as it has words for *you*. Thus English has only one imperative form, e.g. Pay! Carry! Go!

German, on the other hand, has three forms: 1) the singular familiar; 2) the plural familiar; 3) the polite form (identical for singular and plural).

SING. FAMIL.:	Zahle!	Warte!	Trage!	Gehe!
PLUR. FAMIL.:	Zahlt!	Wartet!	Tragt!	Geht!
POLITE FORM:	Zahlen Sie!	Warten Sie!	Tragen Sie!	Gehen Sie!

The singular familiar form, used for a person addressed with **du,** is the **verb stem plus –e.** (In informal, everyday conversation the final **–e** is often dropped.)

The plural familiar form, used with persons addressed individually with **du** or collectively with **ihr,** is **identical with the second person plural of the present tense.** No personal pronoun is used for the two familiar forms of the imperative!

The polite form of the imperative is merely an **inversion of the present tense polite form** in a declarative sentence.

Sie gehen (declarative)—**gehen Sie** (imperative).

Remember: The personal pronoun (**Sie**) is *never* omitted in the polite imperative!

To use our sample verbs in sentences, Frau Löwenzahn would say to Conrad: **Warte auf mich! Zahle für mich!**

Talking to both Conrad and Herbert, she would say: **Tragt diese Dinge! Geht jetzt nach Hause!**

Either Conrad or Herbert, talking to either Herr or Frau Löwenzahn (or to both), would say: **Warten Sie auf mich, bitte** (*please*)! **Bitte, tragen Sie diese Dinge!**

E. Imperatives with Vowel Changes

The rules and examples listed above in Subsection D hold true for all imperatives except those of strong (or vowel-changing)

verbs which in the present tense singular change their stem from
e to i or ie (see Lesson III, Section III,A). **In the singular
familiar imperative only, these verbs change e to i or ie and do
not have the ending –e: Iß! Gib! Hilf! Lies! Nimm! Sieh!
Sprich! Triff! Unterbrich! Wirf!**
The three imperative forms of **werden** are **werde, werdet,
werden Sie;** of **sein** they are **sei, seid, seien Sie!**

IV. Grammatical Exercises

A. Change the following sentences into questions, using *was,
wo,* a form of *wer,* or a *wo–* combination:

Examples: a) Ich warte auf meinen Freund. Auf wen warte
ich? b) Ich warte auf die Zeitung. Worauf warte ich?

1. Das Fleisch liegt auf einem Teller. 2. Die Suppe war in einer
Schüssel. 3. Wir gingen mit der Zeitung nach Hause. 4. Eulenspiegel heilte (*cured*) die Kranken durch Medizin. 5. Herbert
schreibt die Aufgabe an die Tafel. 6. Die Krawatte war von
dir. 7. Wir helfen Frau Löwenzahn. 8. Er zahlte für das
Geschenk. 9. Sie hatten Angst vor der Prüfung. 10. Du trinkst
eine Erdbeerbowle. 11. Gestern war Herrn Löwenzahns Geburtstag. 12. Er wurde traurig über die Geschichte.

B. Address each of the following commands to Herr or Frau
Löwenzahn, or to both:

1. (werfen) das nicht nach mir! 2. (sehen) nicht immer nach
der Bank! 3. (machen) Ihre Arbeit! 4. (sagen) solche Dinge
nicht! 5. (gehen) in die Stadt! 6. (geben) mir etwas Geld!
7. (nehmen) dieses Geld! 8. (rufen) mich in einer halben
Stunde! 9. (sprechen) lauter! 10. (treffen) mich in der Stadt!
11. (unterbrechen) mich nicht! 12. (tragen) dies in das Haus.
13. (tun) das nicht! 14. (laufen) ins Haus!

C. Re-do B, addressing each sentence to Conrad or Herbert.

D. Re-do B, addressing each sentence to *both* students, Herbert and Conrad.

V. Translation Exercise

1. Conrad, read the newspaper! 2. Where did you read the test about history? 3. Whose cigarettes does he smoke? 4. Wait for your friend! (*three forms*) 5. Who interrupted him? 6. In whose car did he ride? 7. Whom are you helping? 8. Help me! 9. What are you waiting for? 10. Are you afraid of this girl? 11. How do you say that in English? 12. He came home every afternoon. 13. Whom do you see now? 14. Give (*three forms*) me something to eat. 15. When are you downtown? 16. How old is Mr. Löwenzahn? 17. Why does he ask this question? 18. For whom did you buy the shirt? 19. Where are you going? 20. In which language did he write the story?

VI. Fragen

1. Wo saß das Mädchen? 2. Was lasen die Studenten in der Zeitung? 3. Wodurch wurde Gutenberg berühmt? 4. Wo leben die Eltern des Mädchens? 5. Was rauchte das Mädchen? 6. Wohin ging Conrad? 7. Was fragte er das Mädchen? 9. Antwortete Conrad auf englisch? 10. Warum sprechen Conrad und Herbert deutsch? 11. Wohin gingen Conrad und Herbert? 12. Wie war Herbert an diesem Abend?

VII. Lesestück

Till Eulenspiegel kauft und verkauft

Till Eulenspiegel kam nach Quedlinburg. Da war gerade Markt, und auf dem Marktplatz saß eine Bauernfrau neben einem Korb. In dem Korb waren fünf Hühner und ein Hahn. „Was kosten die Hühner?" fragte Eulenspiegel.

„Der ganze Korb kostet acht Groschen", antwor
Bauernfrau.

„Ich kaufe die Hühner und den Hahn", sagte Eulenspiegc.,
nahm den Korb und ging weg.

„Halt, junger Mann", rief die Bauernfrau, „du mußt mir
acht Groschen dafür geben."   10

„Ich habe mein Geld vergessen", sagte Eulenspiegel. „Hier,
nimm den Hahn als Pfand. Ich trage den Korb mit den Hühnern
nach Hause und komme mit dem Geld zurück."

Die dumme Bauernfrau nahm ihren Hahn als Pfand und
wartete. Sie saß da noch am Abend und wartete und wartete.

Als die Leute in Quedlinburg die Geschichte hörten, begannen
sie, Eulenspiegel zu suchen.

Aber Till Eulenspiegel war nicht mehr da, und er kam nie
wieder nach Quedlinburg zurück.

.   .   .

Till Eulenspiegel kam nach Leipzig. In Leipzig wohnten viele 20
Pelzhändler, denn die Stadt war berühmt durch ihren Pelzhandel.
Eulenspiegel fing eine dicke, alte Katze, nähte sie in ein schönes
Hasenfell, steckte sie in einen alten Sack und ging auf den Markt.

„Ich habe einen schönen Hasen zu verkaufen", sagte er zu
einem Pelzhändler.

„Gut", antwortete der Pelzhändler, „ich kaufe ihn für sieben
Groschen."

Er gab Eulenspiegel das Geld, nahm den Sack und ging nach
Hause. Dann rief er seine Freunde.

„Kommt in den Hof hinter dem Haus und laßt die Hunde in 30
den Hof. Ich habe einen Hasen in dem Sack. Wir werden eine
lustige Jagd sehen, und am Abend werden wir den Hasen essen.
Und dann habe ich noch das schöne Hasenfell."

Er öffnete den Sack und die Katze kam heraus. Die Hunde
begannen zu bellen, die Katze sprang auf einen Baum, schrie
„miau, miau" und lief weg.

„Wo ist Eulenspiegel?" schrien die Pelzhändler.

Aber Till Eulenspiegel war nicht mehr da, und er kam nie wieder nach Leipzig zurück.

VIII. Wörterverzeichnis

als as, when
der Baum, ⸚e the tree
beginnen; begann (to) begin; began
bellen (to) bark
dick fat
fangen; fing (to) catch; caught
ganz whole, entire
gerade just; just then
der Groschen, – the groschen, dime
der Hahn, ⸚e the rooster
halt! halt! stop!
der Hase, (–n), –n the hare
das Hasenfell the rabbit pelt
heraus out
der Hof, ⸚e the yard
das Huhn, ⸚er the chicken
der Hund, –e the dog
die Jagd the chase, hunt
die Katze, –n the cat
der Korb, ⸚e the basket

lassen, (to) let, permit
der Markt, ⸚e the market
der Marktplatz, ⸚e the market place
du mußt you must
nähen (to) sew
nicht mehr no longer
noch still
öffnen (to) open
der Pelzhandel the fur trade
der Pelzhändler, – the furrier
das Pfand, ⸚er the security
der Sack, ⸚e the sack, bag
schreien; schrie (to) cry; cried
springen; sprang (to) jump; jumped
stecken (to) put
suchen (to) seek, look for
vergessen; vergaß; vergessen; vergißt (to) forget; forgot; forgotten; forgets

AUFGABE NEUN

PRESENT PERFECT · PAST PERFECT
TIME EXPRESSIONS

I. Reading Selection

Nachmittags gehen viele Leute in Deutschland in ein Café.
Im Winter sitzt man drinnen, im Sommer draußen auf dem
Bürgersteig oder im Garten. Heute treffen wir Monika Wenk
und ihre Freundin Vera Sütterlin in einem Café in der Stadt.

Wir sind zu früh gekommen. Wir haben eine Zeitung gekauft, eine Zigarette geraucht, Kaffee und Kuchen bestellt, aber
wir haben noch nicht gegessen. Der Kaffee ist kalt geworden,
die Schlagsahne auf dem Kuchen ist geschmolzen: wir sitzen und
warten.

„Wir sind zu höflich", sage ich. „Das macht das Leben zu 10
schwer."

„Vielleicht ist etwas geschehen", sagt Herbert. „Sie sind noch
nie so spät gekommen."

In diesem Augenblick kommen die Mädchen.

„Es tut uns leid, wir sind wieder zu spät gekommen. Es gab
einen Verkehrsunfall."

„Was ist geschehen?" frage ich. „Erzählen Sie!"

„Ein Volkswagen ist um die Ecke gekommen und ist in unsere
Straßenbahn gefahren. Man hat einen Polizisten gerufen, und er
hat einen Bericht geschrieben. Der Volkswagen war ganz . . ." 20

89

„Kaputt", unterbreche ich schnell. „Sagt man das auf deutsch?"

Monika und Vera lächeln.

„Gewiß, man sagt es", antwortet Vera, „aber man schreibt es nicht."

„Du hast unterbrochen", sagt Herbert. „Wir hatten noch nicht das Ende der Geschichte gehört."

„Sie haben fast alles gehört", berichtet Monika. „Ein Verkehrsunfall mit viel Lärm, aber ohne Blut. Wir haben dann ein
30 Taxi genommen und sind zum Café gefahren."

„Ich sehe, Sie haben eine Zeitung gekauft", sagt Vera. „Was haben Sie darin gelesen?"

„Wir haben sie nur gekauft, aber nicht gelesen", sage ich. „Die Drucktypen in dieser Zeitung sind deutsch. Das ist sehr schwer für uns. Wir haben es heute in der Schule gelernt, aber wir haben es noch nicht geübt."

„Gestern haben wir eine Zeitung gekauft und darin Fragen über deutsche Geschichte gelesen", sagt Herbert.

„O ja", sage ich, „es gab etwas über Maria Theresia. Die
40 Frage war: hat Maria Theresia in Kansas City gewohnt?"

Die Mädchen lachen. Herbert ist rot geworden.

„Nehmen Sie ihn nicht ernst", sagt er, „er ist ein Till Eulenspiegel."

In former centuries a great number of German books (in 1930 still more than 50 per cent) were set in Gothic letters, usually called *Fraktúr*. During the last decades the Gothic print has receded more and more, and today more than 90 per cent of all German publications are set in Roman type, called *Antíqua*. We have used *Antíqua* for this book. However, if anyone wants to read older publications, he will have to familiarize himself with Gothic print, which is considerably easier than it may look at first glance. Many present-day German newspapers use *Fraktur* for their headlines. To give you an idea of how German *Fraktur* looks, we reprint now the Reading Selection of Lesson IX in Gothic letters.

Nachmittags gehen viele Leute in Deutschland in ein Café. Im Winter sitzt man drinnen, im Sommer draußen auf dem Bürgersteig oder im Garten. Heute treffen wir Monika Wenk und ihre Freundin Vera Sütterlin in einem Café in der Stadt.

Wir sind zu früh gekommen. Wir haben eine Zeitung gekauft, eine Zigarette geraucht, Kaffee und Kuchen bestellt, aber wir haben noch nicht gegessen. Der Kaffee ist kalt geworden, die Schlagsahne auf dem Kuchen ist geschmolzen: wir sitzen und warten.

„Wir sind zu höflich“, sage ich. „Das macht das Leben zu schwer.“

„Vielleicht ist etwas geschehen“, sagt Herbert. „Sie sind noch nie so spät 10 gekommen.“

In diesem Augenblick kommen die Mädchen.

„Es tut uns leid, wir sind wieder zu spät gekommen. Es gab einen Verkehrsunfall.“

„Was ist geschehen?“ frage ich. „Erzählen Sie!“

„Ein Volkswagen ist um die Ecke gekommen und ist in unsere Straßen= bahn gefahren. Man hat einen Polizisten gerufen, und er hat einen Bericht geschrieben. Der Volkswagen war ganz . . .“

„Kaputt“, unterbreche ich schnell. „Sagt man das auf deutsch?“

Monika und Vera lächeln. 20

„Gewiß, man sagt es“, antwortet Vera, „aber man schreibt es nicht.“

„Du hast unterbrochen“, sagt Herbert. „Wir hatten noch nicht das Ende der Geschichte gehört.“

„Sie haben fast alles gehört“, berichtet Monika. „Ein Verkehrsunfall mit viel Lärm, aber ohne Blut. Wir haben dann ein Taxi genommen und sind zum Café gefahren.“

„Ich sehe, Sie haben eine Zeitung gekauft“, sagt Vera. „Was haben Sie darin gelesen?“

„Wir haben sie nur gekauft, aber nicht gelesen“, sage ich. „Die Druck= typen in dieser Zeitung sind deutsch. Das ist sehr schwer für uns. Wir 30 haben es heute in der Schule gelernt, aber wir haben es noch nicht geübt.“

„Gestern haben wir eine Zeitung gekauft und darin Fragen über deutsche Geschichte gelesen“, sagt Herbert.

„O ja“, sage ich, „es gab etwas über Maria Theresia. Die Frage war: hat Maria Theresia in Kansas City gewohnt?“

Die Mädchen lachen. Herbert ist rot geworden.

„Nehmen Sie ihn nicht ernst“, sagt er, „er ist ein Till Eulenspiegel.“

II. Vocabulary

*alles (*singular*) everything
*der Bericht, –e the report
*berichten (to) report

*bestellen (to) order
das Blut the blood
der Bürgersteig, –e the sidewalk

das Café, –s the café
draußen outside
drinnen inside
die Drucktypen (*plu.*) the type, type faces
*die Ecke, –n the corner
*das Ende, –n the end
*ernst serious
*erzählen (to) tell, narrate
*fast almost
*früh early
*ganz whole, entire, quite
*geschehen (ie), geschah, ist geschehen (to) happen, occur
*höflich courteous
*der Kaffee the coffee
*kalt cold
kaputt broken, ruined, "all shot"
*der Kuchen, – the cake, pastry, cookie
der Lärm the noise

*das Leben the life
*man one, they, people, (*3rd person indefinite*)
*nachmittags afternoons, in the afternoon, of an afternoon
*neun nine
*nie never
*noch nie never yet
*nur only
der Polizist, (–en), –en the policeman
die Schlagsahne the whipped cream
schmelzen (i), schmolz, ist geschmolzen (to) melt
*der Sommer, – the summer
das Taxi, –s the taxi
der Verkehrsunfall, ⸚e the traffic accident
der Volkswagen, – the Volkswagen
*der Winter, – the winter

Idiom

*es gibt (*takes acc.*) there is, there are

III. Grammar

The present perfect and past perfect tenses are formed in English and German in the same way, by a phrase comprising a finite auxiliary verb (in English it is always "have") and the past participle of the main verb. *The past participle is the third principal part of the verb.*

A. Past Participles of Weak Verbs

The past participle of a weak verb is formed by adding to the verb stem the prefix ge– and the ending –t, thus ge + stem + t. The past participle of the verb frag-en will be gefragt. So the

three principal parts of **fragen** are: **fragen, fragte, gefragt**; of
leben: leben, lebte, gelebt. With verbs whose stem ends in **–t** or
–d, again **–e–** is inserted between stem and ending: **gewartet,
geantwortet.**

B. Past Participles of Strong (or Vowel-Changing) Verbs

The past participle of a strong verb is also formed by prefixing
the verb stem by **ge–,** but in this case the ending **–en** is added,
and the stem vowel is changed. Since there is no way of knowing
how the stem vowel will change, the past participles of strong
verbs must be memorized. *It is imperative to memorize all three
principal parts of strong verbs.*

C. The Auxiliaries of the Perfect Tenses

Unlike English, not all German verbs are used with the same
auxiliary in the perfect tenses. To be sure, for most verbs the
auxiliary is **haben,** but a limited number of verbs require the
auxiliary **sein.** These verbs are all intransitive (i.e., they cannot
take a direct object); most of them are strong verbs, and they
all denote either *change of position* (going, coming, running) *or
change of condition* (growing, becoming, happening). He *has*
come: er **ist** gekommen; they *had* gone: sie **waren** gegangen; you
have grown: du **bist** gewachsen; she *has* become: sie **ist** geworden. To this group also belong the two verbs **sein** and
bleiben, e.g., he *has* been: er **ist** gewesen; we *had* remained: wir
waren geblieben.

D. Principal Parts of Strong (or Vowel-Changing) Verbs

A list of the principal parts of all strong verbs we have had so
far is given below. If there is a vowel change in the second and
third person singular of the present tense, it is given in parentheses

after the infinitive. In the third column, **ist** before the past participle indicates that **sein** is required for the perfect tenses.

INFINITIVE	PAST	PAST PARTICIPLE
bleiben	blieb	ist geblieben
essen (i)	aß	gegessen
fahren (ä)	fuhr	ist gefahren
geben (i)	gab	gegeben
gehen	ging	ist gegangen
geschehen (ie)	geschah	ist geschehen
gießen	goß	gegossen
helfen (i)	half	geholfen
kommen	kam	ist gekommen
laufen (äu)	lief	ist gelaufen
lesen (ie)	las	gelesen
liegen	lag	gelegen
nehmen (nimmt)	nahm	genommen
rufen	rief	gerufen
schlafen (ä)	schlief	geschlafen
schneiden	schnitt	geschnitten
schreiben	schrieb	geschrieben
sehen (ie)	sah	gesehen
sein (ist)	war	ist gewesen
singen	sang	gesungen
sitzen	saß	gesessen
sprechen (i)	sprach	gesprochen
stehen	stand	gestanden
tragen (ä)	trug	getragen
treffen (i)	traf	getroffen
trinken	trank	getrunken
tun	tat	getan
unterbrechen (i)	unterbrach	unterbrochen*
wachsen (ä)	wuchs	ist gewachsen
werden (wird)	wurde	ist geworden
werfen (i)	warf	geworfen

E. Word Order for Perfect Tenses

A very important feature of German word order is that *the past participle stands at the end* of the clause (except after subordinating conjunctions). Examples: sie haben den Kuchen

---

* The absence of the prefix ge– for this form will be explained later.

schwer arbeiten

gegessen; er ist in die Stadt gegangen; gestern habe ich meinem
Freund einen Brief geschrieben.

F. The Present Perfect Tense

Here is a table of the conjugation of two verbs in the present
perfect tense (one weak, one strong—one with **haben**, one with
sein):

1. ich habe ein Buch gekauft	ich bin nach Hause gekommen
2. du hast ein Buch gekauft	du bist nach Hause gekommen
3. er hat ein Buch gekauft	er ist nach Hause gekommen
1. wir haben ein Buch gekauft	wir sind nach Hause gekommen
2. ihr habt ein Buch gekauft	ihr seid nach Hause gekommen
3. sie haben ein Buch gekauft	sie sind nach Hause gekommen

G. Use of the Present Perfect Tense

In English, the present perfect tense is used to indicate either
an action which began in the past and is still continuing in the
present (*I have lived in this city for five years*) or an action which
began in the past and was completed in the past (*he has bought a
book*). In the latter case, the time element of the present perfect
coincides with that of the simple past (*he bought a book*). Yet in
choosing the present perfect in preference to the simple past, the
English speaker implies that the action which was completed in
the past had effects which are still relevant now for the person
who performed the action. For speakers of German these distinctions are extremely difficult to learn; they are almost "unlearn-
able."

The difference between simple past and present perfect in
German, however, is a different matter and easily learned by the
English speaker. Both denote: past. The choice of the form does
not depend upon meaning (as in English) but rather upon style:
it may roughly be said that in conversation the present perfect
tense is preferred, while in an objective narration of past events

the past tense is indicated. Therefore, when translating from English into German, observe the following rules:

ENGLISH	GERMAN	
	(*colloquial style*)	(*narrative style*)
Simple past ⎫ Present perfect ⎭	Present perfect	Simple past

When translating from German into English, the choice of an English simple past or present perfect depends on the context. You, the student, a native speaker of English, will have to make the decision. Translate German into correct English, and not into an artificial semi-English lingo. For example:

> **Ein Volkswagen ist um die Ecke gekommen und ist in unsere Straßen-bahn gefahren. Man hat einen Polizisten gerufen, und er hat einen Bericht geschrieben.**

> *A Volkswagen came around the corner and smashed into our streetcar. They called a policeman and he wrote a report.*

> (*Not:* A Volkswagen has come around the corner and has smashed into our streetcar. They have called a policeman and he has written a report.)

Remember especially this: In German the present perfect tense can never be used as in English to indicate an action that has started in the past and is still going on. "I have lived in this city for five years" means you are still living there. For this, German must use the present tense, usually in combination with **schon** (*already*). So the above sentence would be: **ich wohne schon seit fünf Jahren in dieser Stadt.** The German sentence **ich habe fünf Jahre in dieser Stadt gewohnt** means you are no longer living there and is equal to *I lived for five years in this city.*

H. The Past Perfect Tense

The German past perfect tense corresponds exactly to the English (except that some verbs, as noted, use **sein** as their auxiliary). Again we give you the full conjugation for two verbs:

1. ich hatte eine Zigarette geraucht   ich war schnell gegangen
2. du hattest eine Zigarette geraucht   du warst schnell gegangen
3. er hatte eine Zigarette geraucht   er war schnell gegangen

1. wir hatten eine Zigarette geraucht   wir waren schnell gegangen
2. ihr hattet eine Zigarette geraucht   ihr wart schnell gegangen
3. sie hatten eine Zigarette geraucht   sie waren schnell gegangen

In both languages, the past perfect denotes an action that occurred prior to another action in the past. It occurs only in such contexts. In isolation the past perfect makes no sense. Thus our examples above must be imagined in a wider context. For example: **Am Abend war er krank, denn er hatte am Tage zu viele Zigaretten geraucht.**

I. The Idiom **es gibt**

Statements of general existence or of broad general truth are often introduced in English by the phrase *there is* (*are*), e.g., "there is no park in this town," "there are many parks in this town." To this phrase corresponds the German phrase **es gibt.**

es gibt keinen Park in dieser Stadt
es gibt viele Parke in dieser Stadt

Note, however, that the German construction is entirely different from the English: **es** is the subject, **gibt** a transitive verb, and the following noun the object. From this it follows, too, that in the phrase **es gibt** the verb is always in the singular, whether the object is in the singular or in the plural.

J. Time Expressions

1. Time adverbs referring to parts of the day in statements about customary actions are: **morgens, vormittags, nachmittags, abends, nachts.** Examples: Ich gehe morgens (*or* vormittags) in die Schule. Nachmittags gehe ich in die Stadt. Ich schreibe abends meine Aufgabe in mein Heft. Nachts schlafen wir.

2. Time expressions indicating a span of time or extent of time are expressed by the accusative case. *This evening:* **diesen Abend;** *every day:* **jeden Tag;** *the entire day:* **den ganzen Tag.**

3. A fixed point in time is expressed by a prepositional phrase with the dative. With the names of days the preposition is **an,**

with months and seasons **in.** Examples: **an diesem Tag**: *on this day;* **am Dienstag**: *on Tuesday;* **am Mittwoch**: *on Wednesday;* **im April**: *in April;* **im Winter**: *in the winter.*

All the names of days, months, and seasons are masculine. All are regularly used with the definite article (which is omitted in most cases in English). In such time expressions preposition and definite article are contracted.

IV. Grammatical Exercises

A. Put into the present perfect tense:

1. Viele Leute gehen in ein Café. 2. Im Winter sitzt man drinnen. 3. Heute trafen wir die Freundinnen in der Stadt. 4. Wir warten auf sie. 5. Wir sind zu höflich. 6. Das macht das Leben zu schwer. 7. Dann kommen die Mädchen. 8. Es tat ihnen leid. 9. Es gab einen Verkehrsunfall. 10. Er lief über die Straße. 11. Schreibt er das auf englisch? 12. Was brauchen Sie? 13. Was sieht Vera? 14. Herbert bleibt im Haus. 15. Conrad fährt in die Stadt. 16. Herr Löwenzahn liest in der Zeitung. 17. Dann liegt er auf dem Sofa und schläft. 18. Später ruft ihn seine Frau. 19. Dann nimmt er zwei Pfund Erdbeeren, steht vor dem Tisch und schneidet sie in eine Schüssel. 20. Er gießt Wein darüber. 21. Du hilfst ihm bei dieser Arbeit. 22. Wir gehen in den Garten, trinken etwas und sprechen über dies und das.

B. Re-do some of the sentences in A, putting the verbs into the past perfect tense. This is a "grammatical exercise"; remember that in isolation the past perfect tense makes little sense.

V. Translation Exercise

(Use the present perfect where English has the past.)

1. A girl sat on a bench. 2. She smoked a cigarette and read a newspaper. 3. I saw a quiz in it. 4. Herbert read the questions. 5. He did not shake hands with him, for he had never been his

friend. 6. Herbert gave me the paper. 7. What did Luther throw? 8. What did Herbert ask the girl? 9. Where had his parents lived? 10. I had taken Herbert by the arm. 11. Then we ran home. 12. It had become very late. 13. Every night we slept well. 14. We stayed in Germany one year. 15. Herbert had eaten too much and grown too fast. 16. Many things had happened after this day. 17. Then a salesman had come to us. 18. We went home by trolley. 19. Yesterday we met the girls downtown. 20. They were standing and talking, and we had been waiting for them. 21. In the afternoon I worked, but at night I slept. 22. In the winter it was not warm, but cold. 23. What did Monika do yesterday? 24. We have bought an easy chair for Mrs. Löwenzahn.

VI. Fragen

1. Wohin gehen viele Leute nachmittags? 2. Wo sitzen sie im Sommer? 3. Und im Winter? 4. Wen treffen die Studenten heute? 5. Wo treffen sie sie? 6. Was haben sie gekauft? 7. Und was haben sie bestellt? 8. Warum haben sie nicht sofort gegessen? 9. Warum sind die Mädchen wieder spät gekommen? 10. Was war geschehen? 11. Wen hat man gerufen? 12. Was ist mit dem Volkswagen geschehen? 13. Womit sind die Mädchen zum Café gefahren? 14. Gibt es ein Café in Ihrer Stadt? 15. Stehen da die Tische und Stühle auch auf dem Bürgersteig?

VII. Lesestück

Die Schweiz

In drei Ländern spricht man die deutsche Sprache: in Deutschland, in Österreich und in der Schweiz. In Deutschland und Österreich sprechen alle Leute deutsch. In dem Lande zwischen Deutschland, Frankreich, Italien und Österreich sprechen nur dreiviertel der Schweizer deutsch, die anderen sprechen französisch oder italienisch.

Im deutschen Teil der Schweiz finden wir einen Unterschied zwischen geschriebener und gesprochener Sprache. Die geschriebene Sprache ist die gleiche, die man in Deutschland und 10 Österreich braucht; die gesprochene Sprache in der Schweiz ist verschieden. Es ist ein Dialekt, das sog. „Schwyzerdütsch." Alle Schweizer im deutschen Teil des Landes verstehen Hochdeutsch, sie lesen auch hochdeutsche Bücher und Zeitungen, aber sie sprechen ihr Schwyzerdütsch. Es gibt in der Schweiz viele Leute, die mehr als eine Sprache fließend sprechen. Sie wissen, daß es sehr wichtig ist, viele Sprachen zu lernen.

Im Mittelalter war die Schweiz ein Teil des Deutschen Reiches. Die Trennung begann im 14. (vierzehnten) Jahrhundert, aber erst in der Mitte des 17. (siebzehnten) Jahr- 20 hunderts wurde die Schweiz ein selbständiger Staat. In früheren Jahrhunderten waren die Schweizer berühmt als die besten Soldaten in ganz Europa. Bis heute hat der Papst in Rom eine Garde von Schweizer Soldaten. Die Schweiz aber ist seit 1815 (achtzehnhundertfünfzehn) ein neutrales Land. Seit der Zeit von Napoleon sind die Schweizer in allen Kriegen neutral geblieben.

Es hat in der Schweizer Geschichte nie einen Kaiser oder König gegeben. Die Schweiz ist heute die älteste Republik Europas. In der Verfassung des Landes findet man viele Ähn- 30 lichkeiten mit der Verfassung der Vereinigten Staaten. Die Schweiz ist ein Bundesstaat. In unserem Lande haben wir 50 (fünfzig) Staaten, in der Schweiz gibt es 22 (zweiundzwanzig) Kantone. Hier sind ein paar Namen von Schweizer Kantonen: Uri, Glarus, Aargau, Luzern, Basel, Graubünden, Genf. Jeder Kanton hat eine Hauptstadt. Bern ist die Hauptstadt des Kantons Bern und die Hauptstadt des ganzen Landes. Von dem Kanton Schwyz hat das ganze Land seinen Namen und seine Fahne genommen: ein weißes Kreuz in einem roten Feld.

Eine berühmte internationale Organisation wurde von dem 40 Schweizer Henri Dunant gegründet. Diese Organisation brauchte die Schweizer Farben für ihre Fahne: ein rotes Kreuz in einem weißen Feld. Es gibt heute gewiß nicht viele Leute auf der Welt, die noch nie vom Roten Kreuz gehört haben.

VIII. Wörterverzeichnis

die **Ähnlichkeit**, **–en** the similarity
als as
die **älteste** the oldest
die **anderen** the others
beginnen; begann; begonnen (to) begin; began; begun
die **besten** the best
der **Bundesstaat**, **–en** the federated state
das **Deutsche Reich** the German Empire
der **Dialekt**, **–e** the dialect
dreiviertel three-quarters
erst only, not until
die **Fahne**, **–n** the flag
das **Feld**, **–er** the field
fließend fluently
Frankreich France
französisch French
früher former
die **Garde**, **–n** the guard
wurde . . . gegründet was . . . founded
das **gleiche** the same
die **Hauptstadt**, **⸚e** the capital
Hochdeutsch High German
Italien Italy
italienisch Italian
das **Jahrhundert**, **–e** the century
der **Kaiser**, **–** the emperor
der **Kanton**, **–e** the canton
der **König**, **–e** the king

das **Kreuz**, **–e** the cross
der **Krieg**, **–e** the war
mehr more, **mehr als** more than
das **Mittelalter** the Middle Ages
der **Name**, **(–ns)**, **–n** the name
neutral neutral
oder or
die **Organisation**, **–en** the organization
Österreich Austria
der **Papst**, **⸚e** the Pope
die **Schweiz** Switzerland
der **Schweizer**, **–** the Swiss
Schwyzerdütsch Swiss German
seit since, for
selbständig independent
sogenannt, *abbr.* **sog.** so-called
der **Soldat**, **(–en)**, **–en** the soldier
der **Staat**, **–en** the state
der **Teil**, **–e** the part
die **Trennung**, **–en** the separation
der **Unterschied**, **–e** the difference
die **Verfassung**, **–en** the constitution
verschieden different
verstehen; verstand; verstanden (to) understand; understood; understood
die **Welt** the world
wichtig important
wissen (to) know

AUFGABE ZEHN

MODAL AUXILIARIES
IN THE PRESENT AND PAST

I. Reading Selection

Wir blieben mit den Mädchen bis fünf Uhr im Café. Dann machten wir einen Spaziergang durch den Park und kamen zum Zoologischen Garten.

„Sollen wir in den Zoo gehen?" fragte Herbert.

„Ich muß um sieben Uhr zu Hause sein", sagte Monika. „Haben wir genug Zeit?"

„Gewiß", sagte ich. „In einer Stunde können wir viel sehen."

Vor dem Käfig mit dem Affen stand eine Frau mit ihrem Sohn. Der Junge war vielleicht zehn Jahre alt. Er warf mit
10 einem Stein nach dem Affen. Ein Mann kam und sagte: „Du darfst nicht nach den Tieren werfen." Der Junge sagte: „Der Affe soll etwas tun. Er sitzt da und tut nichts."

Der Affe beachtete weder die Mutter noch den Sohn. Er saß still in einer Ecke, sah in die Luft und fraß eine Banane.

Wir gingen durch den Zoo und sahen Elefanten, Tiger und Löwen. Wir kamen dann an einen Teich. Herbert las laut: „Es ist verboten, die Tiere zu füttern." In dem Wasser schwamm ein Walroß.

Herbert und ich mußten lachen.

„Warum lachen Sie?" fragte Vera Sütterlin. 20

„Das Walroß gleicht Herrn Löwenzahn", sagte ich.

„Sie sind nicht sehr höflich", meinte Monika.

„Ich wollte nicht unhöflich sein", sagte ich. „Ich mag Herrn Löwenzahn. Ich mag auch das Walroß."

„Ich wollte Sie und Herbert immer etwas fragen", sagte Monika. „Sie beide sind achtzehn Jahre alt. Da soll man in Deutschland die Sie-Form brauchen. Warum sprechen die Löwenzahns zu Ihnen in der Du-Form?"

„Ich will es Ihnen erklären", antwortete Herbert. „Nur unser Lehrer und die Löwenzahns sprechen zu uns in der Du-Form. 30 Wir wollen die Du-Form üben. Nach drei Monaten und nach Aufgabe vierzehn sprechen sie alle in der Sie-Form zu uns."

Wir waren wieder zu dem Käfig mit dem Affen gekommen. Der Affe fraß jetzt eine Tomate. Sie war groß, rot und sehr reif. Der Junge stand noch vor dem Käfig und rief: „Er soll etwas tun! Komm aus deiner Ecke! Ich will dich sehen."

„Darf man zu einem Affen ‚du' sagen?" fragte ich Monika.

„Nein", antwortete sie. „Vor Darwin durfte man es. Jetzt muß man ‚Sie' sagen."

Wieder warf der Junge einen Stein in den Käfig. Plötzlich 40 nahm der Affe die Tomate und warf sie schnell nach dem Jungen. Sie traf ihn auf den Kopf. Er schrie laut.

„Sagtest du nicht, er sollte etwas tun?" fragte seine Mutter.

II. Vocabulary

NOTE: In this lesson, new meanings are used for three words: **da,** *then, in that case;* **meinen,** *(to) say;* **treffen,** *(to) hit.* Such meanings will be given in the end vocabulary.

achtzehn eighteen

der Affe, (–n), –n the ape, monkey

die Banane, –n the banana

beachten (to) notice, pay attention to

beide (plu.) both

*dürfen (darf), durfte, gedurft (to) be permitted; may

der Elefant, (–en), –en the elephant

*erklären (to) explain, declare

fressen (i), **fraß**, **gefressen** (to) eat (*used of animals*)
füttern (to) feed
gleichen, **glich**, **geglichen** (*takes dative*) (to) resemble, be like
*__der Junge__, (–n), –n the boy
der Käfig, –e the cage
*__können__ (**kann**), **konnte**, **gekonnt** (to) be able; can
*__laut__ loud
der Löwe, (–n), –n the lion
*__mögen__ (**mag**), **mochte**, **gemocht** (to) like; may
*__der Monat__, –e the month
*__müssen__ (**muß**), **mußte**, **gemußt** (to) have to; must
*__die Mutter__, ⸚ the mother
reif ripe
*__schreien__, **schrie**, **geschrieen** (to) cry, shout
*__schwimmen__, **schwamm**, **ist geschwommen** (to) swim
*__der Sohn__, ⸚e the son

*__sollen__ (**soll**), **sollte**, **gesollt** (to) be supposed to, be to, ought to; shall, should
*__der Spaziergang__, ⸚e the walk
*__der Stein__, –e the stone
der Teich, –e the pond
*__das Tier__, –e the animal
der Tiger, – the tiger
die Tomate, –n the tomato
unhöflich impolite, discourteous
*__verboten__ forbidden
*__vielleicht__ perhaps
vierzehn fourteen
das Walroß, **Walrosse** the walrus
*__das Wasser__ the water
*__weder . . . noch__ neither . . . nor
*__wollen__ (**will**), **wollte**, **gewollt** (to) want to, wish to
*__zehn__ ten
*__die Zeit__, –en the time
der Zoo, –s (*abbreviation*) the zoo
*__der Zoologische Garten__ the zoological garden

Idioms

*__er macht einen Spaziergang__ he takes a walk
*__zu Hause__ home (*only in the sense of* at home)

III. Grammar

Modal Auxiliaries

A small but important group of verbs indicate that the realization of an action depends upon some particular attitude or condition such as compulsion, ability, permission, volition, intention, assumption, etc. This condition is called a "mode," and for this reason the verbs which convey it are called "modal auxiliaries." For example, *I must go* in English means that the realization of the action *go* depends upon compulsion.

Note and remember three important facts about this representative sentence:

1. *must* (the modal auxiliary) is the finite verb of the sentence,
2. *go* (the main verb) is an infinitive,
3. the infinitive is *not preceded by "to."*

We find the same sentence structure in German: **ich muß gehen.**

However, English and German modal auxiliaries do not always match in meaning and function. English *will,* for example, indicates that an action is going to take place in the future: *he will go.* German **will** denotes volition, intention, wish. **Er will gehen** has to be translated into English as *he wants to go* (*he intends, wishes to go*).

Since *want, intend, wish* are not modal auxiliaries in English, the infinitive *go* is here preceded by *to.*

Note and remember this carefully, because it has relevance to another problem:

The German modal auxiliaries are "full-fledged" verbs, i.e., they have all finite forms, an infinitive, and a past participle. The English modals, however, are defective, i.e., most of them have only present-tense forms (and a subjunctive, which we cannot treat yet). The missing grammatical forms are expressed by circumlocutions. Moreover, these circumlocutions can also be used instead of the existing auxiliary forms. An example may illustrate this:

	ENGLISH		GERMAN
	AUXILIARY	SUBSTITUTE	AUXILIARY
INFINITIVE:	—	(to) have to	müssen
PRESENT:	he must	he has to	er muß
PAST:	—	he had to	er mußte

A. Forms and Meanings of the German Modal Auxiliaries

1. Infinitive: **müssen**

PRESENT:	ich muß	PAST:	ich mußte
	du mußt		du mußtest
	er muß		er mußte
	wir müssen		wir mußten
	ihr müßt		ihr mußtet
	sie müssen		sie mußten

ENGLISH EQUIVALENTS

INFINITIVE:	—	(to) have to
PRESENT:	I must	I have to
PAST:	—	I had to

2. Infinitive: **können**

PRESENT: ich kann   PAST: ich konnte
du kannst   du konntest
er kann   er konnte
wir können   wir konnten
ihr könnt   ihr konntet
sie können   sie konnten

ENGLISH EQUIVALENTS

INFINITIVE:	—	(to) be able to
PRESENT:	I can	I am able to
PAST:	I could	I was able to

3. Infinitive: **dürfen**

PRESENT: ich darf   PAST: ich durfte
du darfst   du durftest
er darf   er durfte
wir dürfen   wir durften
ihr dürft   ihr durftet
sie dürfen   sie durften

ENGLISH EQUIVALENTS

INFINITIVE:	—	(to) be permitted to
PRESENT:	I may	I am permitted to
PAST:	—	I was permitted to

4. Infinitive: **wollen**

PRESENT: ich will   PAST: ich wollte
du willst   du wolltest
er will   er wollte
wir wollen   wir wollten
ihr wollt   ihr wolltet
sie wollen   sie wollten

ENGLISH EQUIVALENTS

INFINITIVE:	—	(to) want to
PRESENT:	—	I want to
PAST:	—	I wanted to

5. Infinitive: **sollen**

PRESENT:		PAST:	
	ich soll		ich sollte
	du sollst		du solltest
	er soll		er sollte
	wir sollen		wir sollten
	ihr sollt		ihr solltet
	sie sollen		sie sollten

ENGLISH EQUIVALENTS

INFINITIVE:	—	(to) be supposed to
PRESENT:	—	I am supposed to
PAST:	—	I was supposed to

B. The Verb **mögen**

Formally, this verb belongs in the category of modal auxiliaries:

Infinitive: **mögen**

PRESENT:		PAST:	
	ich mag		ich mochte
	du magst		du mochtest
	er mag		er mochte
	wir mögen		wir mochten
	ihr mögt		ihr mochtet
	sie mögen		sie mochten

However, **mögen** can also function as a "transitive verb," i.e., it requires an object. It corresponds to English *like*. Examples:

ich mag ihn	I like him
mögen Sie Rheinwein?	do you like Rhine wine?
sie mochte ihn nicht	she did not like him

As a modal auxiliary, **mögen** is used only in negative sentences,

ich mag nicht warten	I do not like to wait
er mochte nicht arbeiten	he did not like to work

Mögen corresponds to English *may* only in statements like **das mag sein** *that may be*. We shall have little use for **mögen** in this function. The forms

ich möchte	wir möchten
du möchtest	ihr möchtet
er möchte	sie möchten

mean *I would like to,* etc. Examples:

Ich möchte hier bleiben	I would like to stay here
Möchten Sie ein Glas Wein?	Would you like a glass of wine?

C. Negation of Permission and Negation of Compulsion: Negation of Permission is Prohibition

Compare:

er darf nach Hause gehen *he is permitted to go home; he may go home* (permission).

er darf nicht nach Hause gehen *he is not permitted to go home; he may not go home* (prohibition).

In English, prohibition can be expressed also by *he must not go home.* This, actually, is a strong prohibition. It cannot be paralleled in German. **Er muß nicht nach Hause gehen** is negation of compulsion and corresponds to English *he does not have to go home.*

D. The Infinitive

Word order

The infinitive stands at the end of a clause.

Herbert will heute nach der Schule mit seiner Freundin auf den Tennisplatz **gehen.** Er konnte die ganze Nacht nicht **schlafen.**

Plain infinitive and connected infinitive

When dependent upon a modal auxiliary, the plain infinitive is used. When dependent upon a "full" verb, the infinitive is connected with *zu:*

Herbert möchte Monika **treffen.** Herbert hofft, Monika **zu treffen.**

The same rule is valid for English, but as has been pointed out in the introduction to this chapter, German statements with a modal are often paralleled by English statements with a "full" verb:

Er muss **gehen**—he must *go* (both languages use a modal auxiliary).
Er hofft, sie **zu treffen**—he hopes *to meet* her (both languages use a "full" verb).

Er will **gehen**—he wants *to go* (modal auxiliary in German, "full" verb in English).

Note: Infinitives are traditionally listed in vocabularies and dictionaries without **zu** in German but with *to* in English. To lessen the confusion to which this tradition may lead in our vocabulary, we list English infinitives with *to* in parenthesis: (to) go, (to) see, (to) write, etc.

E. Omission of Infinitive

Frequently in German the infinitive (the main verb) is omitted in sentences with modal auxiliaries. This is done whenever the meaning of the sentence is quite clear (to the German!) without the main verb, and corresponds to the German-English colloquialism "The dog wants out." Examples:

> Ich muß in die Stadt. Mußt du schon nach Hause? Er will mit. Ich kann es.

Most frequently it is *gehen, kommen,* or *tun* which is omitted. The matter is highly idiomatic and must be learned through practice.

Remember also expressions with **möchte** (see above) in which the infinitive is omitted:

> **Ich möchte ein Stück Kuchen** *I would like to have a piece of cake*
> **Möchten Sie ein Glas Wein?** *Would you like a glass of wine?*

The sentence **er kann Deutsch** is translated into English as *he knows German*. To the German the sentence means "he can (speak) German." This is again one of those instances where the infinitive is omitted.

IV. Grammatical Exercises

A. Supply the proper present tense of the verb in parentheses:

1. Du (sollen) etwas tun. 2. Er (dürfen) mit den Mädchen bis fünf Uhr bleiben. 3. Ich (wollen) einen Spaziergang machen.

4. Das (mögen) ich nicht. 5. In einer Stunde (können) der Student nicht viel sehen. 6. Er (müssen) sein Haus verkaufen. 7. Der Junge (wollen) einen Stein nach dem Affen werfen. 8. Das (dürfen) du nicht. 9. Der Junge (können) die Tiere füttern, aber er (sollen) es nicht. 10. Der Student (wollen) nicht unhöflich sein, aber er (müssen) in einer halben Stunde zu Hause sein.

B. Re-do A, putting all the subjects and verbs into the plural by changing 1st person singular to 1st person plural, etc.

C. Re-do A, putting all the verbs into the past tense.

D. Translate the words in parentheses:

1. Sie (doesn't have to) so bald nach Hause gehen. 2. Sie (is supposed to) noch eine halbe Stunde hier bleiben. 3. Er (can) nicht lauter rufen. 4. Man (mustn't) hier rauchen. 5. (You may) die Zeitung lesen (*three forms*). 6. (Are you able to) mit ihm einen Spaziergang machen? 7. Sie (must) für ihr Kind ein Kleid kaufen. 8. Er (wants to) mit. 9. Das Mädchen (likes) diese Geschichte nicht.

V. Translation Exercise

1. Conrad can tell stories in German very nicely. 2. He is not permitted to smoke in the dining room. 3. You must not (do) it. 4. He is supposed to go to bed every evening at ten o'clock. 5. I can read it, you don't have to explain it to me. 6. He does want to speak German with them. 7. He is not able to talk it very well. 8. He does not want to work, but he has to. 9. Perhaps he doesn't like it. 10. You are not supposed to ask so many questions. 11. She does not like to stay at home. 12. I am supposed to write this letter in German. 13. He is allowed to sit on the easy chair. 14. She wants to take a walk with him, but she is not permitted to.

Re-do the above sentences (except 5 and 10) in the past tense.

VI. Fragen

1. Bis wann sind die Studenten mit den Mädchen im Café geblieben? 2. Wohin sind sie dann gegangen? 3. Wann muss Monika zu Hause sein? 4. Wer hat vor dem Käfig mit dem Affen gestanden? 5. Wie alt war der Junge? 6. Was hat er nach dem Affen geworfen? 7. Wer ist gekommen? 8. Was hat der Mann gesagt? 9. Was hat der Affe getan? 10. Wohin sind die Freunde dann gegangen? 11. Warum mußten die Studenten lachen? 12. Warum sprechen die Löwenzahns zu Conrad und Herbert in der Du-Form? 13. Was hat der Affe am Ende der Geschichte getan? 14. Was tat der Junge?

VII. Lesestück

Wilhelm Tell schießt zwei Pfeile

Am Anfang der Schweizer Geschichte steht die Figur von Wilhelm Tell. Damals gehörte das Land um den Vierwaldstättersee den Herzögen von Österreich. Der Landvogt Geßler herrschte für den Herzog. Geßler war ein Tyrann, der die Schweizer grausam unterdrückte. Sie alle hofften auf das Ende seiner Herrschaft.

Eines Tages sagte der Landvogt zu seinen Soldaten: „Stellt eine Stange auf die Straße in der Mitte der Stadt Altdorf und hängt meinen Hut darauf. Jeder Schweizer, der den Hut sieht, muß ihn grüßen. Wenn ein Mann den Hut nicht grüßen will, 10 werft ihn ins Gefängnis."

An diesem Tage kam Wilhelm Tell mit seinem jungen Sohn in die Stadt. Er sah die Stange und den Hut, aber er tat nichts.

„Halt!" riefen die Soldaten. „Willst du den Hut des Landvogts nicht grüßen?"

„Nein", sagte Tell. „Ich bin ein freier Mann, ich grüße weder den Landvogt noch seinen Hut."

In diesem Augenblick kam Geßler selbst, und die Soldaten erzählten ihm, was geschehen war.

20   „Ich kann dich ins Gefängnis werfen, ich kann dich für deinen Ungehorsam töten", sagte Geßler zu Tell. Er sah, daß ein Junge neben Tell stand, und fragte: „Ist dies dein Sohn?"

„Ja", antwortete Tell und legte seinen Arm um den Jungen, „dies ist mein Sohn."

„Ich habe gehört, daß du als guter Schütze berühmt bist. Du sollst uns zeigen, ob du schießen kannst. Wenn du diesen Apfel vom Kopf deines Sohnes schießen kannst, darfst du dein Leben behalten."

Wilhelm Tell zeigte ihm, daß er ein guter Schütze war. Der 30 Pfeil traf den Apfel auf dem Kopf des Jungen. Tell glaubte, er wäre jetzt ein freier Mann und wollte gehen.

„Halt!", rief Geßler. „Ich sah, du nahmst zwei Pfeile in die Hand, bevor du den Apfel schossest. Was wolltest du mit dem zweiten Pfeil?"

„Der zweite Pfeil war für dich", sagte Tell. „Wenn ich meinen Jungen getroffen hätte, würdest du jetzt nicht mehr leben."

„Werft ihn ins Gefängnis", befahl Geßler seinen Soldaten. „Ich habe ihm sein Leben versprochen, aber nicht seine Freiheit."

40   Aber Wilhelm Tell entkam. Auf einer engen Straße im Wald wartete er auf den Landvogt, und nun schoß er den zweiten Pfeil. Er traf den Tyrannen mitten ins Herz.

Dies war der Anfang der Schweizer Freiheit.

VIII. Wörterverzeichnis

der Anfang, ⁼e the beginning
der Apfel, ⁼ the apple
der Augenblick, –e the moment
befehlen (ie), befahl, befohlen (*with dat.*) (to) command
behalten (ä), behielt, behalten (to) keep
bevor before

damals then
daß that
eng narrow
entkommen, entkam, ist entkommen (to) escape
die Figur, –en the figure
frei free
die Freiheit the freedom

das Gefängnis, –se the jail
gehören (*with dat.*) (to) belong to
grausam cruelly
grüßen (to) greet
Halt! Halt! Stop!
hängen (to) hang
ich hätte (*subjunctive*) I would have
die Herrschaft the rule, dominion
herrschen (to) rule
das Herz, (–ens), –en the heart
der Herzog, ⸚e the duke
der Hut, ⸚e the hat
der Landvogt, ⸚e the governor
legen (to) place
mitten in in the middle of
nicht mehr no longer
ob if, whether
Österreich Austria
der Pfeil, –e the arrow
schießen, schoß, geschossen (to) shoot

der Schütze, –n the marksman, shot
der Schweizer, – the Swiss
(Schweizer *is also used as adjective*)
der Soldat, (–en), –en the soldier
die Stange, –n the pole
eines Tages one day
töten (to) kill
treffen (trifft), traf, getroffen (to) hit
der Tyrann, (–en), –en the tyrant
der Ungehorsam the disobedience
unterdrücken (to) oppress
versprechen (i), versprach, versprochen (to) promise
der Vierwaldstättersee Lake Lucerne
er wäre (*subjunctive*) he would be
wenn if
Wilhelm William
du würdest you would
der zweite the second

AUFGABE ELF

FUTURE TENSES · ADVERBS
IRREGULAR WEAK VERBS

I. Reading Selection

Wir saßen mit den Löwenzahns im Garten hinter dem Haus.
„In ein paar Wochen werdet ihr Ferien haben", sagte Frau
Löwenzahn. „Was werdet ihr dann tun? Wollt ihr hier bleiben
oder eine Reise machen?"

„Wir werden eine Radtour durch das Rheinland machen",
antwortete Herbert. „Wir wollen von Mainz bis Köln mit dem
Rad fahren."

„Ihr werdet eine schöne Landschaft sehen", sagte Herr Löwenzahn. „Dort wächst der beste Wein in Deutschland."

10 Frau Löwenzahn lächelte. „Daran denkt unser Papa immer
zuerst", meinte sie.

„Du weißt", sagte er, „der Wein ist sehr wichtig für die
Ausfuhr unseres Landes."

„Natürlich", sagte seine Frau, „nur daran hast du gedacht.
Doch es ist richtig: das Rheinland ist ein Weinland. Dort
brennt die Sonne bis spät im Herbst heiß auf die Berge. Davon
wird der Wein so gut. Werdet ihr auch zur Loreley gehen?"

„Wer ist die Loreley?" fragte ich.

Courtesy of Deutsche Zentrale für Fremdenverkehr

Lausbuben an einem Koblenzer Brunnen

„Conrad!" rief Herbert. „Willst du sagen, du kennst die
20 Geschichte von der Loreley nicht?"

„Ich kenne ein Restaurant Loreley in Philadelphia", antwortete ich.

„Die Loreley war eine sehr schöne Frau. Sie saß auf einem Berg über dem Rhein, kämmte ihr Haar, sang und brachte die Schiffer auf dem Rhein in Gefahr. Sie dachten nur an die Frau und nicht an die Felsen im Wasser. Später hat man den Berg Loreley genannt."

„Die Geschichte ist sehr traurig", sagte ich. „Vielleicht werden auch wir die Loreley sehen. Ich hoffe, sie wird dann
30 nicht singen und dich in Gefahr bringen."

„Ihr dürft nicht die ganze Reise mit dem Rad machen", sagte Frau Löwenzahn. „Von Rüdesheim bis Koblenz müßt ihr mit einem Dampfer fahren. In Koblenz kenne ich eine Familie. Dort könnt ihr über Nacht bleiben. Morgen werde ich den Leuten schreiben und ihnen von euch erzählen."

Herr Löwenzahn war ins Haus gegangen. Jetzt kam er zurück. Er trug eine Flasche Wein und zwei Gläser. „Ihr habt zu viel vom Rhein und vom Wein gesprochen", meinte er. „Das hat mich durstig gemacht." Er goß Wein in ein Glas und gab
40 es seiner Frau. „Prost, Mutter!"

„Prost", antwortete sie. „Ich dachte, der Wein ist für die Ausfuhr unseres Landes. Darum sollten wir ihn nicht trinken."

„Gewiß", sagte Herr Löwenzahn. „Das ist alles richtig, aber dies hier nennt man den inneren Markt."

II. Vocabulary

die Ausfuhr the export, foreign trade
der beste the best
*__brennen, brannte, gebrannt__ (to) burn
*__bringen, brachte, gebracht__ (to) bring
der Dampfer, – the steamer

*__darum__ therefore, for this reason
*__denken, dachte, gedacht__ (**an** *with acc.*) (to) think (of)
*__doch__ yet, still; but, however; really
*__dort__ there
*__durstig__ thirsty
*__elf__ eleven

der Felsen, – the rock
*die Ferien (*plu.*) vacation
*die Gefahr, –en the danger
*heiß hot
*der Herbst, –e the fall, autumn
der innere Markt the domestic market, local consumption
kämmen (to) comb
*kennen, kannte, gekannt (to) know, be acquainted with
*die Landschaft, –en the scenery, landscape
*natürlich naturally, of course
*nennen, nannte, genannt (to) name, call
der Papa, –s papa
*Prost (*abbreviation of Latin prosit*) Here's to your health!

*das Rad, –er the wheel, bicycle
die Radtour, –en the bicycle tour
*die Reise, –n the trip
*das Restaurant, –s the restaurant
*der Rhein the Rhine (River)
*das Rheinland the Rhineland
der Schiffer, – the boatman
*die Sonne the sun
*später later
über Nacht bleiben (to) stay overnight
das Weinland, –er the wine country
*wichtig important
*wissen (weiß), wußte, gewußt (to) know
*die Woche, –n the week
*zuerst first, at first

Idioms

*er macht eine Reise, he takes a trip
*er fährt mit (dem Rad, dem Auto, der Straßenbahn etc.) he travels by *or* with

III. Grammar

A. The Future Tense

1. The future tense is formed both in English and German by using a finite auxiliary verb (in English *shall* and *will*) and the infinitive of the main verb. The German auxiliary is **werden**:

1. ich werde   nach Hause gehen
2. du wirst   nach Hause gehen
3. er wird   nach Hause gehen

1. wir werden nach Hause gehen
2. ihr werdet   nach Hause gehen
3. sie werden nach Hause gehen

The infinitive stands at the end of the clause, as explained in Lesson X, Section III,D.

2. Just as, in English, the phrase with *shall* and *will* is not the only means for conveying the idea of action in the future, so in German the phrase with **werden** is not a compulsory grammatical category. In both languages, the present tense is frequently used to express the future, especially when a time adverb is used:

Morgen fahre ich nach Frankfurt
I am going to Frankfurt tomorrow

3. The future perfect tense is rarely used in English or German:

ich werde das Buch gelesen haben *I shall have read the book*
er wird in die Stadt gegangen sein *he will have gone into the city*

Note the difference in word order.

B. Irregular Weak Verbs

A small group of weak verbs deviates from the regular pattern of weak verbs inasmuch as the present tense forms have a stem vowel different from the stem vowel in the past tense and past participle. Therefore the three principal parts of such verbs must be memorized.

Our active vocabulary (up to this lesson) contains the following:

bringen	**brachte**	**gebracht**	(to) bring
denken	**dachte**	**gedacht**	(to) think
brennen	**brannte**	**gebrannt**	(to) burn
kennen	**kannte**	**gekannt**	(to) know, be acquainted with
nennen	**nannte**	**genannt**	(to) name, call

(There are three other verbs in this group which we have not used so far: rennen, rannte, gerannt, [*to*] *run;* senden, sandte, gesandt, [*to*] *send;* wenden, wandte, gewandt, [*to*] *turn.*)

C. wissen, kennen, können

1. The verb **wissen** (*to*) *know* is conjugated like a modal auxiliary:

Infinitive: **wissen**

PRESENT:		PAST:	
ich weiß		ich wußte	
du weißt		du wußtest	
er weiß		er wußte	
wir wissen		wir wußten	
ihr wißt		ihr wußtet	
sie wissen		sie wußten	

PAST PARTICIPLE: **gewußt**

2. In Subsection B we listed **kennen** (*to*) *know*. The two verbs **kennen** and **wissen** cannot be used interchangeably: **kennen** requires a direct object, **wissen** a dependent clause:

Ich kenne seinen Vater; ich weiß, wo er wohnt

In the sentences **ich kenne es** and **ich weiß es**, to be sure, both verbs govern a direct object (**es**). The first one, however, can only stand for a noun, for example **das Buch**. The second one can only stand for the content of an entire phrase, for example **wo er wohnt**.

3. Remember that **können** also may convey the meaning of *comprehend*: **er kann Deutsch; er kann Algebra**. This was explained in Lesson X, Section III,E.

D. German Adverbs

In English the adverb usually is formed from the adjective by adding the suffix *–ly*.

In German, the uninflected form of the adjective functions also as the adverb. Examples:

Dieser Wein ist schlecht (*this wine is bad*).
Wir haben heute schlecht gespielt (*we played badly today*).
Monika ist sehr schön (*Monika is very beautiful*).
Sie singt auch sehr schön (*she also sings beautifully*).

In English, the pair adjective-adverb sometimes consists of two different words, for example *good—well*. This is not the case in German: **gut** serves both as the adjective (*good*) and the adverb (*well*).

IV. Grammatical Exercises

A. Put sentences 1–12 into the future tense:

1. Wir sitzen im Garten hinter dem Haus. 2. Ich mache eine Reise durch das Rheinland. 3. Dort trinkt man guten Wein. 4. Im Sommer brennt die Sonne heiß auf die Berge. 5. In diesem Jahr wird der Wein gut. 6. Woran denkt Herr Löwenzahn zuerst? 7. Wer trinkt den Wein? 8. Machst du die ganze Reise mit dem Rad? 9. Nein, wir fahren auch mit dem Dampfer. 10. Herr Löwenzahn kommt in den Garten. 11. Er trägt eine Flasche Wein. 12. Er gießt Wein in ein Glas und gibt es seiner Frau. 13. Was weiß er? 14. Die Loreley sitzt auf einem Berg. 15. Sie kämmt ihr Haar und singt sehr schön. 16. Damit bringt sie die Schiffer in Gefahr.

B. Put the sentences in A (except number 8) into the past tense.

C. Put the sentences in A into the present perfect tense.

D. Supply the proper present-tense form for the verb in parentheses:

1. Was (bringen) Herr Löwenzahn? 2. Er (denken) zuerst an den Wein. 3. Dort (brennen) die Sonne sehr heiß. 4. Wie (nennen) man diesen Berg am Rhein? 5. Das (wissen) er so gut wie ich. 6. (Können) du Deutsch? 7. (Kennen) Sie meinen Freund Herbert?

E. Re-do D, putting the sentences into the past tense.

F. Re-do D, putting the sentences into the present perfect tense.

G. Re-do D, putting the sentences (except 6 and 7) into the past perfect tense.

V. Translation Exercise

1. The trip through the Rhineland will be very beautiful. 2. In summer the sun will burn very hot on the mountains. 3. Then it will get very warm. 4. It will be good for the wine. 5. Are you going to take a trip by bicycle? 6. What do you know about the Loreley? 7. You knew the story about her, didn't you? 8. He knows where he is going (to). 9. Later they named this mountain the Loreley. 10. The men thought only of her, for she sang so beautifully. 11. People were afraid of her. 12. We shall have our vacation in a couple of days. 13. Later we shall go into a restaurant and eat something. 14. What kind of a cigarette do you want to smoke? 15. He knows neither my wife nor my son. 16. She will bring me a glass of water.

VI. Fragen

1. Wo sitzen die Studenten? 2. Bei wem sitzen sie? 3. Wessen Garten ist das? 4. Was werden die Studenten in ein paar Wochen tun? 5. Wohin wollen sie gehen? 6. Wie ist die Landschaft am Rhein? 7. Was wächst dort auf den Bergen? 8. Warum wird der Wein im Rheinland so gut? 9. Wer ist die Loreley? 10. Wo hat sie gesessen? 11. Was hat sie dort getan? 12. An wen haben die Schiffer gedacht? 13. Womit werden unsere Studenten von Rüdesheim bis Koblenz fahren? 14. Wo werden sie über Nacht bleiben? 15. Was wird Frau Löwenzahn tun?

VII. Lesestück

Basel

Basel liegt an der nördlichen Grenze der Schweiz. Hier kommen die Grenzen von drei Ländern zusammen, von Deutschland, Frankreich und der Schweiz. Vom Marktplatz der Stadt

kann man in einer halben Stunde mit der Straßenbahn nach
Frankreich oder nach Deutschland fahren.

Basel war im Mittelalter eine sehr berühmte Stadt. Noch
in unserer Zeit gibt es hier viele Häuser, die 300 (dreihundert)
oder 400 (vierhundert) Jahre alt sind. Auf einem Felsen über
dem Rhein steht eine schöne, alte Kirche, das Münster. Von
10 dem Platz hinter dem Münster hat man eine wunderbare Aussicht
über die Stadt, den Fluß und die Schwarzwaldberge. Viele
berühmte Männer haben in Basel gewohnt, z.B. die Maler
Conrad Witz, Albrecht Dürer und Hans Holbein und der größte
Gelehrte des 16. (sechzehnten) Jahrhunderts, Erasmus von
Rotterdam.

Seit dem Mittelalter ist Basel eine wichtige europäische
Handelsstadt gewesen. Hier kreuzten sich zwei große europäische
Handelswege, von Osten nach Westen und von Süden nach
Norden. Darum wurde Basel auch eine wichtige Industriestadt.
20 Im 16. (sechzehnten) Jahrhundert war Basel bekannt als die
Stadt der Buchdrucker, im 19. (neunzehnten) Jahrhundert
wurde die Seidenindustrie sehr wichtig, und in unserer Zeit ist
die Stadt berühmt als ein Zentrum der chemischen Industrie.
Auch in den Vereinigten Staaten kennen wir die Produkte der
Ciba. CIBA ist nur eine Abkürzung für C hemische I ndustrie
B a sel. Durch den Rhein hat Basel eine gute Wasserverbindung
mit dem Atlantischen Ozean.

Der Rhein fließt durch die Mitte der Stadt. Auf fünf Brücken
kann man über den Fluß gehen. Wenn man viel Zeit hat, kann
30 man auch mit der Fähre über den Rhein fahren. Dann erzählt
der Fährmann vielleicht eine Geschichte. Man nennt diese Geschichten in der Schweiz „Baseler Fährmannsgeschichten." Hier
ist eine der berühmten Geschichten, die der Fährmann auf dem
Rhein erzählt.

Eine Baseler Fährmannsgeschichte

In der Gerbergasse in Basel steht noch heute ein altes Haus,
das im Mittelalter plötzlich berühmt wurde. Dort geschah es
im Jahre 1479 (vierzehnhundertneunundsiebzig), daß ein Hahn

Courtesy of Basel Tourist Office, Basel

Basel: Die Fähre am Münster

ein Ei legte. Wenn ein Hahn ein Ei legt—so glaubte man im Mittelalter—dann wird aus diesem Ei ein großes Ungetüm kommen, das allen Leuten Tod und Verderben bringt. Darum wurde 40 der Hahn vor Gericht gestellt und wegen Hexerei zum Tode verurteilt. Das Ei wurde verbrannt und der Hahn wurde öffentlich enthauptet. So wurde die Stadt Basel gerettet.

VIII. Wörterverzeichnis

die Abkürzung, –en the abbreviation
der Atlantische Ozean the Atlantic Ocean
die Aussicht über the view of
bekannt known

die Brücke, –n the bridge
der Buchdrucker, – the book printer
chemisch chemical
daß that
ein Ei legen (to) lay an egg

enthaupten (to) behead
europäisch European
die Fähre, –n the ferry
der Fährmann the ferryman
die Fährmannsgeschichte, –n the ferryman's tale
der Felsen, – the cliff
fließen, floß, ist geflossen (to) flow
der Fluß, Flüsse the river
Frankreich France
der Gelehrte, (–n), –n the scholar
die Gerbergasse Gerber St., Tanner St.
vor Gericht before the court
die Grenze, –n the border
der größte the greatest
der Hahn, ⸚e the rooster
halb half
die Handelsstadt, –e the commercial city
der Handelsweg, –e the trade route
die Hexerei the witchcraft
die Industrie industry
die Industriestadt, –e the industrial city
das Jahrhundert, –e the century
sich kreuzen (to) cross
der Maler, – the painter
der Marktplatz, ⸚e the market place
das Mittelalter the Middle Ages

das Münster, – the minster, cathedral
der Norden the north
nördlich northern
öffentlich public
der Osten the east
der Platz, ⸚e the square
das Produkt, –e the product
retten (to) save
die Schwarzwaldberge the Black Forest Mountains
die Schweiz Switzerland
die Seidenindustrie the silk industry
der Süden the south
der Tod the death
zum Tode verurteilt condemned to death
das Ungetüm, –e the monster
verbrennen, verbrannte, verbrannt (to) burn
das Verderben the destruction, ruin
die Wasserverbindung, –en the water connection
wegen on account of
wenn if
der Westen the west
wunderbar wonderful
z.B.; zum Beispiel e.g., for example
das Zentrum the center
zusammen together

AUFGABE ZWÖLF

CONJUNCTIONS
DEPENDENT CLAUSES

I. Reading Selection

Am Sonntag haben Herbert und ich eine Reise nach Frankfurt gemacht. Da wir so viel von der Stadt gehört hatten, wollten wir sie einmal sehen. Obgleich es vormittags regnete, wurde es später ein sehr schöner Tag. Am Bahnhof kauften wir einen Führer, um darin zu lesen, was man über Frankfurt wissen muß. Dann gingen wir durch die Stadt, um alles zu sehen.

Frankfurt war bis vor hundert Jahren eine Freie Reichsstadt. Reichsstädte waren frei, weil sie nicht unter einem Fürsten standen, sondern direkt unter dem Kaiser. In diesen Städten regierte nicht ein Graf oder ein Herzog, sondern die Bürger selbst, 10 d.h. sie wählten einen Bürgermeister und einen Rat. Wenn der Bürgermeister die Räte zu einer Sitzung rief, kamen sie in das Rathaus, um dort über die Geschäfte der Stadt zu sprechen. Das Rathaus in Frankfurt ist sehr berühmt. Wenn ein Kaiser gestorben war, kamen die sieben Kurfürsten des Reiches im Rathaus von Frankfurt zusammen, um den nächsten Kaiser zu wählen. Weil früher hier ein „Gasthaus zum Römer" gestanden hatte, nannte man das Rathaus den „Römer." Nachdem die Kurfürsten gewählt hatten, ging der neue Kaiser auf den Balkon des

125

Courtesy of Deutsche Zentrale für Fremdenverke

Der Frankfurter Römer

Courtesy of Deutsche Zentrale für Fremdenverkehr

Frankfurter Spezialität: Frankfurter Würstchen, Brötchen,
Salzbretzel und Äpfelwein

Courtesy of German Tourist Information Office, Chicago

Rathauses, um sich dem Volk zu zeigen. Alle Leute schrieen 20
„Hurra" oder „Vivat" und zeigten damit dem Kaiser, daß sie
mit der Wahl zufrieden waren. Ich weiß nicht, ob sie auch etwas
tun konnten, wenn sie den Kaiser nicht mochten. Darüber stand
nichts in unserm Führer, obwohl wir zwei Mark dafür gezahlt
hatten.

Nicht alles in Frankfurt ist alt. Als wir einen Spaziergang
durch die Stadt machten, sahen wir, daß viele Häuser ganz neu
und modern sind.

Nachdem wir alles gesehen hatten, gingen wir zum Essen
in ein Restaurant. Ehe wir mit der Straßenbahn zum Bahnhof 30
fuhren, schrieben wir eine Ansichtskarte an Herberts Vater. Er
hat vor vielen Jahren in Frankfurt an der Universität studiert.

Als wir an diesem Abend nach Hause kamen, waren die
Löwenzahns noch im Wohnzimmer. Ehe wir zu Bette gingen,
erzählten wir ihnen von Frankfurt, vom Römer und vom Heiligen
Römischen Reich.

„Nichts ist geblieben", sagte Herr Löwenzahn, „kein Kurfürst,
kein Kaiser, kein Reich."

„Aber das deutsche Verb steht auch heute noch am Ende
des Nebensatzes", sagte ich. „Gute Nacht!"   40

II. Vocabulary

*als when
die **Ansichtskarte, –n** the picture
postcard
*der **Bahnhof, ⸚e** the railroad station
der **Balkon, –e** the balcony
der **Bürger, –** the citizen; *plu.:*
citizens, people
der **Bürgermeister, –** the mayor
*da (*conj.*) since
*daß (*conj.*) that
direkt direct
*ehe before
Frankfurter of Frankfurt (**–er** *is
usually added to names of cities*

*in German to mean pertain-
ing to. Cf. New Yorker in English*)
*frei free, independent
die **Freie Reichsstadt** the Independent Imperial City
*früher formerly
der **Führer, –** the guide; leader;
guide book
der **Fürst, (–en), –en** the prince
(*i.e., a ruling prince*)
das **Gasthaus zum Römer** the
Roman Inn
die **Geschäfte** (*plu.*) the business
der **Graf, (–en), –en** the count

*heilig holy
das **Heilige Römische Reich** the Holy Roman Empire
der **Herzog,** ̈-e the duke
hundert a hundred
hurra hurrah
der **Kaiser,** – the emperor
der **Kurfürst,** (–en), –en the elector
modern modern
*nachdem after
der **nächste** the next
der **Nebensatz,** ̈-e the dependent clause
*neu new
noch still
*ob whether, if
*obgleich although
*obwohl although
*oder or
der **Rat,** ̈-e the council, councillor
*das **Rathaus,** ̈-er the city hall
*regieren (to) reign, rule, govern
*regnen (to) rain
das **Reich,** –e the empire, nation
der **Römer** the Römer (*old city hall of Frankfurt*)

*selbst even; –self, e.g., himself, herself, etc.
sich himself
die **Sitzung,** –en the session, meeting
*der **Sonntag,** –e Sunday
*sterben (i), starb, ist gestorben (to) die
*studieren (to) study
*um . . . zu in order to
die **Universität,** –en the university
*der **Vater,** ̈ the father
das **Verb,** –en the verb
vivat (*Latin word*) Long may he live!
*das **Volk,** ̈-er the people, folk, nation
*vormittags mornings, in the morning
die **Wahl,** –en the choice, selection, election
wählen (to) choose, select, elect
*weil because
*wenn when(ever)
*zufrieden content, satisfied
zusammen together
*zwölf twelve

Idioms

*d.h. (*abbreviation for* das **heißt**) that is, i.e.
*vor vielen Jahren (*dat.*) many years ago (vor *with time expressions always means* ago: vor hundert Jahren, vor zwei Monaten, vor vier Wochen)

III. Grammar

A. Subordination

Statements like "She knows everything" or "She reads a lot" do not require a wider context to be meaningful.

One such statement can, however, be made dependent upon another, e.g., "She knows everything, because she reads a lot." The combined statement now consists of two clauses, a *main clause* ("She knows everything") and a *dependent* or *subordinate clause* ("because she reads a lot"). The dependent clause is introduced by a *subordinating conjunction* (in this case: *because*).

The two clauses may also be arranged in reverse order in the sentence: "Because she reads a lot, she knows everything."

In German, the dependent clause has a different word order: *the finite verb is at the end.* **Sie weiß alles, weil sie viel liest.** Note that the main clause has normal word order: the finite verb takes the second place.

If, however, the main clause follows the dependent clause, the main clause begins with the verb: **Weil sie viel liest, weiß sie alles.** We call this *inversion.*

The subordinating conjunctions in German are: **als, da, daß, ehe, nachdem, obgleich, obwohl, weil, wenn.** Examples:

Herbert war sehr hungrig, da er schwer gearbeitet hatte.
Conrad war nicht hungrig, obwohl er schwer gearbeitet hatte.
Obgleich Conrad schwer gearbeitet hatte, war er nicht hungrig.

Indirect questions beginning with **wer, was, wann, wo, wohin, wie,** or **ob** are dependent clauses, i.e., the finite verb stands at the end:

Fragen Sie ihn, was er will.
Monika fragte uns, wo wir wohnèn.
Der Lehrer fragte mich, ob ich meine Aufgabe habe.

Interpunctuation

All dependent clauses in German are set off by commas. Never forget to put in these commas; they act as a sort of reminder, calling attention to where the dependent clause starts or ends.

B. Infinitive Phrases

1. In German, the infinitive phrase functions as a dependent clause. It is set off by a comma, and the verb—here an infinitive—stands at the end of the clause:

Ich hoffe, Monika am Tennisplatz zu treffen
I hope *to meet* Monika at the tennis court .

2. To express purpose, the infinitive phrase begins with **um**:

Wir gingen durch die Stadt, **um** alles **zu sehen**
We walked through the city *in order to see* everything

Ich fahre in die Stadt um ein Kleid zu kaufen.

C. Coordination

Two statements can be coordinate, and in such a case neither statement is dependent upon the other. We have then two main clauses, e.g., "Mr. Löwenzahn does not hear well and Mrs. Löwenzahn does not see well." The two clauses are connected by a coordinating conjunction (in this case: *and*).

In German, the two (main) clauses both have normal word order:

Herr Löwenzahn hört nicht gut, und Frau Löwenzahn sieht nicht gut.

The coordinating conjunctions in German are: **und, aber, sondern, denn, oder.** Examples:

Die Aufgabe ist schwer, aber die Geduld des Lehrers ist groß.
Wir aßen sehr viel, denn wir waren sehr hungrig.

Note: Confusion of main-clause word order with dependent-clause word order can be easily avoided if the smaller group of coordinating conjunctions is carefully memorized. Remember: **und, aber, sondern, denn, oder** are coordinating. From this it follows that any other conjunction will be subordinating.

The conjunctions **weil** and **denn** are almost as freely exchangeable as *because* and *for*. However, **weil** introduces a *dependent clause*, whereas **denn** introduces a *main clause*.

D. wann, als, wenn, ob

1. **wann** (*when*) is an interrogative and asks for a point in time, a date: Wann ist er nach Hause gegangen? Können Sie mir sagen, wann er nach Hause gegangen ist?
2. **als** (*when*) is a subordinating conjunction and refers to a

single event in the past (when once at a certain time . . .) : Als wir nach Frankfurt fuhren, regnete es.

3. **wenn** (*when*) is a subordinating conjunction and refers to repeated or customary action in the present, past or future (*whenever*) : Wenn sie diese Geschichte las, wurde sie immer traurig.

4. **wenn** also means *if* (in a conditional sense) : Wenn ich Zeit habe, werde ich Ihnen schreiben.

5. But in statements in which *if* can be replaced by *whether*, the German equivalent is **ob**: Können Sie mir sagen, ob Herr Löwenzahn zu Hause ist?

E. selbst, selber

Note the following usages of **selbst, selber**:

> Herbert **selbst** hat die Aufgabe geschrieben.
> Herbert hat die Aufgabe **selbst** geschrieben.
> Herbert *himself* wrote the lesson.
> Herbert wrote the lesson *himself*.

The words **selbst** and **selber** are interchangeable.
In the meaning of *even*, **selbst** cannot be replaced by **selber**.

> **Selbst** Herbert wußte das.
> *Even* Herbert knew that.

F. Verbs ending in –ieren

There is a considerable number of verbs whose stem ends in –ier–, such as **regieren, studieren**. Their past participle does not have the prefix **ge–**:

> Der Kaiser regiert; der Kaiser hat **regiert**.
> Ich studiere; ich habe **studiert**.

All these verbs are of foreign origin and they are all weak. When you come across them, you will never have trouble in knowing their meanings: alarmieren, atomisieren, experimentieren, illuminieren, produzieren, reformieren, etc.

IV. Grammatical Exercises

A. Combine the following simple sentences into meaningful compound sentences, using the German conjunctions equivalent to the English in parentheses:

1. Wir haben ein Zimmer bei einer deutschen Familie. Wir sind nun in Deutschland. (*since, for, because*) 2. Ich sehe ein Schulbuch. Ich bin sofort krank. (*when, for, and, because*) 3. Er hatte einen Spaziergang gemacht. Er ging früh zu Bett. (*after*) 4. Die Fenster waren offen. Die Luft kam ins Zimmer. (*because, since*) 5. Conrads Aufgabe ist schwer. Die Geduld des Lehrers ist groß. (*but*) 6. Ich ging zu Bett. Ich schrieb meiner Mutter einen Brief. (*before*) 7. Es wird jetzt spät. Ich werde sehr hungrig. (*and, because, since*) 8. Ich frage Frau Löwenzahn: „Werden wir bald essen?" (*whether*) 9. Ich frage sie: „Werden wir essen?" (*when*) 10. Ich frage Herbert: „Liest Herr Löwenzahn in der Zeitung?" (*what*) 11. Er trägt eine Brille. Er sieht nicht gut. (*because, for, since*) 12. Wir hatten Tennis gespielt. Wir wurden durstig und bestellten ein Glas Limonade. (*since, after, because*) 13. Ich will dieses Kleid nicht kaufen. Es kostet zu viel. (*for, because*) 14. Wir waren auf den Balkon gegangen. Herr Löwenzahn brachte uns etwas zu trinken. (*after*) 15. Er wurde alt. Er konnte ganz gut hören. (*before*) 16. Ich sage: „Ich muß um sieben Uhr zu Hause sein." (*that*)

B. Use **wenn, wann, als,** or **ob**:

1. _____ es spät wird, wird Conrad hungrig. 2. _____ die Studenten an diesem Sonntag nach Frankfurt fuhren, sahen sie den Römer. 3. Ich möchte wissen, _____ man im Bahnhof ein Glas Limonade bestellen kann. 4. Im Führer steht nichts darüber, _____ der Kaiser gestorben ist. 5. _____ machen wir wieder einen Spaziergang? 6. _____ Herr Löwenzahn etwas Wein trank, dann sang er immer.

V. Translation Exercise

1. Since Herbert and Conrad don't have any (= *have no*) school on Sunday, they will go to Frankfurt on this day. 2. I believe that they will travel by car. 3. Although he has never studied in Germany, he knows German. 4. The students went downtown to buy something for Mrs. Löwenzahn. 5. We can ask the boy if he knows where the Römer is. 6. He says that it is situated in the middle of the city. 7. Her parents died many years ago. 8. When my father was a student in Frankfurt, he knew many people in the city. 9. Can you tell me when your father studied here? 10. After they had taken a walk through the city, they went into a restaurant in order to eat something. 11. Before they went home, they also drank a glass of Coca Cola. 12. Although it was raining, we took a walk in the afternoon. 13. Because the city hall is so famous, we wanted to see it. 14. The father of my friend told us that many years ago he had studied in Frankfurt. 15. When he sat in his garden, smoked a cigar and drank a glass of wine, he was always very content. 16. Do you know who this man is? 17. Can you tell me when he went to the station?

VI. Fragen

1. Warum wollten Conrad und Herbert Frankfurt sehen? 2. An welchem Tage fuhren sie dahin? 3. Wie wurde es an diesem Tag? 4. Warum haben sie einen Führer gekauft? 5. Warum sind sie durch die Stadt gegangen? 6. Warum nennt man eine Reichsstadt "frei"? 7. Wer hat in diesen Städten regiert? 8. Warum kamen die Räte in das Rathaus? 9. Wie nennt man das Frankfurter Rathaus? 10. Warum ist der neue Kaiser auf den Balkon des Römers gegangen? 11. Wieviel hatten die Studenten für ihren Führer gezahlt? 12. Was taten sie, ehe sie zum Bahnhof

gingen? 13. Wann hat Herberts Vater an der Universität Frankfurt studiert? 14. Wo waren die Löwenzahns am Abend?

VII. Lesestück

Münchhausen erzählt

Wenn man in Deutschland von einem Mann sagt: „Er erzählt
wie der Freiherr von Münchhausen", dann will man damit
sagen: „Er kann viele gute Geschichten erzählen, aber sie sind
alle nicht wahr. Er ist ein unterhaltsamer Lügner."

Münchhausen, so hören wir, lebte im 18. (achtzehnten)
Jahrhundert. Er war in vielen Kriegen, machte lange Reisen,
er war oft in großer Gefahr, aber er wußte immer Rat.

Hier mag er selbst uns eine seiner Geschichten erzählen. Wir
wollen daran denken, daß das Wort „lügen" nicht in seinem
10 Wörterbuch steht.

„Vor vielen Jahren war ich ein Matrose in der Flotte des
Kaisers. Der Kaiser und seine Flotte waren in großer Gefahr,
denn der Feind hatte mehr Matrosen als wir, mehr Schiffe und
eine große Kanone. Am Abend vor der Schlacht kam der Kaiser
zu mir. Als er in mein Zimmer kam, war er sehr besorgt und
traurig. Nachdem er mit mir gesprochen und meinen Rat gehört
hatte, ging er glücklich nach Hause, denn er wußte, daß wir
morgen den Feind schlagen würden.

Als die Schlacht begann, stand ich hinter unserer großen
20 Kanone und wartete auf den ersten Schuß des Feindes. Ich schoß
im gleichen Augenblick wie der Feind. Die beiden großen
Kanonenkugeln trafen sich in der Mitte zwischen uns und dem
Feind. Weil unsere Kugel stärker war, ging die Kugel des Feindes
zurück; sie enthauptete den Kanonier des Feindes und zwölf
andere Matrosen, die in einer Reihe hinter ihm standen, zerstörte
die Maste von drei Schiffen und fiel dann auf das Dach eines
Hauses auf dem Land. In dem Haus war nur eine alte Frau. Sie
lag auf einem Bett und schlief mit offenem Munde. Es war ein

altes Haus, ein altes Dach und eine schwere Kugel. Weil die Kugel zu schwer war, brach sie durch das Dach, fiel in den offenen 30 Mund der alten Frau und zerstörte ihren letzten Zahn.

Unsere Kugel aber zerstörte die große Kanone des Feindes und das Schiff des Admirals mit 1000 (tausend) Matrosen. Sie alle ertranken. Muß ich noch sagen, daß wir die Schlacht gewannen, und daß ich ein Admiral in der Flotte des Kaisers wurde?"

VIII. Wörterverzeichnis

der **Admiral, –e** the admiral
ander other
beginnen, begann, begonnen (to) begin
besorgt worried, apprehensive
brechen (i), brach, gebrochen (to) break
das **Dach, –̈er** the roof
enthaupten (to) behead
der **erste** the first
ertrinken, ertrank, ist ertrunken (to) drown
fallen (ä), fiel, ist gefallen (to) fall
der **Feind, –e** the enemy
die **Flotte, –n** the fleet
der **Freiherr, (–n), –en** the baron
gewinnen, gewann, gewonnen (to) win
im gleichen Augenblick in the same moment
glücklich happily
das **Jahrhundert, –e** the century
der **Kaiser, –** the emperor
die **Kanone, –n** the cannon
die **Kanonenkugel, –n** the cannonball
der **Kanonier, –e** the gunner
der **Krieg, –e** the war

die **Kugel, –n** the ball
der **letzte** the last
lügen, log, gelogen (to) lie, tell a lie
der **Lügner, –** the liar
der **Mast, –e** the mast
der **Matrose, (–n), –n** the sailor
mehr . . . als more . . . than
der **Mund, –̈er** the mouth
noch still, in addition
oft often
der **Rat** the counsel, advice
Rat wissen (to) know what to do
die **Reihe, –n** the row
das **Schiff, –e** the ship
die **Schlacht, –en** the battle
schlagen (ä) schlug, geschlagen (to) defeat
der **Schuß, Schüsse** the shot
sich themselves, each other
stärker stronger
unterhaltsam entertaining
wahr true
wie as
das **Wort, –e** *or* –̈er the word
das **Wörterbuch, –̈er** the dictionary
wir würden we would
der **Zahn, –̈e** the tooth
zerstören (to) destroy

AUFGABE DREIZEHN

PREFIX VERBS
TIME EXPRESSIONS

I. Reading Selection

Heute ist Monika Wenk abgefahren, um Freunde in Bremen zu besuchen. Wir waren am Bahnhof, weil wir ihr „Auf Wiedersehn" sagen wollten. Wir waren zu spät aufgestanden, und wir mußten laufen, um vor acht am Bahnhof anzukommen.

Als wir dann am Bahnhof waren, wußten wir nicht, auf welchem Bahnsteig der Zug abfuhr. Wir wußten nur, es war der Hansa-Expreß nach Bremen, und er sollte um acht Uhr abfahren. Wir hatten gerade angefangen, den Fahrplan zu lesen, als wir hinter uns Vera Sütterlins Stimme hörten: „Bahnsteig vier.
10 Kommen Sie mit mir! Ich brauche es nicht nachzusehen, weil ich oft mit diesem Zug aus der Schweiz hier angekommen bin."

Gerade als wir auf den Bahnsteig hinausgingen, kam der Zug an. Monika war schon da, und Herbert half ihr nun, ihre Koffer in den Zug hineinzutragen.

Leider blieb Monika nicht allein in ihrem Abteil. Eine Dame kam. Sie war sehr dick und furchtbar aufgeregt. Sie stieg ein und aus, machte das Fenster auf und zu, nahm ihren Hut ab und setzte ihn wieder auf. „Wo sind meine Koffer? Wo ist mein Mann?" schrie sie. Es war alles da: ihre fünf Koffer waren schon

138

im Abteil, und ihr Mann stand vor dem Zug auf dem Bahnsteig. 20
Er sprach gerade mit dem Schaffner: „Meine Frau fährt allein.
Sie muß in Köln umsteigen. Bitte, helfen Sie ihr mit den
Koffern."

„Wir werden Sie vermissen", sagte ich zu Monika. „Herbert
wird Sie sogar sehr vermissen. Wann werden Sie zurück-
kommen?"

„In einer Woche komme ich zurück", sagte sie. „Ich werde
Ihnen auch schreiben." Ich gebe zu, daß sie es mehr zu Herbert
als zu mir sagte.

Die Dame hatte das Fenster aufgemacht und sprach zu ihrem 30
Mann:

„Die Blumen brauchen jeden Tag Wasser.

Vergiß nicht, jeden Abend alle Fenster zuzumachen.

Denk daran, den Staubsauger zu reparieren.

Vergiß nicht, mich morgen anzurufen."

Der Zug fuhr ab, es wurde sehr laut auf dem Bahnsteig. Noch
einmal gaben wir Monika die Hand und riefen „Auf Wiedersehn!
Gute Reise! Kommen Sie bald zurück!" Alle Leute im Zug
und auf dem Bahnsteig winkten.

„Du darfst im Bett nicht rauchen", schrie die dicke Dame 40
noch. „In der Küche darfst du nicht . . ."

Doch dann konnte man sie nicht mehr hören.

„So", sagte ihr Mann laut. „Jetzt fangen meine Ferien an."

II. Vocabulary

NOTE: Separable prefixes will be indicated by a hyphen between the
prefix and the verb for the convenience of the student in both the lesson
and the end vocabularies. Thus we list **ab-fahren** as an aid to the student
who should not make any other use of the hyphen, but should write
abfahren.

*ab-fahren (ä), fuhr ab, ist abge-
fahren (to) leave, depart
*ab-nehmen (nimmt ab), nahm ab,
abgenommen (to) take off
*das Abteil, –e the compartment
*allein alone

*an-fangen (ä), fing an, ange-
fangen (to) begin
*an-kommen, kam an, ist ange-
kommen (to) arrive
*an-rufen, rief an, angerufen (to)
call up, (tele)phone

aufgeregt excited, stirred up

*auf-machen, machte auf, aufge-macht (to) open

auf-setzen, setzte auf, aufgesetzt (to) put on (*glasses, hat, etc.*)

*auf-stehen, stand auf, ist aufge-standen (to) get up, stand up

*aus-steigen aus, stieg aus, ist aus-gestiegen (to) get out, get off

*der Bahnsteig, –e the platform, track

*besuchen (to) visit

*bitte please

dick thick, fat

*dreizehn thirteen

*ein-steigen in, stieg ein, ist ein-gestiegen (to) get on, board (*a vehicle*)

der Expreß the express

der Fahrplan, ⸚e the time table

furchtbar frightful, terrible

*gerade just

hinaus-gehen, ging hinaus, ist hinausgegangen (to) go out

*hinein-tragen in (ä), trug hinein, hineingetragen (to) carry in

*der Hut, ⸚e the hat

der Koffer, – the suitcase; trunk; valise

*laufen (äu), lief, ist gelaufen (to) run

*leider unfortunately

*mehr more; nicht mehr no longer, not any more

*nach-sehen (ie), sah nach, nach-gesehen (to) look up (*in a phone book, time table, etc.*)

noch einmal once more, again

reparieren (to) repair, fix

der Schaffner, – the conductor

*die Schweiz Switzerland

*sogar even

der Staubsauger, – the vacuum cleaner

*die Stimme, –n the voice

um-steigen, stieg um, ist umge-stiegen (to) transfer, change trains

*vergessen (i), vergaß, vergessen (to) forget

vermissen (to) miss

wieder-sehen (ie), sah wieder, wiedergesehen (to) see again

winken (to) wave

*der Zug, ⸚e the train

zu-geben (i), gab zu, zugegeben to admit

*zu-machen, machte zu, zugemacht (to) shut, close

*zurück-kommen, kam zurück, ist zurückgekommen (to) come back, return

Idioms

*Auf Wiederseh(e)n good-bye

*Gute Reise pleasant journey, have a good trip

sehr *is used in German often when we say* very much: Ich vermisse Sie sehr, I miss you very much.

III. Grammar

A. Compound Verbs

In English, a large number of verbs are derived from other verbs. These derivations are formed in two ways:

1. a prefix is joined to the verb;
2. the verb is used in conjunction with a modifier, usually an adverb or a preposition.

For example:

1. pose: compose, dispose, expose, impose, propose, etc.
2. get: get up, get in, get out, get on, get off, etc.

Such verbs are called *compound verbs;* both types occur frequently in German. However, the second type is arranged in the sentence differently in German from the way it is in English.

B. Inseparable Prefixes

1. The prefixed elements in German compound verbs of type No. 1 are called *inseparable prefixes,* because they exist only as integral elements of verbs. They can never stand alone. The inseparable prefixes are:

 be–, ent–, emp–, er–, ge–, ver–, zer–

2. The inseparable prefixes are never accented (just as in English).

3. The participial prefix **ge–** is never added to the past participle of a compound verb with an inseparable prefix.

The compound verbs of this type so far listed in our active vocabulary are:

berichten, bestellen, besuchen, erklären, erzählen, geschehen, vergessen, verkaufen.

We have also used **beachten** (*notice*), **vermissen** (*miss*), **verstehen** (*understand*).

Their past participles are: **berichtet, bestellt, besucht, erklärt, erzählt, (ist) geschehen, vergessen, verkauft, beachtet, vermißt, verstanden.**

Here is an example of the complete usage:

PRES.   ich **bestelle** ein Glas Limonade
PAST   ich **bestellte** ein Glas Limonade

Fut.	ich **werde** ein Glas Limonade **bestellen**
Pres. Perf.	ich **habe** ein Glas Limonade **bestellt**
Past Perf.	ich **hatte** ein Glas Limonade **bestellt**

Imperative: **bestelle, bestellt, bestellen Sie!** Infinitive phrase: **Ich ging in ein Restaurant, um ein Glas Limonade zu bestellen.**

Note that the conjugational pattern differs from that of the simple verbs *only* in the past participle.

C. Separable Prefixes

1. The modifiers in German compound verbs of type No. 2 are called *separable prefixes.* They are so called because in an independent clause they are separated from the main body of the verb in the simple tenses (present tense, past tense,) as well as in the imperative, and are moved to the very end of the clause. Most prepositions and also some adverbs may serve as separable prefixes. In our active vocabulary we have had so far the following separable-prefix verbs: **abfahren, abnehmen, anfangen, ankommen, anrufen, aufmachen, aufstehen, aussteigen, einsteigen, zumachen, zurückkommen.**

2. Separable prefixes are always accented (just as the modifiers in English).

3. In the past participle, these verbs use the **ge–**prefix, but the **ge–** is placed between the prefix and the stem. Thus the past participles of the above-mentioned verbs are **abgefahren, abgenommen, angefangen, angekommen, angerufen, aufgemacht, aufgestanden, ausgestiegen, eingestiegen, zugemacht, zurückgekommen.**

4. In infinitive phrases the preposition **zu** of the infinitive is placed between the prefix and the stem, and all three elements are written as one word. Thus, in infinitive phrases, the verbs appear as **abzufahren, abzunehmen, anzufangen, anzukommen, anzurufen, aufzumachen, aufzustehen, auszusteigen, einzusteigen, zuzumachen, zurückzukommen.**

5. In dependent clauses, separable-prefix verbs never separate. Here the prefix remains "prefixed" to the finite verb.

Here is an example of the complete usage:

MAIN CLAUSES

Pres.	Conrad **nimmt** den Hut **ab**
Past	Conrad **nahm** den Hut **ab**
Fut.	Conrad **wird** den Hut **abnehmen**
Pres. Perf.	Conrad **hat** den Hut **abgenommen**
Past Perf.	Conrad **hatte** den Hut **abgenommen**
Imperative	**nimm** den Hut **ab!**
	nehmt den Hut **ab!**
	nehmen Sie den Hut **ab!**

DEPENDENT CLAUSES

Pres.	**Wenn** Monika den Hut **abnimmt** . . .
Past	**Als** Monika den Hut **abnahm** . . .
Fut.	**Ehe** Monika den Hut **abnehmen wird** . . .
Pres. Perf.	**Weil** Monika den Hut **abgenommen hat** . . .
Past Perf.	**Nachdem** Monika den Hut **abgenommen hatte** . . .
Infinitive Phrase	Monika ging ins Schlafzimmer, **um** den Hut **abzunehmen**

6. Compare the following two sentences:

Die Dame **steigt aus**	The lady *gets off*
Die Dame **steigt aus** dem Zug **aus**	The lady *gets off* the train

The first sentence is constructed the same way in German as in English, but the second sentence is not. It can be seen from the second sentence that the German "separable prefix" cannot function as a preposition. A sentence like „Die Dame steigt dem Zug aus" does not contain a preposition and is wrong. More examples:

Monika **steigt in** den Zug **ein.**
Monika *gets on* the train.

Der Zug **kommt am** Bahnhof **an.**
The train *arrives at* the station.

D. Doubtful Prefixes

The prefixed element of some verbs may be either separable or inseparable. With the separable prefix the verb has a literal meaning, with the inseparable prefix it has a figurative meaning.

Let's take the verb **übersetzen.** In its literal meaning, pronounced **ü'bersetzen,** it stands for (*to*) *ferry over.* **Der Fährmann setzte sie über,** *The ferryman ferried them over.* The past participle would be **ü'bergesetzt.** In its figurative meaning **übersétzen** stands for (*to*) *translate.* **Herbert übersétzte den Satz,** *Herbert translated the sentence.* The past participle is now **übersétzt.**

Likewise **wiéderholen** has a literal meaning: (*to*) *get back;* past: **er holte es wieder;** past participle: **wiédergeholt.** The figurative (and much more frequently used) verb is **wiederhólen,** *to repeat;* past tense: er **wiederhólte;** present perfect: er hat **wiederhólt.**

Often the literal verb does not exist, and only the figurative one is used. We have used actively the verb **unterbréchen,** (*to*) *interrupt,* which belongs in this category. Examples: **Er unterbrícht mich; unterbrích mich nicht!; er hat mich unterbróchen,** etc.

Fortunately the number of these doubtful prefix verbs is very limited. Our vocabulary will always clearly indicate the character of the prefix verbs.

E. hin—her, aus—ein, auf—ab

The prefixes **hin–** and **her–** are directional signals. **Hin** means *away from the speaker;* **her** means *toward the speaker.* They are used a great deal, both alone, and in combination with **ein** and **aus** (*in* and *out*) and **auf** and **ab** (*up* and *down*).

Suppose I am in a room and you are outside of it, and Conrad enters the room. I say: **Conrad kommt in das Zimmer herein.** You say: **Conrad geht in das Zimmer hinein.**—But Herbert leaves the room. I say: **Herbert geht aus dem Zimmer hinaus.** You say: **Herbert kommt aus dem Zimmer heraus.**

F. Time Expressions

1. When no preposition is used, **indefinite time takes the genitive case: Eines Tages (eines Abends)** fuhren die Freunde

nach Frankfurt, *One day (one evening)* the friends went to Frankfurt.

2. When no preposition is used, **definite time** or **duration of time takes the accusative**: Die Blumen brauchen **jeden Tag** Wasser, The flowers need water *every day.* Parallel expressions are: **alle Tage, jeden Abend, jede Nacht.** Sie arbeiteten **eine Stunde (lang),** They worked *(for) an hour.* Sie saßen **den ganzen Abend** auf dem *Balkon,* They sat on the balcony *(for) the whole evening.*

For other time expressions see Lesson IX, Section III,J.

G. Telling Time with **um, vor, nach**

In telling the hour of the day, **um** means *at;* **nach** means *after;* and **vor** means *before, until,* or *to.*

Wie spät ist es? or **Wieviel Uhr ist es?** *What time is it?* **Es ist fünf Minuten vor acht,** *It is five minutes to eight.* **Es ist gerade sieben (Uhr),** *It is exactly seven (o'clock).* **Kommt der Zug um neun (Uhr) an?** *Does the train arrive at nine (o'clock)?* **Es ist schon zehn Minuten nach zwölf,** *It is already ten minutes after twelve.*

H. Infinitives As Nouns

Practically any German infinitive can be used as a neuter noun. **Das Arbeiten macht mich hungrig,** *Working makes me hungry.* **Sein Beten half,** *His praying helped.* **Rauchen verboten,** *Smoking forbidden.* **Sehen ist Glauben,** *Seeing is Believing.* So **Auf Wiedersehen** means literally *until seeing (each other) again.*

IV. Grammatical Exercises

A. Put the following into the present, past, future, and perfect tenses:

1. Heute (abfahren) Monika Wenk. 2. Sie (hoffen), Freunde zu besuchen. 3. Sie (besuchen) Freunde in Bremen. 4. Wir (auf-

stehen) zu spät. 5. Wir (ankommen) vor acht am Bahnhof. 6. Auf welchem Bahnsteig (abfahren) der Zug? 7. Wir (anfangen), den Fahrplan zu studieren. 8. Wir (lesen) den Fahrplan. 9. Was (geschehen) nun? 10. Ich (ankommen) oft aus der Schweiz hier. 11. Er (hinausgehen) auf den Bahnsteig. 12. Dann (ankommen) der Zug. 13. Herbert (hineintragen) Monikas Koffer in den Zug. 14. Die Dame (einsteigen) sofort. 15. Sie (aufmachen) das Fenster. 16. Dann (zumachen) sie es wieder. 17. Wir (bestellen) etwas. 18. Wann (zurückkommen) Sie? 19. Herbert (unterbrechen) mich. 20. Er (vergessen) das nicht.

B. Make one sentence dependent upon the other with the help of the conjunction given in parenthesis:

1. Sie kam in Berlin an. Sie rief ihren Mann an. (als) 2. Meine Frau steigt in Hamburg um. Sie müssen ihr helfen. (wenn) 3. Der Zug war abgefahren. Sie machte den Koffer auf. (nachdem) 4. Wir standen zu spät auf. Wir kamen zu spät am Bahnhof an. (weil) 5. Er machte das Fenster zu. Es blieb kalt im Zimmer. (obgleich)

C. Make sentences with three forms of the imperative of the following verbs (with the words given in parenthesis):

1. besuchen (mich); 2. aufstehen (früher); 3. abnehmen (den Hut); 4. aufmachen (das Fenster); 5. vergessen (nicht den Koffer); 6. zurückkommen (bald); 7. erzählen (eine deutsche Geschichte); 8. unterbrechen (nie den Lehrer).

D. Use **zu** with the infinitive given in parenthesis, if and when needed:

1. Ich gehe in ein Restaurant, um etwas (bestellen). 2. Wir müssen in Frankfurt nicht (umsteigen). 3. Er kam gestern zu mir, um mir das (erzählen). 4. Hier darf man nicht (rauchen). 5. Er stand auf, um das Fenster (aufmachen). 6. Ich möchte das zu Hause (nachsehen). 7. Sie stellte ihre Frage nur, um ihn (unterbrechen).

V. Translation Exercise

1. We must not get up too late, for Monika is leaving early today. 2. We must get up earlier in order to say good-bye to her. 3. Do you know when the train leaves? 4. Don't get up too early! (*three forms*) 5. Herbert was on the platform in order to carry Monika's suitcase (*Koffer*) into the compartment. 6. When he arrived at the station, the train had just left. 7. It happened one day. 8. Do you know her? 9. Before she got into the compartment she bought a newspaper for the trip. 10. He is to open the windows every afternoon. 11. We hoped to arrive in Düsseldorf at nine o'clock (*Uhr*). 12. Please help me (to) close the windows (*three forms*). 13. I called him up before I visited him. 14. He became sick because he opened the window. 15. The lady gets on the train and then she gets off again. 16. When is Herbert's girl friend coming back? 17. She is visiting friends of her family in Bremen. 18. After she had returned, she began to learn English.

Re-do sentences 1, 10, and 15 in the past tense; sentences 13, 16, and 17 in the future and present perfect tenses.

VI. Fragen

1. Warum ist Monika nach Bremen gefahren? 2. Warum sind wir zum Bahnhof gegangen? 3. Warum mußten wir laufen? 4. Wann sollte der Zug abfahren? 5. Auf welchem Bahnsteig fuhr der Zug ab? 6. Was geschah, als wir auf den Bahnsteig gingen? 7. Was hat Herbert getan? 8. Wer ist auch in Monikas Abteil gestiegen? 9. Wieviele Koffer hatte die Dame? 10. Wo stand ihr Mann? 11. Mit wem sprach er? 12. Wo sollte die Dame umsteigen? 13. Muß Monika auch umsteigen? 14. Was sagte die Dame zu ihrem Mann, ehe der Zug abfuhr? 15. Was sagte der Mann, nachdem der Zug abgefahren war?

VII. Lesestück

Der Rattenfänger von Hameln

Nicht viele Leute in Deutschland kennen die kleine, alte Stadt Hameln an der Weser, aber jedes deutsche Kind kennt die Geschichte vom Rattenfänger von Hameln.

Es geschah im Mittelalter, daß die Zahl der Ratten in Hameln erschreckend wuchs. Man sah sie in allen Häusern und auf allen Straßen. Nicht nur in der Nacht, sondern auch am hellen Tage liefen sie durch die Stadt. Die Bürger von Hameln legten Gift, sie töteten Hunderte und Tausende von Ratten, doch ihre Zahl wuchs mit jedem Tage.

10 An einem schönen Tag im Sommer kam ein junger Mann in die Stadt, den niemand kannte. Er ging zum Rathaus und fragte den Bürgermeister: „Wieviel wollt ihr mir zahlen, wenn ich euch von den Ratten befreie?"

Der Bürgermeister rief seine Räte und erzählte ihnen von dem Angebot des jungen Mannes.

„Wenn du uns von den Ratten befreien kannst", sagte der Bürgermeister dann zu dem jungen Mann, „werden wir dir tausend Gulden zahlen und ich, meine Räte und alle Bürger der Stadt werden dir ewig dankbar sein."

20 Der junge Mann war damit zufrieden. Er nahm aus seiner Tasche eine Flöte und, während er langsam durch alle Straßen von Hameln ging, spielte er seltsame Melodien darauf. Aus allen Häusern kamen nun die Ratten und folgten ihm. Als alle Ratten aus den Häusern herausgekommen waren, ging der junge Mann zur Weser, gefolgt von Tausenden von Ratten. Er führte sie ins Wasser, und alle Ratten ertranken in der Weser.

Am Abend ging der junge Mann zum Rathaus, um sein Geld zu holen. Doch der Bürgermeister und die Räte lachten. „Wir wußten nicht, daß es so einfach war. Tausend Gulden? Hier, 30 nimm zehn Gulden, das ist genug für dein Flötenspiel."

Der junge Mann sagte nichts. Er warf die zehn Gulden auf den Tisch und ging.

Doch an einem Abend im Herbst kam er zurück. Wieder ging er langsam durch die Straßen von Hameln, und wieder spielte er auf seiner Flöte seltsame Melodien. Jetzt kamen die Kinder von Hameln aus ihren Häusern, alle Kinder zwischen sechs und dreizehn. Sie alle folgten dem jungen Mann mit seiner Flöte. Sie hörten nicht die Stimmen der Eltern, sie hörten nur das Flötenspiel des jungen Mannes. Er führte sie aus der Stadt, in den Wald und in die Berge über der Weser. Sie kamen nie 40 zurück, und niemand weiß, was aus ihnen geworden ist.

VIII. Wörterverzeichnis

das **Angebot,** –e the offer
befreien (to) free
der **Bürger,** – the citizen
der **Bürgermeister,** – the mayor
dankbar grateful
einfach simple
erschreckend frightfully, startlingly
ertrinken, ertrank, ist ertrunken (to) drown
ewig forever, eternally
die **Flöte,** –n the flute
das **Flötenspiel** the flute-playing
folgen (*with dative*) (to) follow
führen (to) lead
genug enough
das **Gift,** –e the poison
der **Gulden,** – the guilder
hell bright
heraus-kommen, kam heraus, ist herausgekommen (to) come out

holen (to) get
Hunderte hundreds
klein small
langsam slowly
legen (to) place, set out
die **Melodie,** –n the melody, tune
das **Mittelalter** the Middle Ages
niemand no one
der **Rat,** ⁼e the councillor, alderman
die **Ratte,** –n the rat
der **Rattenfänger,** – the rat catcher
seltsam strange
spielen (to) play
Tausende thousands
töten (to) kill
während (*conj.*) while
die **Weser** the Weser (River)
wieviel how much
die **Zahl,** –en the number

AUFGABE VIERZEHN

RELATIVE PRONOUNS
GENITIVE PREPOSITIONS

I. Reading Selection

Liebe Vera!

Gestern bin ich nach einer Reise, von der man nicht viel berichten kann, hier in Bremen angekommen. Die Dame, deren Mann mit Euch auf dem Bahnsteig stand, wurde später sehr nett. Während der Reise machte sie vier Schachteln mit Süßigkeiten auf und bot allen Leuten im Zug davon an. „Bitte essen Sie", sagte sie immer wieder. „Ich selbst sollte wegen meiner Figur nichts davon nehmen. Ich weiß nicht, warum ich so viel Schokolade esse. Mein Arzt sagt, es ist alles psychologisch, aber was
10 wissen die Ärzte?"

Unser Zug kam um drei Uhr in Bremen an. Meine Freundin Anna und ihre Eltern, die ich bis jetzt noch nicht kannte, waren am Bahnhof. Sie haben ein neues Auto, womit wir sofort eine Rundfahrt durch die Stadt machten. Es ist eine Stadt, die viele Jahrhunderte alt und sehr interessant ist, mit einem Hafen, von dem Schiffe in alle Länder der Welt fahren. Annas Vater hat mir viel aus der Geschichte Bremens erzählt, wovon ich leider nicht alles verstanden habe. Ich bin in Geschichte nicht so gut wie Herbert. Heute sind wir in die Stadt gegangen, um das

150

Courtesy of German Tourist Information Office, New York

Das alte Rathaus und der St. Petri Dom in Bremen

20 Rathaus zu sehen. Unten im Rathaus ist der Ratskeller, wo wir zu Mittag gegessen haben. Vor dem Rathaus steht eine Statue, ein Mann, der in den Händen ein Schwert hält. Diese Statue ist der Roland von Bremen, ein Symbol der Gerechtigkeit. Ich mußte an etwas denken, was ich in der Schule gelernt hatte:

> Roland, der Riese, am Rathaus zu Bremen,
> Steht er ein Standbild, standhaft und starr.[1]

Vom Rathaus gingen wir zum Dom, dessen Dach im Lauf der Zeit ganz grün geworden ist, was mir sehr gut gefällt.

Die Landschaft ist nicht wie zu Hause. Anstatt der Berge und 30 Wälder, wie wir sie kennen, gibt es hier Felder und Wiesen, die alle ganz flach sind. Weil das Land so flach ist, fahren fast alle Leute mit den Rädern. Herbert (Du weißt, er kommt von Colorado) sagt immer, eine Landschaft ohne Berge gefällt ihm nicht.

Wie geht es Dir? Wie geht es unseren Freunden aus Amerika? Hilfst Du ihnen, wenn sie ihre Aufgaben übersetzen müssen? Hast Du Herbert gesehen? Hat er von mir gesprochen? Schreib mir darüber. (Ich weiß nicht, warum Du jetzt lächelst. Kann ich nicht fragen, was meine Freunde tun?)

Es ist spät in der Nacht, und ich will zu Bett gehen. Ich hoffe, 40 von Dir zu hören, ehe ich hier wieder abfahre.

Herzlich, Deine Monika.

II. Vocabulary

*an-bieten, bot an, angeboten (to) offer

*anstatt (*prep. with gen.*) instead of

*der Arzt, ⸚e the physician, doctor

das Dach, ⸚er the roof

der Dom, –e the cathedral

*das Feld, –er the field

die Figur, –en the figure

*flach flat, level

*gefallen (ä), gefiel, gefallen (*takes dative*) (to) be pleasing to

die Gerechtigkeit justice

der Hafen, – the harbor, port

*halten (hält), hielt, gehalten (to) hold

*herzlich cordial

*interessant interesting

*das Jahrhundert, –e the century

der Lauf the course

---

[1] Roland, the giant, at Bremen's town hall
Stands as a statue, steadfast and stern.

*lieb dear
nett nice
psychologisch psychological
der Ratskeller the *rathskeller,* basement restaurant in city hall
die Rundfahrt, –en the drive, sightseeing trip
die Schachtel, –n the box
*das Schiff, –e the ship
die Schokolade the chocolate
das Schwert, –er the sword
die Statue, –n the statue
die Süßigkeiten (*plu.*) sweets, candies

das Symbol, –e the symbol
*übersetzen, übersetzte, übersetzt (to) translate
*unten downstairs, below
*verstehen, verstand, verstanden (to) understand
*vierzehn fourteen
*während (*prep. with gen.*) during
*wegen (*prep. with gen.*) on account of
*die Welt the world
*wie (*conj.*) as, like
*die Wiese, –n the meadow

Idioms

*es gefällt mir, es gefällt ihm, etc. I like it, he likes it, etc.
*immer wieder again and again.
*Wie geht es dir? Es geht mir gut. How are you? I'm fine.
*er ißt zu Mittag he has (*eats*) dinner (*at noon*)

III. Grammar

A. Relative Clause and Relative Pronoun

A relative clause modifies a noun by further identification or specification: the man *who bought the car* had much money.

The relative clause is introduced by a relative pronoun (in our example: *who*). The noun to which the relative pronoun refers (in our example: *the man*) is called the antecedent.

B. Definite Relative Pronouns

1. In German, the definite relative pronoun is identical with the definite article, except in all forms of the genitive, and in the dative plural.

	Masculine	Feminine	Neuter	Plural
Nom.	der	die	das	die
Gen.	dessen	deren	dessen	deren
Dat.	dem	der	dem	denen
Acc.	den	die	das	die

In place of **der, die, das** German sometimes uses **welcher, welche, welches,** etc., which, however, has no forms for the genitive case (singular and plural). For the genitive we must always use **dessen** and **deren.** In present-day German the **der** forms are preferred.

2. In English, there are three different relative pronouns: *who,* referring to a person; *which,* referring to a "thing"; and *that,* which can be used for both. No such distinction exists in German. The same set of relative pronouns is used, no matter whether you wish to express *who, which,* or *that* in English.

3. **In German the relative pronoun must agree with its antecedent in gender and number.** The antecedent determines whether the relative pronoun is masculine, feminine, or neuter; singular or plural.

4. The case of the relative pronoun is determined by its grammatical function in the relative clause.

Der   Mann,   der   mit ihm sprach, war sein Lehrer.
      masc. *masc.*
      subj.   *subj.*

Ich kenne den   Mann,   der   da sitzt.
        masc.   *masc.*
          obj.   *subj.*

Der   Mann,   den   Sie sahen, war unser Arzt.
      masc.   *masc.*
      subj.   *direct obj.*

Die   Frau,   der   Herbert die Zeitung gibt, ist Frau Löwenzahn.
      fem.   *fem.*
      subj. *indir. obj.*

5. **The relative clause is a dependent clause. Consequently the finite verb stands at the end of the clause.**

6. German relative clauses are always set off by commas.

7. In English the relative pronoun can be omitted. This can never be done in German.

The car he bought was new: Das Auto, **das** er kaufte, war neu.
The man you saw was my friend: Der Mann, **den** Sie sahen, war mein Freund.

8. The relative pronoun, like any noun or pronoun, may be governed by a preposition. In German the preposition always precedes the relative pronoun.

The house *in* which we live is very old
The house which we live *in* is very old
The house we live *in* is very old:
Das Haus, **in** dem wir wohnen, ist sehr alt.

9. **If the relative pronoun is preceded by a preposition and refers to an inanimate antecedent, a** *wo* + *preposition* **combination may be used,** similar to the one explained for interrogative pronouns in Lesson VIII, Section III,B. So we may say: Der Bleistift, **womit** ich schreibe, ist grün. Das Zimmer, **worin** ich schlafe, ist groß. Die Gläser, **woraus** wir trinken, sind schön. However, these relative **wo–** combinations are less frequently used than the interrogative **wo–** combinations (see Lesson VIII) or the personal pronoun **da–** combinations (see Lesson V).

10. In English the word *that* can be used as a relative pronoun. The book *that* (= *which*) he gave me was interesting. Das Buch, **das** er mir gab, war interessant. However, the English word *that* can also serve to introduce a dependent finite clause. In this usage *that* parallels the German **daß,** the subordinating conjunction (see Lesson XII, Section III,A).

Do not forget that I shall leave tomorrow.
Vergiß nicht, **daß** ich morgen abfahren werde.

C. Indefinite Relative Pronouns

1. The German indefinite relative pronouns are **wer** and **was.** They are identical with the interrogative pronouns (see Lesson VIII). They correspond to the English compounds *whoever* and *whatever* (or *he who* and *that which*). The indefinite relative pronoun shows neither gender nor number, but it carries the distinction of persons (**wer**) and "things" (**was**):

Wer krank ist, kann nicht arbeiten *Whoever is sick, cannot work*
Wer das getan hat, ist nicht mein Freund *Whoever has done that, is not my friend*

Wen wir mögen, (den) besuchen wir *Who(m)ever we like, we visit*
Was schön ist, ist auch gut *Whatever is beautiful is also good*

2. If the antecedent is **alles, etwas, nichts, viel,** the relative pronoun is **was: Er erzählte mir nichts, was ich nicht schon wußte;** *He told me nothing that I didn't know already.*

3. If the antecedent is the content of an entire clause, the relative pronoun is also **was: Er lag zwei Stunden in der Sonne, was ihn sehr durstig machte;** *He was lying in the sun for two hours, which made him very thirsty.* In our example it is not the *sun, which* made him thirsty, rather his lying in it did so.

D. Prepositions with the Genitive

A few prepositions in German take the genitive case: **anstatt** or **statt** (*instead of*) and **während** (*during*). Also the prepositions **wegen** (*on account of*) and **trotz** (*in spite of*) traditionally take the genitive, but in modern German are frequently followed by the dative case.

E. Capitals in Correspondence

In writing letters, not only the polite form but also the familiar forms of personal pronouns and possessive adjectives are capitalized (**Du, Ihr, Dein, Euer,** etc.).

IV. Grammatical Exercises

A. Fill in the proper relative pronoun:

1. Der Mann, _____ mit Ihnen sprach, ist ein Arzt. 2. Der Student, _____ ich das Geschenk gab, hatte gestern Geburtstag. 3. Die Leute, _____ ich diesen Brief schreibe, sind Freunde meiner Eltern. 4. Der Mann, _____ Frau auf Ferien ist, soll jeden Morgen die Fenster im Hause aufmachen. 5. Der Stuhl, _____ in meinem Zimmer steht, gefällt mir. 6. Ist das alles, _____ Sie von ihm wissen? 7. Der Schüler, _____ Sie da sehen, ist der Sohn meines

Freundes. 8. Die Aufgabe, _____ wir heute schreiben müssen, ist schwer. 9. Der Sessel, auf _____ ich sitze, ist neu. 10. Die Mädchen sprechen sehr gut deutsch, _____ uns sehr gut gefällt. 11. Der Mann, in _____ Haus wir wohnen, ist ein Lehrer. 12. Das Buch, in _____ ich lese, ist sehr interessant. 13. Unsere Studenten haben eine Reise gemacht, von _____ ich Ihnen etwas erzählen will. 14. Die Kirche, vor _____ wir jetzt stehen, ist sehr alt. 15. Der Kaffee, _____ er mir brachte, war kalt. 16. Nun stieg eine Dame in das Abteil ein, in _____ Monika saß. 17. Dieser Zug, mit _____ ich oft fahre, kommt aus der Schweiz. 18. Die Frau, _____ Familie wir sehr gut kennen, wird mit Monika nach Bremen fahren. 19. Er hat nichts vergessen, _____ er gelernt hat. 20. _____ mir hilft, ist mein Freund. 21. Er zeigte mir etwas, _____ ich noch nie gesehen hatte. 22. Das Zimmer, aus _____ ich komme, ist unser Wohnzimmer. 23. Die Mädchen, mit _____ wir Tennis gespielt haben, sind Freundinnen. 24. Frau Löwenzahn, _____ Kinder gestern abgefahren sind, ist heute sehr traurig.

B. Re-do sentences 12 and 13 of Exercise A, using a **wo–** combination instead of the relative pronoun.

V. Translation Exercise

1. The physician told a story that had happened many years ago. 2. The lady with whom she took the trip was not very beautiful. 3. The man whose wife was on the train had gone home. 4. Whoever takes a trip to Germany must see the Rhineland. 5. The city hall, in which we ate dinner, is many centuries old. 6. Is that all you know about it? 7. The woman who called us up is a friend of my mother. 8. Anna's parents, in whose house we are living, are friends of my father. 9. The doctor I visited knows almost everything. 10. The student with whom I talked during the trip told me something that I didn't know yet. 11. The pencil with which I write is not very good. 12. On account of his birthday the pupil had no time to translate his lesson. 13. She talked about her family, which did not happen very often. 14. Do you

know the man whose house we bought? 15. The lady whose husband stood on the platform opened the window and offered him a cigarette. 16. He translates much every day, which is very good for him.

VI. Fragen

1. Wohin ist Monika gestern gefahren? 2. Was tat die dicke Dame während der Reise? 3. Warum soll sie keine Süßigkeiten essen? 4. Wann kam der Zug in Bremen an? 5. Wer war am Bahnhof? 6. Was haben sie dann alle gemacht? 7. Was wissen Sie über Bremen? 8. Wo steht der Roland in Bremen? 9. Was steht neben dem Rathaus? 10. Warum gefällt Monika das Dach des Domes? 11. Was sagt Monika über die Landschaft bei Bremen? 12. Worüber soll Vera ihr berichten?

VII. Lesestück

Deutsche Klöster

Bis zum 8. (achten) Jahrhundert waren die deutschen Stämme, die in dem Land zwischen Weser und Rhein wohnten, heidnisch. Sie verehrten heidnische Götter, deren Namen noch heute in den Namen der Wochentage leben, z.B. in den deutschen Namen Donnerstag und Freitag oder in den englischen Namen W e d n e s d a y und T h u r s d a y.

In der Mitte des 8. (achten) Jahrhunderts kam Bonifatius nach Deutschland, ein englischer Mönch, dem die deutsche Geschichte den Namen „Apostel der Deutschen" gegeben hat. Er
10 predigte die christliche Religion und bekehrte Tausende von Heiden zum Christentum. In den Wäldern von Deutschland gab es oft große, alte Bäume. Viele dieser Bäume (so glaubten die heidnischen Deutschen) waren heilig und den Göttern geweiht. Es war ein wichtiger Tag in der deutschen Geschichte, als Bonifatius eine große, alte, heilige Eiche fällte. Er wollte den

Courtesy of Landesverkehrsverband Hessen, Wiesbaden

Kloster Eberbach im Rheingau

Courtesy of German Tourist Information Office, New York

Deutschen zeigen, daß kein heidnischer Gott protestierte oder ihn strafte, und daß darum ihre heidnische Religion falsch war.

Es dauerte noch mehr als 100 (hundert) Jahre, bis alle Deutschen das Christentum angenommen hatten. Die christlichen Mönche gründeten Klöster in allen Gegenden Deutschlands. 20 Diese Klöster wurden bald die Zentren christlicher Kultur. In diesen Zeiten vor der Erfindung der Buchdruckerkunst war es sehr wichtig, daß in allen Klöstern die Mönche alte Manuskripte abschrieben. So retteten sie viele Werke der alten, deutschen Literatur. Fast alle Klöster hatten Schulen, in denen die Mönche lehrten. Man hat oft die 200 (zweihundert) Jahre von 900 (neunhundert) bis 1100 (elfhundert) „die Zeit der Klosterkultur" genannt. Berühmt waren das Kloster St. Gallen in der Schweiz, das Kloster Reichenau auf einer Insel im Bodensee, oder die Klöster Fulda, Hersfeld, Gandersheim, Tegernsee, Maulbronn, 30 Weißenburg, St. Blasien, Eberbach. Dies sind nur ein paar Namen aus der Geschichte berühmter deutscher Klöster.

Eine Klostergeschichte

Die Mönche des alten Klosters Eberbach waren berühmt, nicht nur wegen ihrer Frömmigkeit und Gelehrsamkeit, sondern auch weil in ihrem Weinberg der beste Wein am Rhein wuchs. Eberbach gehörte zu dem großen Kloster Fulda. Jedes Jahr, wenn der Wein zu reifen anfing, mußte ein Bote zum Abt nach Fulda gehen und fragen, ob sie jetzt die Trauben schneiden dürften. Für die Reise von Eberbach nach Fulda brauchte man drei oder vier Tage. Es geschah in einem Herbst, daß der Bote auf dieser Reise 40 krank wurde. Die Trauben wurden reif und überreif, aber der Bote kam nicht. Es war nun Ende Oktober. Die meisten Trauben waren in der warmen Sonne trocken geworden oder halbverfault. Die guten Mönche waren verzweifelt, als endlich, endlich der Bote aus Fulda ankam. Die Eberbacher Mönche schnitten traurig ihre überreifen und halbverfaulten Trauben, doch sieh da: nie zuvor hatte man einen so guten Wein getrunken. Seit dieser Zeit wissen die Leute am Rhein, daß man aus den späten, überreifen Trauben den besten Wein macht.

VIII. Wörterverzeichnis

ab-schreiben, schrieb ab, abgeschrieben (to) copy
der Abt, ∸e the abbot
an-nehmen (nimmt an), nahm an,
angenommen (to) accept
der Apostel, – the apostle
der Baum, ∸e the tree
bekehren (to) convert
der beste the best
der Bodensee Lake Constance
Bonifatius Boniface
der Bote, (–n), –n the messenger
die Buchdruckerkunst the art of
printing
das Christentum Christianity
christlich Christian
dauern (to) last, take
der Donnerstag Thursday
die Eiche, –n the oak (tree)
endlich finally
die Erfindung, –en the invention
fällen (to) fell, cut down
falsch false
der Freitag Friday
die Frömmigkeit piety
die Gegend, –en the region
die Gelehrsamkeit learning
geweiht dedicated
der Gott, ∸er the god
gründen (to) found
halbverfault half rotten
der Heide, (–n), –n the heathen,
pagan
heidnisch heathen
die Insel, –n the island

das Kloster, ∸ the cloister, monastery
die Klosterkultur the cloister culture
die Kultur the culture
die Literatur the literature
die meisten most of the
der Mönch, –e the monk
der Name, (–ns), –n the name
nie zuvor never before
noch still
predigen (to) preach
protestieren (to) protest
reif ripe
reifen (to) ripen
die Religion, –en the religion
retten (to) save
St.; Sankt St.; Saint
sieh da lo and behold
der Stamm, ∸e the tribe
strafen (to) punish
Tausende thousands
die Traube, –n the grape
trocken dry
überreif over-ripe
verehren (to) venerate
verzweifelt desperate, in despair
der Weinberg, –e the vineyard
das Werk, –e the work (of art)
der Wochentag, –e the day of the
week
das Zentrum; Zentren the center;
centers
z.B.; zum Beispiel e.g.; for example
zuvor before

AUFGABE FÜNFZEHN

DECLENSION OF ADJECTIVES
TIME EXPRESSIONS

I. Reading Selection

„Wollen Sie heute abend mit mir kommen?" fragte mich Herr
Löwenzahn. „Ich gehe zur Probe meines Gesangvereins."
„Das ist nichts Interessantes", sagte Frau Löwenzahn.
„Es ist etwas sehr Deutsches", meinte Herr Löwenzahn. „Wir
singen alte deutsche Volkslieder, und manchmal haben wir ein
großes Fest, zu dem wir unsere Familien und Freunde einladen."
„Ich komme gern", sagte ich.
Wir gingen zusammen in die Stadt. Der Gesangverein hatte
seine Proben in einem alten Wirtshaus. Als wir ankamen, hatte
die Probe schon angefangen. Weil Herr Löwenzahn zu spät kam, 10
mußte er sofort fünfzig Pfennig Strafe zahlen. „Wir haben hier
sehr strenge Gesetze", sagte er ernst. Dann ging er auf die Bühne,
wo seine Freunde schon standen. Sie fingen gerade ein neues Lied
an. Es berichtete eine traurige Geschichte von einem grünen
Wald, in dem viele freundliche Tiere lebten, unter ihnen ein
hübsches, junges Reh. Ein böser Mann kam in den Wald, ein
Jäger mit einem Gewehr. Sein Hut hatte die grüne Farbe des
Waldes, doch er hatte ein schwarzes Herz. In der Mitte des
dunklen Waldes traf der Jäger das junge Reh, und nun geschah,

20 was geschehen mußte: er schoß es und brachte damit das Leben
des Rehes und das traurige Lied zu einem schnellen Ende. Die
Männer sangen die letzten Worte des Liedes mit solch leiser
Stimme, daß man sie kaum verstehen konnte. Doch sofort danach
wurden sie sehr laut, kamen von der Bühne und bestellten Bier.
„Nichts macht so durstig wie ein trauriges Lied", sagten sie.

Es gab eine Pause von fünfzehn Minuten, in der ich mit einem
alten Mann sprach, der vor vielen Jahren in Baltimore gelebt
hatte. „Ich habe gern in Baltimore gewohnt", erzählte er mir,
„aber wegen der heißen, feuchten Monate im Sommer konnte ich
30 dort nicht leben. Hier in Deutschland ist es zu kalt, und es regnet
zu viel. Man ist nie zufrieden."

Nun gingen die Männer wieder auf die Bühne und sangen
einige berühmte deutsche Lieder, traurige und lustige, Lieder von
schönen Mädchen, von gutem Wein, von heißer Liebe, von hohen
Bergen, von einer blauen Blume und immer wieder von dunklen,
grünen Wäldern. Dann sangen sie auch das Lied von der Loreley,
von dem wir in Aufgabe elf sprachen.

Wieder ein sehr trauriges Lied, dachte ich, es wird sie wieder
sehr durstig machen. Doch sofort danach kam das letzte Lied des
40 Abends, „Das Schweigen im Walde", in dem sie so laut und hoch
schrieen, daß sie alle rote Köpfe hatten.

„Wie hat Ihnen unser letztes Lied gefallen?" fragte mich Herr
Löwenzahn, als wir später nach Hause gingen.

„Es war ein sehr lautes Schweigen", sagte ich.

II. Vocabulary

das **Bier** the beer
*__blau__ blue
__böse__ bad, evil
die **Bühne, –n** the stage
*__dunkel__ dark
*__einige__ some, a few
ein-laden (ladet ein or lädt ein),
  lud ein, eingeladen (zu) (to)
  invite (to)

das **Fest, –e** festival, celebration
__feucht__ humid
__freundlich__ friendly, kind
*__fünfzehn__ fifteen
__fünfzig__ fifty
der **Gesangverein, –e** the singing
  society, choral group
das **Gesetz, –e** the law, rule
das **Gewehr, –e** the gun

*das Herz, (–ens), –en the heart
*hoch high
der Jäger, – the hunter
*kaum scarcely, hardly
*der letzte the last
*das Lied, –er the song
*manche some (*plu.*)
*manchmal sometimes
*mehrere several
die Pause, –n the pause, recess, intermission
die Probe, –n the rehearsal, trial
das Reh, –e the deer

schießen, schoß, geschossen (to) shoot
das Schweigen the silence
die Strafe, –n the punishment, fine
streng strict
*unter among
das Volkslied, –er the folksong
*wenig little, not much
*wenige few
das Wirtshaus, ¨er the inn, tavern
*das Wort, ¨er or –e the word
*zusammen together

Idioms

*ich komme gern I like to come, I'd like to come
*heute abend this evening

III. Grammar

Adjectives are used **predicatively** (*the shirt is blue*) or **attributively** (*the blue shirt is in the laundry*). Predicate adjectives, as in English, do not have declensional endings. The attributive adjective, however, is declined in German so that it agrees with the number, case and gender of the noun to which it is attributed. There are three declensional patterns according to the following three syntactical patterns:

A. **der-**word—adjective—noun
B. **ein-**word—adjective—noun
C.   adjective—noun

A. Declension of Adjectives after **der**–Words

	MASCULINE	FEMININE	NEUTER
NOM.	der gute Mann	diese gute Frau	jedes gute Kind
GEN.	des guten Mannes	dieser guten Frau	jedes guten Kindes
DAT.	dem guten Mann	dieser guten Frau	jedem guten Kind
ACC.	den guten Mann	diese gute Frau	jedes gute Kind

PLURAL

Nom.	die guten Leute
Gen.	der guten Leute
Dat.	den guten Leuten
Acc.	die guten Leute

In Lesson IV we classified as **der-words: der, dieser, jeder, mancher, solcher, welcher.** Review Lesson IV, Section III, and make sure you have full command of the declension of **der words.**

B. Declension of Adjectives after **ein**–Words

	MASCULINE	FEMININE	NEUTER
Nom.	ein guter Mann	deine gute Frau	ihr gutes Kind
Gen.	eines guten Mannes	deiner guten Frau	ihres guten Kindes
Dat.	einem guten Mann	deiner guten Frau	ihrem guten Kind
Acc.	einen guten Mann	deine gute Frau	ihr gutes Kind

PLURAL

Nom.	keine guten Leute
Gen.	keiner guten Leute
Dat.	keinen guten Leuten
Acc.	keine guten Leute

Again we refer to Lesson IV where we classified as **ein-words: ein, kein, mein, dein, sein, ihr, sein; unser, euer, ihr, Ihr.** (Remember: **ein** has no plural.)

Comparing the declensional patterns A and B, we find that in both patterns the adjective ending is **–en** in the genitive and dative singular and in all cases of the plural. That is easy to remember. We have to concentrate mainly on the nominative and accusative singular:

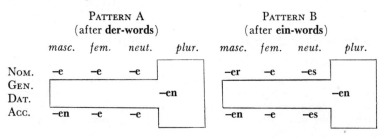

	PATTERN A (after **der-words**)				PATTERN B (after **ein-words**)			
	masc.	*fem.*	*neut.*	*plur.*	*masc.*	*fem.*	*neut.*	*plur.*
Nom.	–e	–e	–e		–er	–e	–es	
Gen.				–en				–en
Dat.								
Acc.	–en	–e	–e		–en	–e	–es	

C. Declension of "Plain" Adjectives

	MASCULINE	FEMININE	NEUTER
NOM.	guter Wein	schwere Arbeit	kaltes Wasser
GEN.	guten* Weines	schwerer Arbeit	kalten* Wassers
DAT.	gutem Wein	schwerer Arbeit	kaltem Wasser
ACC.	guten Wein	schwere Arbeit	kaltes Wasser

	PLURAL
NOM.	gute Leute
GEN.	guter Leute
DAT.	guten Leuten
ACC.	gute Leute

Attributive adjectives not preceded by a **der** or **ein word** are called "plain." Examples: **Guter Wein kostet viel; schwere Arbeit macht hungrig; er trinkt kaltes Wasser.** Note that the "plain" adjective is declined like the **der word** except in the genitive singular, masculine and neuter(*), where instead of the expected ending –es we have –en. Actually, these forms are rarely used.

D. Declensional Details

1. Any number of adjectives attributed to the same noun take the same ending: **ein schönes, gutes, altes Haus; guter, alter, roter Wein.**

2. In the indefinite singular the attributive adjective has an ending of pattern B, but in the indefinite plural it has an ending of pattern C: **ein kleines Kind,** but **kleine Kinder.**

3. The noun to which an adjective is attributed may be "understood," i.e., if it was mentioned before. In such cases the noun is replaced by the word *one* in English: *The men were singing a song; it was a very gay one.*

In German no such "crutch" is used, but the adjective has the ending which would be required if the noun were not omitted: **Die Männer sangen ein Lied; es war ein sehr lustiges** (Lied).

4. In the case of the adjectives ending in –el, –en, –er, the –e– is dropped before the adjectival endings: Die Nacht ist **dunkel,** but: Die **dunkle** Nacht. Das Fenster ist **offen,** but: Das **offne** Fenster.

5. Adjectives which function syntactically as nouns, such as *the blind, the deaf, the evil,* etc., are declined as adjectives but capitalized. For example:

> der **Deutsche** (pattern A, nom., masc.) *the German*
> ein **Deutscher** (pattern B, nom., masc.) *a German*
> eine **Deutsche** (pattern B, nom., fem.) *a German (woman)*
> von einem **Deutschen** (pattern B, dat., masc.) *from a German*
> die **Deutschen** (pattern A, nom., plur.) *the Germans*
> der **Kranke** (pattern A, nom., masc.) *the sick man (the patient)*
> die **Alte** (pattern A, nom., fem.) *the old woman*

As our last two examples show, not every German nominal adjective is paralleled by an English nominal adjective.

6. Abstract ideas are rendered by nominal adjectives in the neuter gender. Examples:

> das **Schöne** (pattern A, nom.) *the beautiful, that which is beautiful*
> aus dem **Blauen** (pattern A, dat.) *out of the blue*
> ich tue mein **Bestes** (pattern B, acc.) *I do my best*
> **Altes** und **Neues** (pattern C, nom.) *old and new (things, ideas)*

7. **viel** *much,* **wenig** *little,* **etwas** *something,* **nichts** *nothing* often precede abstract nominal adjectives. The declension of the nominal adjective then follows pattern C, neuter. Examples:

> viel **Interessantes** *much that is interesting*
> wenig **Neues** *little that is new*
> wir sprachen von etwas **Lustigem** *we spoke of something gay*
> er wußte nichts **Neues** *he knew nothing new*

8. **Alles** *everything* is a **der-word** in the neuter gender. It often precedes abstract nominal adjectives. The declension of the nominal adjective follows pattern A, neuter. Examples:

> alles **Neue** *everything that is new*
> sie sangen von allem **Schönen** *they were singing of everything that is beautiful*

9. **alle** *all* is a **der-word** in the plural. Adjectives following **alle** take endings of pattern A, plural. Examples:

alle neuen Häuser *all new houses*
in allen alten Städten *in all old cities*

10. **viele** *many,* **wenige** *few,* **einige** *some, a few,* **mehrere** *several* are adjectives in the plural. Their declension follows pattern C, plural. Subsequent adjectives also take endings of pattern C, plural. Examples:

viele schöne, neue Häuser *many beautiful new houses*
wenige alte, kranke Leute *few old sick people*
die Häuser einiger reicher Leute *the houses of some (a few) rich people*
in mehreren neuen Büchern *in several new books*

E. manche, einige, etwas

All three words, as we have seen, would be rendered as *some* in English. The following examples will show the fine differences in meaning and function:

1. **manche** *some = a certain group or type of*

   manche Leute haben immer Geld *some people always have money*

2. **einige** *some = a few, a limited number of*

   einige Leute warteten auf die Straßenbahn *some people were waiting for the streetcar*

3. **etwas** *some = a small quantity of*

   er trank etwas Kaffee *he drank some coffee*

   But: **er trank etwas** *he drank something*
   er trank etwas Kaltes *he drank something cold*

F. The Adverb gern

The addition of the adverb **gern** to the verb denotes that the doer *likes to* perform the action: **Er arbeitet gern,** *he likes to* *work.* **Sie erzählten gern Geschichten,** *they liked to tell stories.* **Ich habe gern mit ihm gesprochen,** *I liked to talk with him,* or *I was glad to talk with him.*

G. das Herz

Herz appears as a word of the active vocabulary in this lesson. Remember its unusual declension: *Sing.:* **das Herz, des Herzens, dem Herzen, das Herz.** *Plur.:* **die Herzen.**

H. gestern, heute, morgen

Note the similarities and differences between German and English in expressions referring to parts of the present, previous and following day:

heute morgen, heute früh ⎫ **heute vormittag** ⎬	*this morning*
heute nachmittag	*this afternoon*
heute abend	*this evening, tonight*
heute nacht	*tonight*
gestern morgen, gestern vormittag	*yesterday morning*
gestern nachmittag	*yesterday afternoon*
gestern abend	*yesterday evening, last night*
gestern nacht	*last night*
morgen vormittag, morgen früh	*tomorrow morning*
morgen nachmittag	*tomorrow afternoon*
morgen abend	*tomorrow evening, tomorrow night*
morgen nacht	*tomorrow night*

IV. Grammatical Exercises

A. Fill in the proper adjective endings:

1. Diese alt_____ Männer sangen ein alt_____, deutsch_____ Lied.
2. Einig_____ von unsern berühmt_____ Liedern sind sehr traurig.
3. Nach der letzt_____ Probe gingen wir in ein alt_____ Restaurant. 4. Heute abend wird er uns einen interessant_____ Bericht über seine Reise geben. 5. Sie ist eine gut—— Freundin meiner

lieb____ Mutter. 6. Kalt____ Luft kam durch das offen____
Fenster. 7. Ich weiß nichts Gut____ über ihn. 8. Alle höflich____
Kinder nahmen den Hut ab, als sie ins Zimmer kamen. 9.
Weiß____ und rot____ Blumen wuchsen in seinem still____
Garten. 10. Sie dachten an schön____ Mädchen, gut____ Wein
und hoh____ Berge. 11. Meine Eltern haben ein Haus gekauft,
das in einem schön____, grün____ Wald steht. 12. Er erzählte
mit laut____ Stimme eine interessant____ englisch____ Geschichte. 13. Unser neu____ Rathaus ist nicht so schön wie das
alt____. 14. „Nichts Neu____ ist schön", sagen viele alt____
Leute. 15. „Aber alles Alt____ ist schön."

B. Fill in the proper endings:

1. Wer ist dies____ jung____ Dame? 2. Wir sind die ganz____
Zeit mit ein____ sehr schnell____ Zug gefahren. 3. D____
dumm____ Kind hat laut geschrieen. 4. Einig____ jung____
Leute sangen mit leis____ Stimme alt____ deutsch____ Lieder.
5. Dies____ neu____ Schiffe fahren nach all____ groß____
Ländern d____ Welt. 6. D____ hübsch____ Mädchen, das so
spät ankam, stieg in d____ letzt____ Abteil des Zuges ein.
7. In dies____ frei____ Land wohnt ein zufrieden____ Volk.
8. Obwohl er ein gut____ Schüler ist, hat er ein____ sehr
dumm____ Frage gestellt. 9. Wir haben während unser____
Reise nur wenig____ deutsch____ Studenten getroffen. 10.
All____ gut____ Leute wollten ihm helfen.

C. Decline in the singular and plural:

1. der deutsche Lehrer; 2. diese alte Geschichte; 3. welches
hübsche Mädchen; 4. ein durstiger Gast; 5. unsere alte Kirche;
6. guter Wein; 7. sein letztes Wort. Translate and decline:
8. German students; 9. good physicians; 10. free people.

D. Translate the following expressions:

1. last night; 2. yesterday noon; 3. this morning; 4. tomorrow
afternoon; 5. this evening; 6. tomorrow morning; 7. something

true; 8. everything old; 9. nothing new; 10. little that is interesting; 11. much that is famous; 12. some wine; 13. some boys.

V. Translation Exercise

1. Young man, do you like to play tennis? 2. Tomorrow the doctor will visit our sick friend. 3. He told me nothing interesting. 4. They have red heads, for they have been singing too loudly. 5. Many gay songs are very famous. 6. A week ago she wrote me a very sad letter. 7. He read many interesting stories in his German book, gay ones and serious ones. 8. Conrad saw a pretty blond girl in a blue dress, who was sitting on a bench in the park. 9. We wanted to swim in the warm water, but unfortunately it was forbidden. 10. The children of my friend asked me: "Do you have something good for us in your pocket?" 11. Although it was not yet late, the old lady got on the train quickly. 12. Tomorrow morning we shall meet an important man from America. 13. Our beautiful flowers need some water every day. 14. After my dear friend had arrived in Bremen, he wrote me a very cordial letter. 15. The sick (man) was sitting in an easy chair in front of his house near (*bei*) the beautiful, old, green forest. 16. The old church stands on a high mountain. 17. A free people lives in this great country.

VI. Fragen

1. Wohin geht Herr Löwenzahn heute abend? 2. Was sagt Frau Löwenzahn darüber? 3. Was singt man im Gesangverein? 4. Wer kommt zu den Festen des Gesangvereins? 5. Warum muß Herr Löwenzahn eine Strafe zahlen? 6. Wo standen schon Herrn Löwenzahns Freunde? 7. Welche Geschichte berichtete das neue Lied, das sie gerade angefangen hatten? 8. Wie sangen die Männer die letzten Worte dieses Liedes? 9. Was taten die Männer in der Pause? 10. Wo hatte der alte Mann, mit dem Conrad sprach, früher gelebt? 11. Warum mochte er es dort

nicht? 12. Wie gefällt es ihm jetzt in Deutschland? 13. Wie waren die Lieder, die die Männer nach der Pause sangen? 14. Welches Lied haben sie auch gesungen? 15. Können Sie uns die Geschichte von der Loreley erzählen? 16. Wie haben sie das letzte Lied gesungen? 17. Was haben Conrad und Herr Löwenzahn nach dem letzten Lied getan? 18. Singt ihr gern deutsche Lieder?

VII. Lesestück

Deutsche Universitäten

Unter den deutschen Universitäten, die heute noch existieren, ist die Universität Heidelberg die älteste. Sie wurde im Jahre 1386 (dreizehnhundertsechsundachtzig) gegründet. In den Vereinigten Staaten haben oft reiche Leute das Geld für die Gründung einer Schule oder einer Universität gegeben. Darum tragen viele amerikanische Universitäten die Namen ihrer Gründer: Harvard, Yale, Cornell, Stanford und viele andere. In Deutschland wurden alle frühen Universitäten von Fürsten gegründet, deren Namen noch heute in den Namen der Unversitäten leben: die Ludwig-Maximilians Universität in München, die Ruprecht- 10 Karls Universität in Heidelberg, die Philipps Universität in Marburg. Die Johann Wolfgang Goethe Universität in Frankfurt und die Johannes Gutenberg Universität in Mainz tragen die Namen von zwei großen Söhnen der beiden Städte.

Viele deutsche Universitäten entstanden in der Zeit der Renaissance oder in der Zeit der Aufklärung, d.h. im 15. (fünfzehnten) oder im 18. (achtzehnten) Jahrhundert. Später übernahmen die deutschen Staaten die Universitäten. Einige der neuen Universitäten, die im 20. (zwanzigsten) Jahrhundert entstanden, wurden von Städten gegründet. So geschah es in Hamburg, Frankfurt 20 oder Köln. Es gibt in Deutschland keine privaten Universitäten.

Während des 19. (neunzehnten) Jahrhunderts wurden die deutschen Universitäten sehr berühmt. Einige von ihnen waren führend in Philosophie, Geschichte, Philologie, Naturwissen-

Courtesy of Deutsche Zentrale für Fremdenverkehr

schaften und Medizin. Von den großen Professoren nennen wir
nur solche Namen wie den Philosophen Friedrich Hegel, die Historiker Leopold von Ranke und Theodor Mommsen, die Philo-
logen Jacob und Wilhelm Grimm, die Mediziner Rudolf Virchow
und Paul Ehrlich, den Chemiker Robert Bunsen, den Physiker
Wilhelm Röntgen, der die Röntgenstrahlen entdeckte.   30

Studenten kamen aus allen Ländern der Welt, um in Deutschland zu studieren. Bei amerikanischen Studenten war besonders
die Universität Göttingen beliebt. Viele der jungen Intellektuellen
von Neu-England haben im frühen 19. (neunzehnten) Jahrhundert an der Universität Göttingen studiert. Auch in unserer
Zeit studieren noch viele junge Amerikaner an deutschen Universitäten, doch ehe sie nach Deutschland gehen, müssen sie an
ihren amerikanischen Universitäten die deutsche Sprache lernen.

Deutsche Universitäten liegen meistens in der Mitte der Stadt.
Sie haben nicht das, was wir in Amerika den „Campus" nennen. 40
Deutsche Studenten wohnen nicht in der Universität. Ein Stu-
dent in Deutschland hat ein Zimmer bei einer Familie in der
Stadt, oder er wohnt bei seinen Eltern. Von dort fährt er jeden
Tag mit der Straßenbahn oder mit dem Zug zur Universität.

In vielen anderen Einrichtungen und Gewohnheiten sind
deutsche Universitäten anders als amerikanische. Doch das kann
man nicht in wenigen Worten erklären. Vielleicht können Sie ein
Buch darüber lesen oder noch besser: studieren Sie an einer
deutschen Universität!

VIII. Wörterverzeichnis

der älteste the oldest
anders als different from
die Aufklärung the Enlightenment
beliebt bei popular with
besonders especially
der Chemiker, – the chemist
die Einrichtung, –en the institution, arrangement

entdecken (to) discover
entstehen, entstand, ist entstanden
(to) originate
existieren (to) exist
der Fürst, (–en), –en the ruling
prince
die Gewohnheit, –en the custom
gründen (to) found

der Gründer, – the founder
die Gründung, –en the foundation, founding
der Historiker, – the historian
der Intellektuelle, (–n), –n the intellectual
Köln Cologne
der Mediziner, – the medical man
meistens mostly, usually, for the most part
der Name, (–ns), –n the name
die Naturwissenschaften the natural sciences
noch still
oft often
der Philologe, (–n), –n the philologist
die Philologie language and literature, philology

der Philosoph, (–en), –en the philosopher
die Philosophie philosophy
der Physiker, – the physicist
privat private
der Professor, –en the professor
reich rich
die Röntgenstrahlen the X-rays
der Staat, –en the state
übernehmen (übernimmt), übernahm; übernommen (to) take over, assume
die Universität, –en the university
wurde, wurden *plus past participle form passive voice; translate* was *and* were

COMPARISON OF ADJECTIVES

I. Reading Selection

Eines Abends besuchte uns Klaus Ebert, ein Neffe von Frau Löwenzahn, der an der Universität Heidelberg Physik studiert. Er ist ein freundlicher, junger Mann, vielleicht zwei oder drei Jahre älter als Herbert und ich. Er ist noch nie in Amerika gewesen, doch er wollte viel über unser Land wissen.

„In Europa hat man Amerika oft das Land der Superlative genannt", sagte er. „Ich weiß nicht, ob es so ist, aber viele Amerikaner, die uns besucht haben, haben uns erzählt, daß zu Hause alles am besten, am schönsten, am größten und am höchsten ist."

„Wir sind ein jüngeres Volk als die Völker Europas", meinte 10 Herbert. „Wir sind vielleicht noch nicht so skeptisch wie Sie. Sie lesen in der Zeitung, daß ein Bäcker den größten Kuchen der Welt gebacken hat, aber Sie fragen sofort: hat nicht (vielleicht zur Zeit von Nebukadnezar oder später) ein anderer Bäcker einen noch größeren gebacken? Wir in Amerika lesen es und glauben es."

„O nein", widersprach ich. „Auch wir sind nicht so naiv, alle Superlative ernst zu nehmen. Wir lesen in der Politik, daß dies ‚der beste Mann' ist oder daß ein anderer ‚die größte Tat des Jahrhunderts' getan hat, aber wir wissen, daß wir davon nur die 20 Hälfte oder noch weniger glauben dürfen. Doch weil wir, wie

Herbert sagt, ein junges Volk sind, haben wir ein größeres Interesse für alles, was in die frühste Geschichte unseres Landes zurückgeht. Wir sind stolz auf das älteste Haus in Massachusetts oder die älteste Kirche in Maryland."

„Das kann ich verstehen", meinte Klaus Ebert. „Hier ist so viel alt, älter und am ältesten, daß das Alte für uns nichts Neues und nichts Interessantes ist."

„Wir sprechen auch oft in Superlativen, ohne darauf stolz zu 30 sein", sagte ich. „Immer wieder nennt man Rhode Island den kleinsten Staat des Landes. Wir sagen von einem Sommer: es war der heißeste des Jahrhunderts. In meinem Staat Pennsylvania gibt es einen großen Fluß, auf dem keine Schiffe fahren können, und wir sagen darum: der Susquehanna ist der längste nutzlose Fluß der Welt. Wir wollen damit nicht sagen, daß wir stolz darauf sind. Wir lächeln darüber, anstatt es ernst zu nehmen."

„Wenn wir vom Klima sprechen", meinte Herbert, „können wir vielleicht sagen: Amerika ist nicht das Land des ‚am meisten', aber das Land des ‚mehr'. Wir haben kältere Winter und 40 wärmere Sommer. In Chicago ist der Wind stärker, in Seattle regnet es öfter, in Texas brennt die Sonne heißer als in anderen Städten und Ländern der Welt.—Da wir von Texas sprechen", fragte Herbert mich, „kennst du Leute aus Texas, die über ihren Staat nicht im Superlativ sprechen?"

„Halt!" unterbrach ich ihn schnell. „Sprich freundlich über die Leute in Texas, sonst werden die Studenten und Lehrer dort dieses Buch nicht kaufen."

„Nun", sagte Klaus Ebert, als er aufstand, um nach Hause zu gehen, „es war ein höchst interessanter Abend. Sie haben die 50 längsten, schönsten und schwersten Superlative geübt, und ich habe viel über Ihr Land gelernt. Auf Wiedersehen!"

II. Vocabulary

*als (*after comparative*) than
*(der) ander(e) (the) other
backen (ä), buk, gebacken (to) bake

der Bäcker, – the baker
*Europa Europe
*der Fluß, (Flusses), Flüsse the river

*freundlich friendly
*die Hälfte (the) half
*höchst highly, very
*klein small, little
das Klima the climate
*lang long
naiv naive
Nebukadnezar Nebuchadnezzar
der Neffe, (–n), –n the nephew
*noch still
nutzlos useless
*oft often
die Physik physics
die Politik politics

*sechzehn sixteen
skeptisch sceptical
*sonst otherwise
*der Staat, –en the state
*stark strong
*stolz auf (with acc.) proud of
der Superlativ, –e the superlative
*die Tat, –en the act, deed
widersprechen (i), widersprach,
   widersprochen (to) contradict
*der Wind, –e the wind
zurückgehen, ging zurück, ist
   zurückgegangen (to) go back

Idioms

*Halt! Halt! Stop!
*zur Zeit at the time
*nun does not always mean now; at the beginning of a sentence, followed
   by a comma, it means well + comma: Nun, was sollen wir tun? Well,
   what shall we do?

III. Grammar

A. Comparison of Adjectives and Adverbs

In English the comparative and superlative of the adjective
end in –er and –st respectively: small—smaller—smallest.

The same holds true for German: klein—kleiner—kleinst.

In English, the comparative and superlative of some adjectives
and of most adverbs are formed by adding the words more and
most: interesting—more interesting—most interesting. This is not
done in German: interessant—interessanter—interessantest.

In the following we list the most important adjectives from
our vocabulary, as so far introduced, with their comparative and
superlative forms:

1. Addition of –er and –st to the simple form:

SIMPLE FORM	COMPARATIVE	SUPERLATIVE
dunkel, dark	dunkler	dunkelst–
durstig, thirsty	durstiger	durstigst–

SIMPLE FORM	COMPARATIVE	SUPERLATIVE
flach, *flat*	flacher	flachst–
freundlich, *friendly*	freundlicher	freundlichst–
früh, *early*	früher	frühst–
grün, *green*	grüner	grünst–
heilig, *holy*	heiliger	heiligst–
herzlich, *cordial*	herzlicher	herzlichst–
höflich, *courteous*	höflicher	höflichst–
klein, *small*	kleiner	kleinst–
lieb, *dear*	lieber	liebst–
lustig, *merry*	lustiger	lustigst–
schnell, *fast*	schneller	schnellst–
schön, *beautiful*	schöner	schönst–
schwer, *hard*	schwerer	schwerst–
still, *quiet*	stiller	stillst–
traurig, *sad*	trauriger	traurigst–
wichtig, *important*	wichtiger	wichtigst–
zufrieden, *contented*	zufriedener	zufriedenst–

2. German adjectives or adverbs ending in t, d, s, z, sch, or sometimes a vowel form the superlative, as in English with –est:

SIMPLE FORM	COMPARATIVE	SUPERLATIVE
berühmt, *famous*	berühmter	berühmtest–
blau, *blue*	blauer	blauest–
blond, *blond*	blonder	blondest–
ernst, *serious*	ernster	ernstest–
frei, *free*	freier	freiest–
heiß, *hot*	heißer	heißest–
hübsch, *pretty*	hübscher	hübschest–
interessant, *interesting*	interessanter	interessantest–
laut, *loud*	lauter	lautest–
leise, *soft*	leiser	leisest–
neu, *new*	neuer	neuest–
spät, *late*	später	spätest–
stolz, *proud*	stolzer	stolzest–
weiß, *white*	weißer	weißest–

3. Some very common adjectives and adverbs of one syllable take umlaut in the comparative and superlative:

SIMPLE FORM	COMPARATIVE	SUPERLATIVE
alt, *old*	älter	ältest–
dumm, *stupid*	dümmer	dümmst–
groß, *big*	größer	größt–

Simple Form	Comparative	Superlative
hoch, *high*	höher	höchst–
jung, *young*	jünger	jüngst–
krank, *sick*	kränker	kränkst–
kalt, *cold*	kälter	kältest–
lang, *long*	länger	längst–
oft, *often*	öfter	öftest–
rot, *red*	röter	rötest–
schwarz, *black*	schwärzer	schwärzest–
stark, *strong*	stärker	stärkst–
warm, *warm*	wärmer	wärmst–

4. A very few are irregular:

Simple Form	Comparative	Superlative
gut, *good*	besser	best–
viel, *much*	mehr	meist–
gern, *gladly*	lieber	am liebsten

B. Use of the Comparative and Superlative

1. In the comparative and superlative, the attributive adjective is declined in accordance with the declensional rules presented in Lesson XV, e.g., **das alte Haus, das ältere Haus, das älteste Haus; mein jüngerer Bruder; bessere Bücher,** etc.

In the comparative and superlative the adjective therefore has

a) a suffix, i.e., **–er** for the comparative, **–(e)st** for the superlative, *and*

b) a declensional ending.

2. It has already been stated that neither the predicate adjective nor the adverb have declensional endings (cf. Lessons XI and XV). This is also true in the comparative, e.g., **mein Auto ist schneller,** *my car is faster;* **mein Auto fährt schneller,** *my car runs faster.*

3. The superlative, however, is used differently. In this case, both the adjective and the adverb are always inflected and may appear in the following constructions:

a) with the definite article, e.g., **Herr Löwenzahn ist der lustigste (von uns allen),** *Mr. Löwenzahn is the gayest* (*of us all*); **Herbert ist der beste** (**von allen Studenten**), *Herbert is the best* (*of all students*), or

b) with the preposition **an** and the dative of the definite article contracted to **am**. The superlative adjective then has the ending **–en**, e.g., **Herr Löwenzahn ist am lustigsten, wenn er Wein trinkt,** *Mr. Löwenzahn is gayest* (or: *the gayest,* or: *at his gayest*) *when he drinks wine.* **Im Winter sind die Tage am kältesten,** *in winter the days are coldest.* **Die Tage sind im Sommer am heißesten,** *the days are hottest in summer.*

The superlative of the adverb is always in this construction, e.g., **Mein Auto fährt am schnellsten,** *my car runs* (*the*) *fastest.* **Herr Löwenzahn sang am lautesten,** *Mr. Löwenzahn sang* (*the*) *loudest.*

4. In making comparisons, German **so . . . wie** corresponds to English *as . . . as;* German **als** corresponds to English *than:* Conrad ist gerade **so** alt **wie** ich; Conrad is just *as* old *as* I. Mein Freund ist **älter als** ich; my friend is *older than I.* Ich laufe **schneller als** er; I run *faster than* he.

5. The comparative and superlative of **gern** are **lieber** and **am liebsten** respectively. The following examples show how to render statements with **lieber** and **am liebsten** in English: Ich trinke **gern** Limonade; I *like to* drink lemonade. Herbert trinkt **lieber** Frau Löwenzahns Kaffee; Herbert *prefers to* drink Mrs. Löwenzahn's coffee. Conrad trinkt **am liebsten** Herrn Löwenzahns Erdbeerbowle; Conrad *likes best of all to* drink Mr. Löwenzahn's strawberry punch. Cf. also: Er hat heiße Tage **gern;** he *likes* hot days. Ich habe kalte Tage **lieber;** I *prefer* cold days. Sie haben warme Tage **am liebsten;** they like warm days *best of all.*

6. The German adverb **höchst** corresponds to the English *highly,* e.g., **das ist höchst interessant,** *that is highly interesting.*

7. **German immer + comparative = English comparative + comparative.** Examples: **immer dunkler,** *darker and darker;* **immer schneller,** *faster and faster;* also **immer wieder,** *again and again.*

C. anstatt . . . zu, ohne . . . zu

We have previously (Lesson XII, Section III,D2) used infinitive phrases with um . . . zu: Conrad ging in die Stadt, um ein Geschenk zu kaufen; Conrad went downtown *in order to buy* a present.

German uses anstatt . . . zu and ohne . . . zu in the same way. Examples: Anstatt eine Reise zu machen, sind die Studenten zu Hause geblieben; *instead of taking* a trip, the students stayed home. Der Mann stand auf dem Bahnsteig, ohne in den Zug einzusteigen; the man stood on the platform *without getting on* the train.

As our examples show, English combines these prepositions with the present participle, German uses the infinitive with zu.

IV. Grammatical Exercises

A. Decline in the singular and plural:

1. sein jüngerer Sohn; 2. eine ältere Dame; 3. die bessere Arbeit; 4. der stärkste Mann; 5. die freundlichste Verkäuferin; 6. das längste Lied.

B. Supply the comparatives:

1. Im Winter ist es (colder than) im Herbst. 2. Coca Cola schmeckt (better than) Limonade. 3. Sommertage sind (hotter than) Wintertage. 4. Der Wind in Chicago ist (stronger than) in Frankfurt. 5. In Seattle regnet es (more often than) in Texas. 6. Die Vereinigten Staaten sind (bigger than) Deutschland. 7. Das Geschenk kostet (more than) ich dachte. 8. Das letzte Lied, das sie sangen, war (more beautiful than) das erste. 9. Am Rhein wächst der Wein (better than) an anderen deutschen Flüssen. 10. Die Amerikaner sind (a younger) Volk als die Deutschen. 11. In Deutschland gibt es (older) Kirchen als in den Vereinigten Staaten. 12. In Amerika machen die Leute (longer) Reisen als in Deutschland. 13. Ich habe noch nie einen

(more polite) jungen Mann gesehen als ihn. 14. Das war eine
(more difficult) Aufgabe als wir zuerst dachten.

C. Supply the superlatives:

1. Unsere Studenten wohnen (gern) bei den Löwenzahns. 2. Sie
haben das (groß) Zimmer in diesem Haus. 3. Sein Vater ist der
(stolz) Mann von allen Leuten, die ich kenne. 4. Das Münchener
Bier ist (gut). 5. Herbert arbeitet (gern) spät in der Nacht. 6.
Rhode Island ist der (klein) Staat in unserm Land. 7. Wissen
Sie, welches Land die (hoch) Berge hat? 8. Der Amerikaner
kaufte mehr als der Deutsche, aber seine Frau kaufte (viel). 9.
Haben Sie in der Schule gelernt, in welcher Stadt das (alt) Haus
in Deutschland steht? 10. Er ist heute der (berühmt) Mann
seines Volkes. 11. Man soll immer die (wichtig) Dinge zuerst
tun. 12. Manchmal denke ich, ich bin der (dumm) von allen
Studenten in der Universität.

V. Translation Exercise

1. This is the longest river in Germany. 2. The best wine grows
on the higher mountains on the Rhine. 3. There one has the
hottest sun until late in autumn. 4. The American (*amerikanisch*)
students like best of all to visit the Rhineland. 5. The Germans
are always happiest, when they sing the saddest songs. 6. Conrad
got more and more thirsty. 7. Instead of going home, he went
back into the restaurant and ordered something to drink. 8.
Herbert went to bed earlier without eating. 9. In fall it is not as
hot as in summer, but it rains more often. 10. In summer the
days are longest. 11. [In the] last year we had the coldest winter
in this century. 12. Ohio is larger than Maryland, but Ohio is a
smaller state than Texas; Rhode Island is the smallest one. 13.
His German friend is the most polite young man I have met on
my trip. 14. Monika will go to Bremen by a later train. 15.
During the last half of their trip they saw the oldest and most
famous churches in Europe. 16. When he was a young man, he

liked to drink beer (*Bier*); in his later years he liked most to drink wine. 17. In her younger years she liked to take long trips; now she prefers to stay at home during her vacation. 18. Instead of calling me up, he wrote me a long letter. 19. He held a cigarette in his hand without smoking it. 20. She told me something that was highly interesting. 21. This is the highest mountain I have seen; I have never seen a more beautiful one.

VI. Fragen

1. Wer besuchte die Studenten eines Abends? 2. Was tut Klaus Ebert in Heidelberg? 3. Wie alt ist er? 4. Ist er schon in Amerika gewesen? 5. Worüber sprachen sie an diesem Abend? 6. Hat Klaus Ebert schon früher andere Amerikaner getroffen? 7. Was haben sie ihm über ihr Land erzählt? 8. Welches Wort gebrauchen die Deutschen oft für Amerika? 9. Was sagt Herbert über die Völker Europas? 10. Nehmen die Amerikaner ihre Superlative immer ernst? 11. Was wissen Sie über Alaska? 12. Was wissen Sie über Rhode Island? 13. Warum ist Klaus sehr zufrieden mit diesem Abend? 14. Warum können Conrad und Herbert mit diesem Abend sehr zufrieden sein?

VII. Lesestück

Das Rheinland

Kein anderer deutscher Fluß hat eine solch lange und ruhmreiche Geschichte wie der Rhein, kein anderer ist heute so wichtig für den Verkehr und den Handel Deutschlands und vieler anderer Länder in Europa.

Auf beiden Ufern ist der Fluß von schönen Landschaften umgeben. Da ist im Süden der Bodensee mit alten Städten, Klöstern und Burgen. Da ist der Schwarzwald mit hohen Bergen und dunklen Wäldern. Viele der alten Städte auf dem linken Ufer des Rheins wurden von den Römern gegründet. Vor 2 000 (zweitausend) Jahren gehörte das Rheinland zum römischen Reich. 10

Es war der erste Teil Deutschlands, in den die römische Kultur eindrang. Noch heute kann man im Rheinland die Überreste römischer Tore, Theater und Bäder sehen. Später, im Mittelalter, war das Rheinland der wichtigste Teil des Heiligen Römischen Reiches. Karl der Große lebte viele Jahre in Aachen; in Frankfurt wurden die Kaiser gewählt; im Dom von Speyer sind die Gräber von acht deutschen Kaisern des Mittelalters; die Erzbischöfe von Mainz, Köln und Trier gehörten zu den wichtigsten Fürsten des Heiligen Römischen Reiches. Im Museum von Mainz

20 steht die alte Buchdruckerpresse von Johannes Gutenberg, der aus einer alten Mainzer Familie kam. Überall sehen wir Zeichen einer großen Vergangenheit: alte Burgen, die von hohen Bergen auf den Fluß herabsehen, alte Klöster, die versteckt in grünen Tälern liegen, alte Tore, Brücken, Kirchen, Städte. „Neu" nennt man im Rheinland ein Haus, das nur 100 (hundert) Jahre alt ist. Das älteste Haus Deutschlands steht in Winkel, einer kleinen Stadt am Rhein. Es ist mehr als 1 000 (tausend) Jahre alt, und noch heute wohnen Leute darin.

Zwischen den Wäldern und dem Fluß, zwischen den alten

30 Burgen und den kleinen Städten liegen die Weinberge. Seit mehr als 1 000 (tausend) Jahren wachsen hier die Weine, deren Namen man in der Welt besser kennt als die Namen der Erzbischöfe und Kaiser des Heiligen Römischen Reiches: der Johannisberger, der Niersteiner, der Marcobrunner. Karl der Große, so erzählt die Sage, hat hier die ersten Weinberge gepflanzt, und noch heute geht der Kaiser in warmen Nächten im Sommer durch die Gärten und Weinberge und segnet die Reben.

Doch der Rhein und das Rheinland leben nicht nur in ihrer Vergangenheit. Auf dem Wasser des Flusses, zwischen seinen

40 Ufern mit den Weinbergen, unter seinen Brücken mit den Toren fahren die Schiffe, von der Schweiz bis zum Atlantischen Ozean. Der Rhein zwischen Mainz und Rotterdam ist der belebteste Fluß der Welt, die wichtigste Nord-Süd-Verbindung in Europa. 300 (dreihundert) Schiffe fahren an jedem Tag im Jahr auf dem Rhein über die Grenze zwischen Holland und Deutschland.

Courtesy of German Tourist Information Office, New York

Burg Katz am Rhein, im Hintergrund die Loreley

Courtesy of German Tourist Information Office, New

Der Dom zu Speyer (11. Jahrhundert)

Courtesy of Deutsche Zentrale für Fremdenverkehr

Die Burg über Runkel an der Lahn

Wir kennen keine andere Landschaft mit einer solch glücklichen Verbindung von Vergangenheit und Gegenwart, von Geschichte und Leben.

VIII. Wörterverzeichnis

der **Atlantische Ozean** the Atlantic Ocean
das **Bad,** ⸚er the bath, spa
belebt busy, crowded
der **Bodensee** Lake Constance
die **Brücke, –n** the bridge
die **Buchdruckerpresse, –n** the printing press
die **Burg, –en** the castle
der **Dom, –e** the cathedral
ein-dringen, drang ein, ist eingedrungen (to) penetrate
der **erste** the first
der **Erzbischof,** ⸚e the archbishop
der **Fürst, (–en), –en** the (ruling) prince
die **Gegenwart** the present
gehören zu (to) belong to
glücklich fortunate, happy
das **Grab,** ⸚er the grave
die **Grenze, –n** the border
gründen (to) found
der **Handel** the commerce
herab-sehen (ie), sah herab, herabgesehen (to) look down
der **Kaiser, –** the emperor
Karl der Große Charles the Great, Charlemagne
das **Kloster,** ⸚ the cloister
Köln Cologne
die **Kultur** the culture
der **linke** the left
Mainzer Mainz, of Mainz
das **Mittelalter** the Middle Ages

der **Name, (–ns), –n** the name
die **Nord-Süd-Verbindung** the north-south connection
pflanzen (to) plant
die **Rebe, –n** the grape
das **Reich** the Empire
der **Römer, –** the Roman
römisch Roman
ruhmreich glorious
die **Sage, –n** the saying, legend
der **Schwarzwald** the Black Forest
segnen (to) bless, give a blessing to
der **Süden** the south
das **Tal,** ⸚er the valley
der **Teil, –e** the part
das **Tor, –e** the gate
überall everywhere
die **Überreste** the remains, ruins
das **Ufer, –** the bank
umgeben (i), umgab, umgeben (to) surround
die **Verbindung, –en** the combination, union
die **Vergangenheit** the past
der **Verkehr** the traffic, communication
versteckt concealed, hidden
wählen (to) choose, elect
der **Weinberg, –e** the vineyard
wurden were (*as in* VIII *of the last lesson*)
das **Zeichen, –** the sign

REFLEXIVE PRONOUNS AND VERBS
MODALS IN COMPOUND TENSES

I. Reading Selection

Während des ganzen Monats Dezember hatten die Löwenzahns Besuch aus Österreich. Ihre Tochter kam mit ihren zwei
kleinen Kindern, einem Jungen von sechs und einem Mädchen
von fünf Jahren. Sie hießen Henning und Henriette. Spät in der
Nacht kamen sie an.

„Wie geht es euch?" fragte Herr Löwenzahn. „Seid ihr alle
gesund?"

„Es geht uns gut", sagte seine Tochter. „Wir sind nur sehr
müde, denn wir mußten schon um fünf Uhr aufstehen, und wir
haben 14 Stunden im Zug gesessen."   10

„Wo ist dein Mann?" wollte Frau Löwenzahn wissen.
„Warum ist er nicht mitgekommen?"

„Er hat die Reise nicht machen können", antwortete die
Tochter, „weil man ihn in seinem Büro braucht. Er wird erst am
Tage vor Weihnachten kommen können."

Am nächsten Tage war Nikolaustag. „Henning und Henriette
müssen einen Nikolaus haben", sagte Herr Löwenzahn. „Wir
haben oben noch den roten Anzug und den weißen Bart. Die
Kinder werden viel Spaß haben."

20   „Soll ich den Nikolaus spielen?" fragte ich.

„Nein, das geht nicht", sagte Herr Löwenzahn. „Die Kinder werden Ihren amerikanischen Akzent erkennen. Ich bin ein guter Nikolaus. Vor vielen Jahren habe ich ihn in einem Kindergarten spielen müssen, und alle Leute waren sehr zufrieden mit mir."

Herr Löwenzahn zog sich oben an. Er trug den roten Anzug, die hohe Mütze und den weißen Bart und ging durch die Hintertür auf die Straße. Es war schon ein wenig dunkel geworden.

Ich sah vom Wohnzimmer durch das Fenster auf die Straße. „Ich glaube, ich habe den Nikolaus jetzt gerade kommen sehen",
30 sagte ich und setzte mich neben die kleine Henriette. „Wirst du ein Gebet sagen können, wenn er kommt?"

Sie war sehr blaß im Gesicht, und ohne zu warten, fing sie sofort an zu beten:

Ich bin klein,
Mein Herz ist rein
Soll niemand drin wohnen
Als Jesus allein.

„Das war zu früh", sagte ich, „ich habe ihn jetzt erst an die Tür klopfen hören."

40   „Herein!" riefen wir alle.

Jetzt machte Herr Löwenzahn-Nikolaus die Tür auf und kam ins Zimmer. Henriette schrie laut und lief zu ihrer Mutter.

„Schämst du dich nicht?" fragte der Nikolaus mit tiefer Stimme. „Warum schreist du? Warum fürchtest du dich vor mir? Freust du dich nicht, daß der Nikolaus hier ist? Komm, setz dich auf meinen Schoß und sag ein kleines Gebet, dann habe ich ein hübsches Geschenk für dich."

Die kleine Henriette schrie immer lauter. Man konnte sehen, daß sie weder an Gebete noch an Geschenke dachte.

50   „Nun", meinte der Nikolaus (seine Stimme war jetzt ein wenig leiser geworden), „dann wollen wir sehen, ob dein Bruder etwas gelernt hat. Kann unser kleiner Freund Henning für den Nikolaus ein Gebet sagen?"

„Großvater, ärgere dich nicht über sie", sagte der kleine Henning freundlich. „Sie ist noch ein Kind."

Wir alle lachten.

Herr Löwenzahn setzte sich auf einen Stuhl und nahm den Bart ab. „Ich verstehe es nicht", sagte er. „Im Kindergarten habe ich ihn so gut gespielt."

II. Vocabulary

der Akzent, –e the accent
*amerikanisch (adj.) American
*sich an-ziehen, zog sich an, hat sich angezogen (to) dress, get dressed
*der Anzug, ⁼e the suit
*sich ärgern über (with acc.) (to) be angry with or about, be mad at
der Bart, ⁼e the beard
der Besuch, –e the visit
der Besucher, – the visitor
blaß pale
*der Bruder, ⁼ the brother
das Büro, –s the office
*der Dezember December
drin = darin in it
erkennen, erkannte, erkannt (to) recognize
*erst (adv.) only, not until
*sich freuen über (with acc.) (to) be glad (happy) about, to rejoice in
*sich fürchten vor (with dat.) to be afraid of
das Gebet, –e the prayer
*das Gesicht, –er the face
*gesund well, healthy
der Großvater, ⁼ the grandfather
*heißen, hieß, geheißen (to) be called

*Herein! Come in!
die Hintertür the back door
der Kindergarten, ⁼ the kindergarten
*klopfen an (to) knock at
*mit-kommen, kam mit, ist mitgekommen (to) come along, come too
*müde tired
die Mütze, –n the cap
*der nächste the next
*niemand no one, nobody
der Nikolaus Santa Claus, St. Nick
der Nikolaustag St. Nicholas' Day (Dec. 6)
*oben upstairs, above
*Österreich Austria
rein pure
*sich schämen über (with acc.) (to) be ashamed of
*schon already
der Schoß the lap
*sich setzen (to) sit down
*siebzehn seventeen
der Spaß, ⁼e (the) fun
*spielen (to) play
*tief deep
*die Tochter, ⁼ the daughter
*die Tür, –en the door
*Weihnachten Christmas

Idioms

er hat Besuch he has a visitor *or* visitors
*__das geht nicht__ that won't do
jetzt erst only now, just now
nichts als nothing but
niemand als no one but
*__Wie heißen Sie?__ What is your name?
*__Ich heiße Conrad__ My name is Conrad

III. Grammar

A. Reflexive Pronouns

1. When the subject and the object of a sentence are one and the same person, we say that the action is reflexive. In the sentence *John washes himself,* John performs the action, but John is also the recipient of his own action. This relationship is expressed by the use of a reflexive pronoun for the direct object (*himself* in our example).

2. The indirect object may also be the same person as the subject. This relationship is expressed in the same way by the use of a reflexive pronoun for the indirect object, e.g., *John buys himself a new shirt,* or *John buys a new shirt for himself.*

3. English has a reflexive pronoun for each grammatical person, e.g., *myself, yourself,* etc.

In German, for the first and second person, singular and plural, the personal pronoun is used—in the accusative for the direct object, in the dative for the indirect object. For the third person (all three genders, singular and plural, dative and accusative), one special reflexive pronoun is used: **sich.**

REFLEXIVE PRONOUNS

SINGULAR	DATIVE	ACCUSATIVE
First pers.	mir	mich
Second pers.	dir	dich
Third pers.	sich	

PLURAL	DATIVE	ACCUSATIVE
First pers.	uns	uns
Second pers.	euch	euch
Third pers.		sich

Here is an illustration for the accusative:

1. ich wasche **mich**   I wash myself
2. du wäschst **dich**   you wash yourself
3. ⎰ er wäscht **sich**   he washes himself
   ⎱ sie wäscht **sich**   she washes herself
   ⎰ es wäscht **sich***   it washes itself

1. wir waschen **uns**   we wash ourselves
2. ihr wascht **euch**   you wash yourselves
3. ⎰ sie waschen **sich**   they wash themselves
   ⎱ Sie waschen **sich**   you wash yourself
                                you wash yourselves

Here is an illustration for the dative:

1. **ich** kaufe **mir** ein Hemd   I buy a shirt for myself
2. **du** kaufst **dir** ein Hemd   you buy a shirt for yourself
3. ⎰ er kauft **sich** ein Hemd   he buys a shirt for himself
   ⎱ sie kauft **sich** ein Hemd   she buys a shirt for herself

1. **wir** kaufen **uns** ein Hemd   we buy ourselves a shirt
2. **ihr** kauft **euch** ein Hemd   you buy yourselves a shirt
3. ⎰ sie kaufen **sich** ein Hemd   they buy themselves a shirt
   ⎱ Sie kaufen **sich** ein Hemd   you buy yourself a shirt
                                        you buy yourselves a shirt

B. Reflexive Verbs

1. As in English, many German verbs can be used either reflexively or non-reflexively. For example:

ich wasche mich   *I wash myself* (refl.)
ich wasche das Auto   *I wash the car* (non-refl.)
ich kaufe mir einen Hut   *I buy myself a hat* (refl.)
ich kaufe ihm einen Hut   *I buy him a hat* (non-refl.)

* We would have to use the personal pronoun **es** also if this pronoun stands for a neuter noun such as **das Kind** or **das Mädchen**.

There are, however, some German verbs which are only used reflexively. For example:

ich schäme mich *I am ashamed,* **wir schämen uns** *we are ashamed;*
sie fürchtet sich *she is afraid,* **fürchtet ihr euch?** *are you afraid?*
ich freue mich *I am glad,* **freust du dich?** *are you glad?*

Such verbs will be listed in our voabulary with **sich**:

sich schämen (*to*) *be ashamed;* **sich fürchten** (*to*) *be afraid;* **sich freuen** (*to*) *be glad.*

2. There are other verbs in German which are used both ways, but in the English translation different verbs and sentence constructions will be required for the reflexive and non-reflexive versions. For example:

ich ärgere mich	*I am angry,* but
ich ärgere den Lehrer	*I annoy the teacher, i.e.,*
	I make the teacher angry.

Such verbs are listed in dictionaries and vocabularies separately:

sich ärgern (*to*) *be angry;* **ärgern** (*to*) *annoy,* (*to*) *make angry*

3. Most reflexive verbs are used with a prepositional phrase, e.g., **Der Lehrer ärgert sich über den dummen Schüler** *The teacher is angry with the stupid student.* The proper preposition and the case it governs will also be listed in our vocabulary:

sich ärgern über (with acc.)   (*to*) *be angry with*
sich fürchten vor (with dat.)   (*to*) *be afraid of.*

4. Although there is nothing new to be said about tenses and word order, the following model may be helpful:

PRES.	Sie fürchtet sich vor dem Nikolaus
PAST	Sie fürchtete sich vor dem Nikolaus
PRES. PERF.	Sie hat sich vor dem Nikolaus gefürchtet
FUT.	Sie wird sich vor dem Nikolaus fürchten
IMPER.	Fürchte dich nicht!
	Fürchtet euch nicht!
	Fürchten Sie sich nicht!
INFIN. PHRASE	Sie sagte ihr Gebet, ohne sich zu fürchten.
DEPEN. CLAUSE	Sie sagte ihr Gebet, obwohl sie sich fürchtete.

C. sitzen—sich setzen; liegen—sich legen; stehen—sich stellen

Er sitzt auf einem Stuhl	he is sitting on a chair
Er setzt sich auf einen Stuhl	he is sitting down on a chair
Er liegt in seinem Bett	he is lying in his bed
Er legt sich auf sein Bett	he is lying down on his bed
Er steht vor der Tafel	he stands in front of the blackboard
Er stellt sich vor die Tafel	he places himself in front of the blackboard.

D. Impersonal Verbs and Dative Constructions

1. With some verbs only *it* can be the subject, e.g., *it happens, it rains, it snows:* **es geschieht, es regnet, es schneit.**

Also, **es gibt** in the sense of *there is, there are,* is used in this way. (See Lesson IX, Section III, I.)

2. Another frequent expression with an "impersonal" subject is **es geht mir gut**   *I am fine* (literally, "it goes well with me"); **wie geht es dir?**   *how are you?* (literally: "how goes it with you?")

More expressions of the same type are: **es gefällt mir**   *I like it* (literally: "it appeals to me"); **es tut mir leid**   *I am sorry* (literally: "it does sorrow to me").

These constructions can also contain a personal subject, e.g., **sie gefällt mir**   *I like her* or *I find her pleasing;* **der arme Mann tut mir leid**   *I am sorry for the poor man.*

3. Remember also the following expressions: **es ist mir kalt** or briefly **mir ist kalt**   *I am cold;* **es ist mir warm** or **mir ist warm**   *I am warm;* **es ist mir schlecht** or **mir ist schlecht**   *I am sick.*

E. The Modal Auxiliary in the Future and Perfect Tenses

1. Remember: In sentences with modal auxiliaries the main verb is always an infinitive, e.g., **ich kann dort bleiben** (present

tense), **ich konnte dort bleiben** (past tense). Compare Lesson **X**.

In the future tense the modal auxiliary will also be an infinitive, dependent on a finite form of **werden**. The sentence will therefore have two infinitives. Examples:

Ich werde dort bleiben können	*I shall be able to stay there*
Er wird das Geld zahlen müssen	*he will have to pay the money*
Sie werden es nicht sagen wollen	*they will not want to tell it*

Note that the two infinitives are always arranged in such a way, that the infinitive of the modal auxiliary comes last.

Note that in English the modal auxiliary does not have an infinitive. Instead we use substitutes: *be able to, have to, want to,* etc. (cf. Lesson X).

2. For the present perfect tense we would expect a construction with the past participle of the modal auxiliary. Instead, however, its infinitive is used. Therefore, also in the present perfect tense the sentence will have two infinitives. Examples:

Ich habe dort bleiben können	*I have been able to stay there*
	or I was able to stay there
Er hat das Geld zahlen müssen	*He has had to pay the money*
	or he had to pay the money
Sie haben es nicht sagen wollen	*They have not wanted to tell it*
	or they did not want to tell it

In the past perfect the past tense form of **haben** is used, e.g., **ich hatte dort nicht bleiben können.**

Note that in English the modal auxiliary does not have a past participle. Again we use substitutes: *has been able to, has had to, has wanted to,* etc.

3. We can now set up the following simple rule: In the perfect tenses and in the future tense the modal auxiliary is in the infinitive, depending upon a finite form of **haben** for the perfect tense, and upon a finite form of **werden** for the future tense. The infinitive of the modal auxiliary always follows the infinitive of the main verb.

4. This double infinitive must always be placed at the very end of its clause, even after a subordinating conjunction. Examples: Weil man dort nicht hat rauchen dürfen, ging ich in ein anderes Abteil.—Nachdem ich diese Tür habe zumachen können, kam die Luft nicht mehr hindurch.

5. If in the perfect tenses the main verb is understood and therefore omitted, the regular past participles of the modal auxiliaries (**gekonnt, gemußt** etc.) are used: **er hat es nicht gedurft;** *he has not been allowed to* (*do it*).

F. hören, sehen, helfen, lassen

The verbs **hören, sehen, helfen, lassen** (*to let*) follow the syntactical patterns treated above in Subsection E:

Ich werde sie singen hören	*I will hear her sing*
Ich habe sie singen hören	*I have heard her sing*
Wir werden ihn spielen sehen	*We will see him play*
Wir haben ihn spielen sehen	*We have seen him play*
Er wird uns tragen helfen	*He will help us carry*
Er hat uns tragen helfen	*He has helped us carry*
Sie wird ihn gehen lassen	*She will let him go*
Sie hat ihn gehen lassen	*She has let him go*

Note that in English the present participle is sometimes used, e.g., *I see him coming.* In German the infinitive would still be required: **Ich sehe ihn kommen.**

IV. Grammatical Exercises

A. Conjugate (all persons and tenses):

1. Ich setze mich auf den Stuhl. 2. Ich bestelle mir einen Anzug.

B. Supply the reflexive pronouns and translate into English:

1. Sie setzten ＿＿＿ auf den Stuhl. 2. Ich freue ＿＿＿ darüber, daß es wärmer geworden ist. 3. Hast du ＿＿＿ ein neues Auto gekauft? 4. Das kleine Mädchen fürchtete ＿＿＿ vor dem Niko-

laus. 5. Wir haben _____ für diese Reise nicht warm genug (*enough*) angezogen. 6. Willst du _____ nicht setzen? 7. „Schämt _____", sagte Frau Löwenzahn zu den Kindern. 8. Ich habe _____ eine Flasche Coca Cola bestellt. 9. Ich frage _____, ob er _____ über meinen Brief geärgert hat.

C. After translating the following sentences into English, change them to the present perfect tense:

1. Ich ärgere mich über meinen Lehrer. 2. Sie fürchtet sich vor dem Tier. 3. Wir freuen uns über unsere Geschenke. 4. Sie schämen sich über ihre Angst.

D. Change the sentences of Exercise C into the future tense.

E. Translate the following sentences into English:

1. Es tut mir leid; es tut ihm leid; es tat uns leid; sie tut mir leid; er tat ihr leid; sie haben uns leid getan. 2. Es gefällt mir; sie gefällt mir; ich gefiel ihr nicht; er hat uns gefallen; das Rheinland wird euch gefallen; wie hat es Ihnen in Deutschland gefallen? 3. Es geht ihm gut; dem Lehrer ging es nicht gut; wie geht es dir? wie geht es ihr? wie geht es Ihnen? es ist ihnen nicht gut gegangen.

F. Put the following sentences into the present perfect tense:

1. Klaus will uns eines Abends besuchen. 2. Wir hören ihn an die Tür klopfen. 3. Er soll um sechs Uhr da sein. 4. Wir dürfen in diesem Zimmer rauchen. 5. Wir sehen unsern Freund in das Haus kommen. 6. Er mag nicht zu Hause bleiben. 7. Er muß früh aufstehen. 8. Von uns kann er sehr viel darüber lernen. 9. Wir können das. 10. Er will das nicht.

G. Put sentences 1, 2, 3, 6, 8, 10 of Exercise F into the past perfect.

H. Put sentences 6, 7, 8, 9, 10 of Exercise F into the future tense.

V. Translation Exercise

1. In the autumn our students will be able to take a trip to Austria. 2. This afternoon we have seen the children play in the garden. 3. I am happy that you help me write this lesson. 4. Her husband had wanted to arrive earlier. 5. Instead of coming along, he had to stay at home in order to work. 6. My brother will be able to come before Christmas. 7. Their daughter was sorry that her husband had not been able to come with them. 8. "Don't be afraid of animals," he said to his little daughter. 9. His younger brother sat down on the chair in the living room. 10. Nobody had been permitted to stand on the platform when the train arrived. 11. Since he had gotten up so late, he had to get dressed very quickly. 12. It rained very little during this summer. 13. He will have to take off his hat because it is getting warmer and warmer. 14. His mother was very proud of him, for nobody had helped him translate the story. 15. His name was Till Eulenspiegel. 16. "You should be ashamed," said the elderly lady, when the young man sat down before she did (it). 17. Don't get angry about him! (*all three forms*). 18. Their daughter was very happy because she had been able to come along. 19. It happens very often that little children want to know too much. 20. I do not like it if pupils smoke during an examination.

VI. Fragen

1. Was geschah in der Familie Löwenzahn im Dezember? 2. Wer sind die Besucher gewesen? 3. Wann sind sie angekommen? 4. Wie heißen die Kinder? 5. Wie alt sind sie? 6. Um wieviel Uhr haben sie an diesem Morgen aufstehen müssen? 7. Warum hat der Mann nicht mitkommen dürfen? 8. Wann wird er kommen können? 9. Warum hat Conrad den Nikolaus nicht spielen dürfen? 10. Wann und wo hat Herr Löwenzahn ihn früher gespielt? 11. Wo zieht er sich jetzt an? 12. Was tat die kleine

Henriette, als der Nikolaus kam? 13. Was sagte der Nikolaus zu
ihr? 14. Was hat der Nikolaus den Kindern geben wollen? 15.
Was hat der kleine Henning zu seinem Großvater gesagt?

VII. Lesestück

Das Ruhrgebiet

Viele Nebenflüsse fließen von rechts und links in den Rhein.
Vom Neckar singt man in deutschen Liedern, der Main ist eine
Mason and Dixon Line in der deutschen Geschichte gewesen, die
Mosel kennt man wegen des Weines, der dort wächst. Über
keinen der Nebenflüsse haben während der letzten Jahre die
Zeitungen der Welt so viel geschrieben wie über die Ruhr.

Seit den Zeiten der Römer hat der Rhein im Mittelpunkt der
Geschichte gestanden. Das Ruhrgebiet war noch vor 120 (hun-
dertzwanzig) Jahren ein stilles, freundliches Tal, wo Blumen in
10 den Gärten wuchsen und zufriedene Kühe auf grünen Wiesen
standen. Heute ist dieses Land, von Duisburg im Westen bis
Dortmund im Osten, e i n e große Stadt. Sie streckt sich über
mehr als 200 (zweihundert) Quadratmeilen, auf denen mehr als
sieben Millionen Leute leben. Von Duisburg bis Dortmund ist
es nicht mehr als 33 (dreiunddreißig) Meilen, aber dieses kleine
Stück Land produziert in einem Jahr mehr als 100 (hundert)
Millionen Tonnen Steinkohle, ungefähr 20 (zwanzig) Prozent
der gesamteuropäischen Kohleproduktion. Vor dem letzten Weltkrieg produzierte die Ruhr jedes Jahr 13 Millionen Tonnen Eisen
20 und 15 Millionen Tonnen Stahl. Nicht nur über die Quantität,
auch über die Qualität müssen wir noch ein Wort sagen: die
Steinkohle aus dem Ruhrgebiet ist die beste Kohle Europas.

Für jedes Industriegebiet ist es nicht nur wichtig, daß man
produziert, sondern auch, daß man transportiert. Man braucht
Grubenholz, Erz und Rohmaterial aus anderen Ländern, und man
muß das, was man produziert hat, schnell und billig an den Verbraucher schicken. Das Ruhrgebiet hat das dichteste Netz von

Eisenbahnen, das es auf der Welt gibt. Außerdem hat man in den letzten 50 (fünfzig) Jahren Kanäle gebaut, die das Ruhrgebiet mit der Nordsee, mit der Elbe und mit dem Rhein ver- 30 binden. Erze und Grubenhölzer aus Schweden kommen auf Schiffen, und Kohle, Eisen, Maschinen und andere Produkte gehen auf Schiffen in alle Länder der Welt. Es ist billiger, auf dem Wasser als auf dem Lande zu transportieren.

Wir nannten das Ruhrgebiet e i n e große Stadt, doch wir sollten das nicht zu wörtlich nehmen. Zwischen Duisburg und Dortmund drängen sich viele große und kleine Städte, die dicht zusammen liegen. Wir nennen nur ein paar: Essen, Bochum, Gelsenkirchen, Hagen, Solingen, Wuppertal, Düsseldorf. Niemand wird sagen, daß sie in einer schönen Landschaft liegen. Ruhr- 40 gebiet: das sind Fabriken, Fördertürme, Kohlenberge, Schornsteine und Rauch. Doch wir wissen, daß hier zwischen Duisburg und Dortmund das wichtigste Stück Land liegt, das es in Deutschland (wir können sagen: in Europa) gibt. Die Ruhr braucht Europa für ihre Produkte, und Europa braucht die Produkte der Ruhr.

VIII. Wörterverzeichnis

bauen (to) build
billig cheaply, inexpensively
dicht dense, close
sich drängen (to) be crowded
das Eisen the iron
die Eisenbahn, –en the railroad
die Elbe the Elbe (River)
das Erz, –e the ore
die Fabrik, –en the factory
fließen, floß, ist geflossen to flow
der Förderturm, ̈-e the transport tower, haul tower
gesamteuropäisch total European
das Grubenholz, ̈-er the wood for the mine
das Industriegebiet, –e the industrial region

der Kanal, ̈-e the canal
der Kohlenberg, –e the pile of coal
die Kohleproduktion the coal production
die Kuh, ̈-e the cow
links left (*adverb*)
der Main the Main (River)
die Maschine, –n the machine
die Meile, –n the mile
die Million, –en the million
der Mittelpunkt, –e the center
die Mosel the Mosel (River)
der Nebenfluß, –flüsse the tributary
der Neckar the Neckar (River)
das Netz, –e the network
die Nordsee the North Sea

der Osten the east
das Produkt, –e the product
produzieren (to) produce
das Prozent, –e the percent
die Quadratmeile, –n the square mile
die Qualität the quality
die Quantität the quantity
der Rauch the smoke
rechts right (*adverb*)
das Rohmaterial the raw material
der Römer, – the Roman
die Ruhr the Ruhr (River)
das Ruhrgebiet the Ruhr district
schicken (to) send

der Schornstein, –e the chimney
Schweden Sweden
der Stahl the steel
die Steinkohle, –n hard coal
sich strecken (to) extend
das Stück, –e the piece, bit
das Tal, –er the valley
die Tonne, –n the ton
transportieren (to) transport, ship
verbinden, verband, verbunden (to) connect
der Verbraucher, – the consumer
der Weltkrieg, –e the World War
der Westen the west
wörtlich literally

AUFGABE ACHTZEHN

NUMERALS · TELLING TIME
DAYS, MONTHS, SEASONS

I. Reading Selection

Zum ersten Mal in meinem Leben bin ich zu Weihnachten
nicht zu Hause gewesen, und zum ersten Mal, seitdem ich nach
Deutschland gekommen bin, habe ich ein wenig Heimweh gehabt.
Trotzdem war es auch hier ein sehr schönes Fest.

Die Kinder wurden jeden Tag unruhiger. „Noch sieben Tage
. . . noch sechs . . . noch fünf . . . noch vier", hörte man sie
jeden Morgen sagen. „Wann ist der vierundzwanzigste?" fragte
die kleine Henriette immer wieder. Dann sagte Herr Löwenzahn:
„Der vierundzwanzigste ist am vierundzwanzigsten", und sie
schien mit dieser Antwort sehr zufrieden zu sein.   10

Jeden Abend, ehe sie zu Bett gingen, stellten die Kinder einen
Schuh vor das Fenster. Am nächsten Morgen lag dann immer
Schokolade oder Weihnachtsgebäck darin.

„Ein Weihnachtsengel muß es in den Schuh gelegt haben",
sagten wir dann.

„Es kann auch der Nikolaus gewesen sein", meinte der kleine
Henning. Hinter dem Rücken seiner Schwester sah er Herrn
Löwenzahn an und lächelte heimlich. Doch die kleine Henriette
dachte lieber an den Weihnachtsengel als an den Nikolaus.

In Amerika ist der 25. Dezember der wichtigste Tag des 20
Festes. In Deutschland ist es der 24. Der Tag heißt Heilig
Abend. An diesem Tag durften die Kinder nach ein Uhr nicht
mehr ins Wohnzimmer gehen, denn die Eltern und Großeltern
fingen nun an, den Christbaum zu schmücken und die Geschenke
in das Zimmer zu tragen.

„Vielleicht schneit es noch", sagte Frau Löwenzahn. Es war
kalt, doch der Himmel war klar und blau.

Um fünf Uhr kamen wir alle ins Eßzimmer. Der kleine Henning wollte sofort ins Wohnzimmer laufen, doch die Tür zum
Wohnzimmer war noch geschlossen. Herbert setzte sich ans 30
Klavier, und wir alle sangen das Lied „Stille Nacht, heilige Nacht."
Dann nahm Herr Löwenzahn die Bibel und las die Weihnachtsgeschichte in der Übersetzung von Martin Luther. Gerade als er
sagte „Friede auf Erden", unterbrach die kleine Henriette und
rief: „Großvater, wann fangen wir mit dem vierundzwanzigsten
an?" Herr Löwenzahn machte das Buch zu und sagte: „In einer
Minute, mein Kind." Er öffnete die Tür: da stand der Christbaum mit vielen brennenden Kerzen, und darunter lagen die
Geschenke. Wir alle riefen „Fröhliche Weihnachten!"

Es gab Geschenke für jeden von uns, auch für Herbert und 40
mich. Ich kann nicht alles aufzählen, sonst muß ich mein deutsch-
englisches Wörterbuch aufmachen, und ich habe versprochen,
diese Geschichten ohne Wörterbuch zu schreiben. Doch da wir
alle das deutsche Wort „Schnee" kennen, will ich noch sagen, daß
es während der Nacht zu schneien anfing. Am nächsten Morgen
war alles weiß. „Wir haben ein Weihnachten wie in der guten
alten Zeit", sagten die Löwenzahns sehr zufrieden.

Am Tage nach Neujahr fuhren die Kinder und Enkel der
Löwenzahns wieder ab. Herr Löwenzahn, Herbert und ich gingen
mit ihnen zum Bahnhof. Der Zug nach Wien sollte um 13 Uhr 50
31 abfahren, aber wir kamen schon um drei Viertel eins am Bahnhof an. Wir standen länger als eine halbe Stunde auf dem Bahnsteig und niemand wußte, was er sagen sollte.

„Zählen Sie in Amerika die Stunden auch von eins bis vierundzwanzig?" fragte uns Herr Löwenzahn, als wir nach Hause gingen.

Courtesy of Deutsche Zentrale für Fremdenverkehr

Weihnachtsabend in einem Städtchen in Hessen

„Nein", sagte Herbert. „Unsere Uhren gehen bis zwölf und fangen dann wieder mit eins an."

„Auch wir haben die vierundzwanzig Stunden nur auf dem Fahrplan für die Züge", erklärte uns Herr Löwenzahn. „Interessant wird es dann um Mitternacht. Ein Zug kommt um 24 60 Uhr an. Ein anderer fährt in dieser Minute ab, aber wir sagen: er fährt um null Uhr ab. Der ankommende Zug schließt den Tag, der abfahrende fängt ihn an. Sind wir nicht ein poetisches Volk?"

II. Vocabulary

*an-sehen (ie), sah an, angesehen (to) look at

*die Antwort, –en the answer

auf-zählen (to) enumerate

*bekommen, bekam, bekommen (to) get, receive

die Bibel, –n the Bible

der Christbaum, ⸚e the Christmas tree

der Enkel, – the grandchild

*der erste (*adj.*) the first; **erst** (*adv.*) not until, only

*der Fahrplan, ⸚e the timetable

das Fest the celebration, holiday

Friede auf Erden peace on earth

*die Großeltern the grandparents

*halb half

Heilig Abend Christmas Eve

*heimlich secretly

das Heimweh the homesickness

*der Himmel the heaven, sky

die Kerze, –n the candle

*klar clear

das Klavier the piano

*legen (to) lay, place, put

*das Mal, –e the time

*die Minute, –n the minute

die Mitternacht the midnight

*der Morgen, – the morning

Neujahr New Year's

*null zero

*öffnen (to) open

poetisch poetic

*der Rücken, – the back

*scheinen, schien, geschienen (to) seem; shine

*schließen, schloß, geschlossen (to) close, end; shut, lock

schmücken (to) decorate

*der Schnee the snow

*schneien (to) snow

die Schokolade the chocolate

*die Schwester, –n the sister

*seitdem (*conj.*) since

*trotzdem in spite of that

*die Uhr, –en the clock; o'clock

unruhig restless

versprechen (i), versprach, versprochen (to) promise

*das Viertel, – the quarter

der Weihnachtsengel, – the Christmas angel

das Weihnachtsgebäck the Christmas cookies

die Weihnachtsgeschichte the Christmas story

Wien Vienna

das Wörterbuch, ⸚er the dictionary

*zählen (to) count

Idioms

Fröhliche Weihnachten! Merry Christmas!
*zum ersten Mal for the first time

III. Grammar

A. Numerals: Cardinal Numbers

We have already used several numerals. Add the new ones to your active vocabulary.

1. We count from 0 to 12: **null, eins, zwei, drei, vier, fünf, sechs, sieben, acht, neun, zehn, elf, zwölf.**

2. We count from 13 to 19: **dreizehn, vierzehn, fünfzehn, sechzehn** (note the difference in pronunciation and spelling between **sechs** –x– and **sechzehn** –ch–), **siebzehn, achtzehn, neunzehn.**

3. We count from 10 to 100 by tens: **zehn, zwanzig, dreißig** (note that **dreißig** has an irregular form as compared with the –**zig** that everywhere else corresponds to English –ty), **vierzig, fünfzig, sechzig** (again the loss of the final s on **sechs** before a following **z**), **siebzig** (**sieben** always loses its final **en** before a z ending, just as in **siebzehn** above), **achtzig, neunzig, hundert.**

4. We count within the tens: **zwanzig, einundzwanzig, zweiundzwanzig, dreiundzwanzig, vierundzwanzig, fünfundzwanzig, sechsundzwanzig, siebenundzwanzig, achtundzwanzig, neunundzwanzig; dreißig, einunddreißig, zweiunddreißig, dreiunddreißig,** etc.; **vierzig, einundvierzig, zweiundvierzig,** etc.; **hundert; hundert(und)eins, hundert(und)zwei, hundert(und)drei, hundert(und)zwanzig, hundert(und)einundzwanzig, hundert(und)zweiundzwanzig,** etc.; **zweihundert(und)eins, zweihundert(und)zwei, dreihundert(und)einunddreißig, vierhundert(und)zweiundfünfzig,** etc.; **tausend, tausend(und)eins, tausend(und)einundsiebzig, zweitausend(und)vierundachtzig,** etc.

5. Note that **hundert** means *one hundred,* and **tausend** means *a thousand*—**ein** is not normally used with either **hundert** or **tausend.**

6. The numeral **eins** is used only in counting. With a noun it is **ein–** and is inflected like the indefinite article: Er braucht **einen** Pfennig. Es kostet **eine** Mark zwanzig. **Ein** Jahr hat zwölf Monate. Von **einer** Stadt zur anderen (from *one* city to the other). Mit **einem** Wort (with *one word*).

B. Numerals: Ordinal Numbers

The numerals *the first, the second, the third, the fourth,* etc. are called ordinal numbers.

1. The German ordinal numbers are adjectives. They are composed of three elements:

   a) the cardinal number, e.g., **fünf–, zwanzig–;**

   b) the suffix **–t–** (from *the 2nd* to *the 19th*) or **–st–** (from *the 20th* on), e.g., **fünft–, zwanzigst–;**

   c) the proper adjectival ending, e.g., **der fünfte Tag, sein zwanzigster Geburtstag, ihr fünftes Kind, nach dem zwanzigsten Glas Wein.**

2. In the following we list the ordinal numbers with the definite article **der.** Note that the German equivalents of *the first* and *the third* are irregular: **der erste, der zweite, der dritte, vierte, fünfte, sechste, sieb(en)te, achte, neunte, zehnte, elfte, zwölfte, dreizehnte, vierzehnte, fünfzehnte, sechzehnte, siebzehnte, achtzehnte, neunzehnte; der zwanzigste, dreißigste, vierzigste, fünfzigste, sechzigste, siebzigste, achtzigste, neunzigste, hundertste, tausendste.** Also **der einundzwanzigste, zweiunddreißigste, dreiundvierzigste, vierundfünfzigste,** etc.; **der hundertunderste, hundertundzweite, zweihundertundzehnte, zweihundertundelfte, dreihundertzwanzigste, vierhundertvierundvierzigste,** etc.

3. A period after a numeral indicates that it is to be read as an ordinal with the proper adjective ending: Heute ist der 17. Februar (der siebzehnte Februar). — Voltaire war ein Freund Fried-

richs II. (Friedrichs des Zweiten). — Mein Freund ist am 29.
Oktober (am neunundzwanzigsten Oktober) angekommen. —
Er sprach über Friedrich III. (Friedrich den Dritten).

C. mal und erst

1. **Das Mal** means *time* in the sense of *occasion, incident,* e.g.,
das erste Mal *the first time;* **zum dritten Mal** *for the third time.*
It can be compounded with certain **der-** and **ein-**words, e.g.,
manchmal, *sometimes;* **jedesmal,** *everytime;* **diesmal,** *this time;*
keinmal, *no time.* It is compounded also with cardinal numerals:
einmal, *once;* **zweimal,** *twice;* **dreimal,** *three times;* **zehnmal,** *ten
times;* **hundertmal,** *a hundred times;* **tausendmal,** *a thousand
times,* etc.

2. As an ordinal number, **erst–** is an adjective and has an ending, e.g., **der erste Monat, sein erstes Auto.** As an adverb **erst**
means *only* in the sense of *not until, as late as:* **Er ist erst gestern
angekommen,** *He arrived only yesterday,* or *He didn't arrive until
yesterday.*

D. Telling Time

1. Remember the expressions we have already used: **Wie spät
ist es?** or **Wieviel Uhr ist es?** *What time is it?*—**Es ist drei Uhr,**
It is three o'clock; **Es ist sechsundzwanzig Minuten nach drei,** *It
is twenty-six minutes after three;* **Es ist sechzehn Minuten vor
vier,** *It is sixteen minutes to four;* **Der Zug kommt um vier Uhr
an,** *The train arrives at four o'clock.*—Note especially the use of
nach, vor, and **um** with expressions relating to the time of day.

2. German counts the quarter hours in an entirely different
manner from English. Starting with 7:00 o'clock to count the
next three quarter hours, the German would be equivalent to the
following: 7:15 one quarter on the way to eight; 7:30 one half
on the way to eight; 7:45 three quarters on the way to eight.
Thus the German would be as follows: 7:00 **sieben Uhr;** 7:15

(ein) Viertel acht; 7:30 halb acht; 7:45 drei Viertel acht, frequently spelled dreiviertel acht; 8:00 acht Uhr.

3. In railroad, bus, and plane timetables, as with the American armed forces, the hours from midnight to noon are 0 to 12, while the p.m. hours are 13 to 24.

Thus, a train leaving at 6:25 p.m., would leave, for the American armed forces, at "eighteen hundred twenty-five hours," or in German at achtzehn Uhr fünfundzwanzig. *I take the train at 3:47 p.m.* Ich nehme den Zug um fünfzehn Uhr siebenundvierzig.

E. Names of Days, Months, and Seasons

Here are complete lists of the names of the days, months, and seasons. All of them are masculine. *All are now to be considered as active vocabulary.*

The days of the week are Sonntag, Montag, Dienstag, Mittwoch, Donnerstag, Freitag, Samstag or Sonnabend.

The months are Januar, Februar, März, April, Mai, Juni, Juli, August, September, Oktober, November, Dezember.

The seasons are Frühling, Sommer, Herbst, Winter.

F. Dates

Dates are given as follows: der 25. (fünfundzwanzigste) Januar; am 17. (siebzehnten) März 1965 (neunzehnhundertfünfundsechzig). On letterheads: 17. 3. 1965 (day-month-year, so it corresponds to 3/17/1965 in American usage).

G. Participles as Adjectives

1. The past participle can be used as an adjective. In die Tür ist geschlossen, *the door is closed,* it is predicative; in die geschlossene Tür, *the closed door,* it is attributive and is thus used with the proper adjectival ending. More examples: In der ge-

sprochenen **Sprache,** *in the spoken language;* **ein handgeschriebener Brief,** *a handwritten letter;* in **einer gegebenen Situation,** *in a given situation.*

2. The present participle is formed by adding the suffix —**end** to the verb stem. It is, except in elevated literary style, used *only* as an attributive adjective. Examples: **Die schlafenden Kinder,** *the sleeping children;* **das singende Mädchen,** *the singing girl;* **der ankommende Zug,** *the arriving train;* **ein brennendes Haus,** *a burning house.* Such participial constructions are very frequently used in scientific writings.

IV. Grammatical Exercises

A. Count in German from 1 to 12; from 13 to 20; from 21 to 29; from 30 to 39; from 60 to 69; from 70 to 79; from 100 to 112; from 120 to 129; from 230 to 239; from 450 to 459; from 890 to 899; from 1000 to 1012; from 5340 to 5349; from 7560 to 7569; from 9780 to 9789.

B. For the following figures use ordinals such as *the first time, the second time,* etc.: 1, 2, 3, 4, 7, 9, 10, 12, 13, 16, 17, 19, 20, 21, 25, 33, 71, 100.

C. Tell the time of day in German with the sentence "My train arrives at _____ o'clock." Use the first six as a.m. hours, and the rest as p.m.: 6:00; 7:02, 8:05; 9:15; 10:22; 11:30; 12:40; 1:43; 2:52; 5:37; 6:30; 7:45.

D. Translate into English:

1. Die spielenden Kinder; 2. wachsende Städte; 3. in dem abfahrenden Zug; 4. ein brennendes Haus; 5. vor einer geschlossenen Tür; 6. ein übersetztes Gedicht; 7. eine gute, aber schlecht erzählte Geschichte; 8. der Unterschied zwischen der gesprochenen und der geschriebenen Sprache; 9. ich bin lieber der Gebende als der Nehmende.

V. Translation Exercise

1. On the day before Christmas the children got up at a quarter to seven. 2. On the twenty-fifth of December they slept until a quarter after eight. 3. Because we had a vacation we could sleep every morning until half past nine. 4. It was the first time that they had not been at home on this day. 5. This happened on the second day of the new year. 6. During the day it was very cold but it did not snow until the next morning. 7. His brother always receives his money on the last day of the month. 8. On the second of January the children and grandchildren had to go home again. 9. Their third child later became a very famous physician. 10. Thomas Jefferson died on July 4, 1826. 11. My grandparents are traveling to Hamburg on the train that left this morning at 10:48. 12. Only when they got off the train did we see them. 13. Come, Conrad, we must not arrive late, otherwise we will not be able to say good-bye to them. 14. Although I asked this question three or four times, I never received an answer from him. 15. We called up his sister a few minutes after seven o'clock. 16. The singing men did not hear us coming. 17. The father carried the sleeping child into the house. 18. Who is that pretty smiling girl? 19. The students sold their used books. 20. This is a well written story. 21. We could not hear them behind the closed doors.

VI. Fragen

1. Wo sind Conrad und Herbert in diesem Jahre zu Weihnachten? 2. Wo ist Conrad in früheren Jahren zu Weihnachten gewesen? 3. Was haben die Kinder jeden Morgen gefragt? 4. Was machen sie dann am Abend? 5. Was lag am nächsten Morgen in dem Schuh? 6. Welches ist der wichtigste Tag des Weihnachtsfestes in Deutschland? 7. Wohin haben die Kinder nach ein Uhr nicht gehen dürfen? 8. Was machten die Eltern

und Großeltern um diese Zeit? 9. Um wieviel Uhr sind sie alle ins Eßzimmer gekommen? 10. Warum konnte Henning nicht ins Wohnzimmer hinein? 11. Was für ein Lied haben sie gesungen? 12. Welche Geschichte hat Herr Löwenzahn dann gelesen? 13. Wissen Sie, wer die Bibel ins Deutsche übersetzt hat? 14. Was lag unter dem Weihnachtsbaum, als sie ins Wohnzimmer kamen? 15. Wie wurde das Wetter während der Nacht? 16. Wann sind die Besucher abgefahren? 17. Wann sollte der Zug nach Wien abfahren?

VII. Lesestück

Der Freiherr vom Stein

In vielen großen deutschen Städten sieht man in der Eingangshalle des Rathauses das Bild eines Mannes im Kostüm des frühen 19. Jahrhunderts. Darunter steht „Karl vom Stein, 1757–1831." Wer war der Freiherr vom Stein, und warum hängt sein Bild so oft in deutschen Rathäusern?

Stein wurde am 26. Oktober 1757 in Nassau geboren. Er studierte in Göttingen und trat, als er 32 Jahre alt war, in den preußischen Staatsdienst ein. Er hatte, als er ein junger Mann war, viele Bücher über englische Geschichte und englische Politik gelesen. „Worin unterscheidet sich das englische Volk von dem 10 deutschen?" fragte er sich. Die Antwort war: „In Deutschland regieren absolute Fürsten. In England interessieren sich die Leute für Politik, sie haben ein Parlament und Gesetze, und darum kann der König nicht immer tun, was er will. Wenn Deutschland nicht hinter den anderen Ländern zurückbleiben will, müssen wir unter den Deutschen das Interesse für Politik wecken."

Im Jahre 1806 wurde Preußen von Napoleon besiegt. Ein Jahr später ernannte der preußische König den Freiherrn vom Stein zum Ministerpräsidenten. Nun begann Stein mit den Reformen, auf die er so lange gewartet hatte. Unter den vielen 20 Reformen, durch die Stein berühmt wurde, nennen wir hier nur die zwei wichtigsten: das Befreiungsgesetz und die Städteordnung.

Der Freiherr vom Stein

Bis zu dieser Zeit gab es noch viele Leute, besonders auf dem Lande, die nicht frei waren. Das Volk war in soziale Kasten eingeteilt, die man nie verlassen konnte. Ein Bauer mußte immer ein Bauer bleiben, ein Adeliger konnte nicht Arzt werden oder ein Geschäft aufmachen. Steins Befreiungsgesetz hob alle diese alten Beschränkungen auf. „Nach dem Martinitag 1810", sagte das Gesetz, „wird es im Lande nur freie Leute geben."

Nicht weniger wichtig war die Städteordnung. Dieses Gesetz 30
gab den Städten Selbstverwaltung. Die Bürger durften sich nun
selbst regieren, d.h. sie durften einen Bürgermeister und ein Stadtparlament wählen. Die Städteordnung gab den Bürgern der
Städte die Verantwortung für die Geschäfte der Stadt. So war es
in Deutschland schon im Mittelalter gewesen, doch in der Zeit des
Absolutismus, d.h. im 17. und 18. Jahrhundert, hatten die Fürsten
den alten Städten ihre Selbstverwaltung genommen. Die neuen
jüngeren Städte hatten Selbstverwaltung nie gekannt. Wir verstehen jetzt, warum Steins Bild noch heute in den Rathäusern der
deutschen Städte hängt. 40

Niemand hat mehr getan als er, aus dem preußischen Untertan einen deutschen Bürger zu machen.

VIII. Wörterverzeichnis

absolut absolute
der Absolutismus the absolutism
der Ad(e)lige, (–n), –n the nobleman
auf-heben, hob auf, aufgehoben
(to) remove
der Bauer, –n the peasant
das Befreiungsgesetz the Liberation
Edict
die Beschränkung, –en the limitation
besiegt conquered
besonders especially
das Bild, –er the picture, portrait
der Bürger, – the citizen
der Bürgermeister, – the mayor
die Eingangshalle, –n the entrance
hall
ein-teilen (to) divide
ein-treten (tritt ein), trat ein, ist
eingetreten (to) enter
ernennen, ernannte, ernannt (to)
name, appoint

der Freiherr, (–n), –en the baron
der Fürst, (–en), –en the (ruling)
prince
geboren born
das Geschäft, –e the business, affairs
das Gesetz, –e the law
hängen, hing, gehangen (to) hang
sich interessieren für (to) be interested in
die Kaste, –n the caste
der König, –e the king
das Kostüm, –e the costume
auf dem Lande in the country
der Martinitag St. Martin's Day
(Nov. 11)
der Ministerpräsident, (–en), –en
the prime minister
das Mittelalter the Middle Ages
das Parlament, –e the parliament
die Politik politics
Preußen Prussia
preußisch Prussian

die **Reform, –en** the reform
die **Selbstverwaltung** the self-government
sozial social
der **Staatsdienst** the state service
die **Städteordnung** the Municipal Autonomy Statute
das **Stadtparlament, –e** the city council
sich unterscheiden von, unterschied, unterschieden (to) be different from

der **Untertan, –en** the subject
die **Verantwortung** the responsibility
verlassen (ä), **verließ, verlassen** (to) leave
wählen (to) choose, elect
wecken (to) awaken
weniger less
zurück-bleiben, blieb zurück, ist zurückgeblieben (to) remain behind

THE PASSIVE VOICE

I. Reading Selection

Gestern abend waren wir im Theater. Da Schillers „Wallenstein" zum 1. Mal gespielt wurde, war das ganze Theater ausverkauft. Wir kamen viel zu früh. Als wir am Theater ankamen,
waren die Türen noch geschlossen. Wir mußten fünf Minuten
warten, und während wir warteten, sprachen wir mit einem alten
Herrn. „Ich war ein Junge von zehn Jahren", erzählte er uns,
„als dieses Theater gebaut wurde. Und ich erinnere mich noch
an den 3. September 1901, als diese Türen zum ersten Mal aufgemacht wurden." Während wir sprachen, wurden die Türen
geöffnet, und wir gingen hinein.   10
Im Theater wurden Programme verkauft, worin ein wenig
über das Leben des Dichters berichtet wurde, dessen Werk heute
abend gespielt wurde. Wir lasen, daß Friedrich Schiller am 10.
November 1759 geboren wurde und am 9. Mai 1805 starb, und
daß sein größtes Drama, der Wallenstein, zwischen Oktober 1796
und März 1799 geschrieben wurde. Das Drama erzählt die Geschichte eines großen Generals aus dem Dreißigjährigen Krieg.
Wallenstein war von dem Kaiser an die Spitze des Heeres gestellt
worden, er wurde von den Soldaten verehrt und geliebt, und seine
Stellung im Reich wurde immer größer und stärker. Als er dann 20

219

so mächtig wurde, daß der Kaiser anfing, sich vor ihm zu fürchten, wurde Wallenstein entlassen. Bald danach wurde das Heer des Kaisers von den Schweden besiegt. „Das Reich wird nur gerettet werden, wenn Wallenstein zurückgerufen wird", sagte der Kaiser nun. Zum zweiten Mal wurde jetzt das Heer von Wallenstein geführt, und wieder wurde der General zu mächtig. Er wußte, daß er zum zweiten Mal entlassen werden sollte, und er dachte nun sogar daran, das Heer des Kaisers gegen den Kaiser zu führen. Doch ehe er das noch tun konnte, wurde er von einem
30 Offizier, der von ihm schlecht behandelt worden war, in der Stadt Eger ermordet. Das geschah im Jahre 1634.

In der Pause trafen wir unsern Lehrer. „Es wird gut gespielt, nicht wahr?" fragte er. „Schillers Wallenstein ist nicht nur ein großes, sondern auch ein langes Drama. Bis jetzt wurde es immer an zwei Abenden gespielt. Es ist das erste Mal, daß ich das ganze Drama in e i n e r Vorstellung gesehen habe. Es ist gekürzt worden, so daß es an einem Abend gespielt werden kann. Ich freue mich, daß Sie heute abend hier sind. Können Sie alles verstehen?"

40   „Alles", antwortete ich. „Ich verstehe jedes Wort."

„Conrad", sagte Herbert, als wir wieder allein waren, „ich verstehe nicht alles. Entweder ist dein Deutsch besser, oder du hast gelogen."

Ich wurde ein wenig rot. „Das zweite. Ich wollte ihn nicht traurig machen. Ich verstehe vielleicht 70 Prozent. Schillers Sprache ist gewiß schöner, aber auch schwerer zu verstehen als Herrn Löwenzahns Deutsch."

Die Vorstellung dauerte bis halb zwölf. Alle Leute im Theater waren sehr begeistert. Die Schauspieler kamen immer wieder vor
50 den Vorhang, auch der Schauspieler, der den Wallenstein gespielt hatte, obwohl er gerade ermordet worden war. Schließlich wurde der eiserne Vorhang herabgelassen.

„Auch dies ist etwas Neues für mich", meinte Herbert. „Wie oft haben wir in der Zeitung vom eisernen Vorhang gelesen. Dies ist der erste, den ich gesehen habe."

II. Vocabulary

ausverkauft sold out
*bauen (to) build
begeistert enthusiastic
behandeln (to) treat
besiegen (to) vanquish, conquer
*dauern (to) last
*der Dichter, – the poet, author
das Drama, Dramen the drama
der Dreißigjährige Krieg the Thirty Years' War
eisern iron
entlassen (ä), entließ, entlassen (to) dismiss, discharge
*entweder . . . oder either . . . or
*sich erinnern an (with acc.) (to) remember
ermorden (to) murder
*führen (to) lead, conduct
*geboren born
der General, ∸e the general
*das Heer, –e the army
herab-lassen (ä), ließ herab, herabgelassen (to) let down, lower
*der Herr, (–n), –en the gentleman, Mr.
hinein-gehen, ging hinein, ist hineingegangen (to) go in

der Kaiser, – the emperor
kürzen (to) shorten
*lieben (to) love
*lügen, log, gelogen (to) lie, tell a lie
*mächtig mighty, powerful
der Offizier, –e the officer
die Pause, –n the intermission
das Programm, –e the program
Prozent percent
das Reich the empire
*retten (to) save
der Schauspieler, – the actor
*schlecht bad
*schließlich finally
der Schwede, –n the Swede
*der Soldat, (–en), –en the soldier
die Spitze, –n the top, head
die Stellung, –en the position
das Theater, – the theater
verehren (to) honor, respect
*von by
*der Vorhang, ∸e the curtain
die Vorstellung, –en the performance
*während (conj.) while
*das Werk, –e the (creative) work
zurück-rufen, rief zurück, zurückgerufen (to) call back

Idioms

*gestern abend last evening, yesterday evening
*nicht nur . . . sondern auch not only . . . but also

III. Grammar

A. Active and Passive Voice

Let it be imagined that two persons observe the same action. One person will say: *the cat eats the mouse*. The other person will say: *the mouse is eaten by the cat*.

Both persons express the same factual relationship between *cat* and *mouse*. However, they choose different starting points for determining the relationship, i.e., they choose different subjects. In the first sentence, *the cat,* the active element, or the one which performs the action, is the subject. Such a sentence is said to be in the active voice.

In the second sentence, *the mouse,* the passive partner of the relation, is the subject, and the sentence is said to be in the passive voice. In this case the element which performs the action is called the agent or instrument and appears in the sentence with the instrumental preposition *by.*

B. The Passive Voice in German

In German the passive voice construction is basically the same as in English. However:

1. In English the auxiliary for the passive voice is *to be.* In German, the auxiliary is **werden.**

2. The word order is, of course, determined by the rule: finite verb in second position; past participle at the end; if both past participle and infinitive appear, the past participle precedes the infinitive.

3. The preposition preceding the agent or instrument is **von** (Eng. *by*) which takes the dative case.

The correspondences between English and German are therefore as follows:

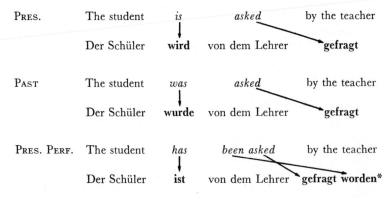

PRES. The student *is* *asked* by the teacher

Der Schüler **wird** von dem Lehrer **gefragt**

PAST The student *was* *asked* by the teacher

Der Schüler **wurde** von dem Lehrer **gefragt**

PRES. PERF. The student *has* *been asked* by the teacher

Der Schüler **ist** von dem Lehrer **gefragt worden***

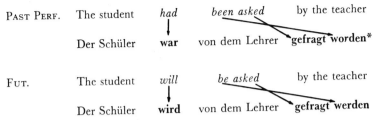

In the dependent clause, here as always, the finite verb is at the end of the clause:

Wenn der Schüler von dem Lehrer gefragt wird, . . .
Da der Schüler von dem Lehrer gefragt worden ist, . . .
Wenn der Schüler von dem Lehrer gefragt werden wird, . . .

Here is an example of an infinitive phrase in the passive:

. . . , ohne von dem Lehrer gefragt zu werden.
. . . , ohne von dem Lehrer gefragt worden zu sein.

C. Substitutes for the Passive Voice

With more experience in German you will find that often the passive voice is used in German, where the English speaker would express himself in the active—and vice versa.

In German quite frequently a reflexive construction is used instead of the passive. For example: **Die Tür öffnet sich** instead of **Die Tür wird geöffnet.** (Cf. English *The door opens* and *The door is opened.*)

Very common in German is the use of an active sentence with the impersonal subject **man,** where in English a passive would be used. For example: **Man fragte uns nicht;** *We were not asked.* **Man konnte ihn nicht sehen;** *He could not be seen.*

D. Static Passive

Strictly speaking, the term "passive voice" is misleading, because, although the sentence is in the passive voice, it is implied that some sort of action does take place. For example: **Das Haus**

---

* Note that the past participle of **werden** as an element of the passive voice construction is **worden** (*not* geworden).

wird verkauft *The house is being sold,* i.e., someone is selling it now; **Die Tür wurde geschlossen** *The door was being closed,* i.e., someone was closing it then; **Das Reich wird gerettet werden** *The empire will be saved,* i.e., some person will be saving it. In all these cases action takes place.

However, in English there is a type of sentence which appears to be in the passive voice, but which expresses no action. If you say, for instance, *The door is closed,* you describe a state or condition of the door. This is what we may call a "static passive," and in this case the German will use **sein** and not **werden.** In German one would say **Das Haus wird verkauft** only if it is implied that the house is being sold. After the purchase is completed and the real estate agent puts his SOLD sign on the front lawn, he would say **Das Haus ist verkauft.** The first sentence describes an action: the selling is being trans-*acted.* The second sentence describes a state. **Verkauft** is here a predicative adjective; it describes a state just as do **alt, neu, groß, klein,** etc.

Another example of the static passive: **Die Tür war geschlossen, als wir ankamen.** *The door was* (already) *closed when we arrived,* i.e., we stood before a closed door; **wir standen vor einer geschlossenen Tür.** (Cf. Lesson XVIII, III,G.)

Since the static passive does not describe a "doing," it will never show any "doer" or agent indicated by the preposition *by* (**von**).

E. Geboren

Geboren (*born*) is used in a past tense passive construction when referring to a historical event:

Schiller wurde 1759 geboren | Wann wurde Mozart geboren?
Schiller was born in 1759 | When was Mozart born?

In referring to the beginning of your own history, as for example in a *curriculum vitae,* this construction is also used: **Ich wurde am 18. April 1935 in Lübeck geboren.** In conversational German

the mere fact of your birthplace or date of birth, however, is
rendered in a static passive in the present tense:

Ich bin im August geboren   Wo sind Sie geboren?
I was born in August   Where were you born?

IV. Grammatical Exercises

A. Change the following sentences into the passive voice:

1. Er schlägt das Tier. 2. Mein Vater bezahlt die Rechnung. 3.
Jeden Abend macht seine Mutter die Tür zu. 4. Unser Nachbar
bringt die Kinder mit dem Auto zur Schule. 5. Wer übersetzt
das Buch?

B. Re-do these sentences in the past, future and present perfect
tenses of the passive voice.

C. Change the following sentences into the corresponding
tense of the passive voice.

1. Die Kinder haben alle Äpfel gegessen. 2. Wir haben das Haus
gekauft. 3. Unser Theater wird Schillers „Wallenstein" spielen.
4. Er hat das Geschenk in unser Haus gebracht. 5. Die Leute
haben viel darüber gesprochen. 6. Im Jahre 1812 führte Napoleon ein großes Heer nach Rußland. 7. So konnte Wilhelm Tell
das Land retten.

D. Translate into English.

1. Wann werden die Warenhäuser in dieser Stadt geschlossen?
2. Ich weiß nicht, ob der Brief schon geschrieben worden ist. 3.
Wenn Sie gefragt werden, sagen Sie nichts. 4. Das Leben wird
immer schwerer. 5. Er ist gestern abend von seinen Großeltern
in San Francisco angerufen worden. 6. Sie will nicht gefragt
werden. 7. Ich glaube, er wird für diese alte Bibel viel Geld bekommen. 8. Das Haus ist vor einer Stunde verkauft worden. 9.
Mir wurde die Geschichte von meinem Professor anders erzählt.
10. Ich hoffe, von Ihnen allen verstanden zu werden.

V. Translation Exercise

1. I was asked by our teacher today; who will be asked tomorrow? 2. The cake which stood on the table was eaten either by my little brother or my little sister. 3. Something had been thrown through the window. 4. Yesterday Monika and her friend Vera were driven downtown by their friends. 5. The door is being opened. 6. After the windows had been opened, cold air came into the room. 7. English is spoken in many countries of the world. 8. When the city hall was built in the year 1630, only 15,000 people lived in the city. 9. The letter has not yet been written. 10. This work must be done before it gets dark. 11. Their army is being led by the greatest soldier in their country. 12. Wallenstein was played for the first time in Weimar in April 1799. 13. When our house was built, the city was still small. 14. When we arrived, the house was already sold. 15. He remembered the day when the great poet died. 16. Only German is spoken here!

VI. Fragen

1. Wo sind die Studenten gestern gewesen? 2. Konnten sie sofort ins Theater gehen, als sie ankamen? 3. Warum nicht? 4. Wie lange haben sie warten müssen, ehe sie hineingehen konnten? 5. Was wurde im Theater verkauft? 6. Was wurde an diesem Abend gespielt? 7. Von wem war dieses Drama? 8. In welchem Jahrhundert hat der Dichter gelebt? 9. Wer war Wallenstein? 10. Warum hat ihn der Kaiser an die Spitze des Heeres gestellt? 11. In welchem Jahre ist der General ermordet worden? 12. Was hat man getan, sodaß man den „Wallenstein" an e i n e m Abend spielen kann? 13. Wen haben Conrad und Herbert im Theater getroffen? 14. Versteht Conrad Schillers Deutsch ganz? 15. Warum hat er gelogen? 16. Wie lange hat die Vorstellung gedauert? 17. Was ist schließlich herabgelassen worden?

VII. Lesestück

Salzburg und Bayreuth

Man hat die Deutschen oft das Volk der Dichter und Denker
genannt. Man kann sie auch das Volk der Komponisten und Musiker nennen. Ob man ein Konzertprogramm in Hamburg oder
Cleveland, in Stockholm oder San Francisco öffnet: immer
wieder sehen wir darin Namen wie Bach, Beethoven, Schumann,
Brahms. Zu den berühmtesten deutschen Komponisten zählt man
Wolfgang Amadeus Mozart (1756–1791) und Richard Wagner
(1813–1883).

Auch ihre Musik wird in der ganzen Welt gespielt. Doch in
zwei Städten wird das Werk dieser beiden Komponisten besonders 10
geehrt: Mozart in Salzburg und Wagner in Bayreuth.

Mozart war kein Deutscher, er war Österreicher. Er wurde
am 27. Januar 1756 in Salzburg geboren, er starb am 5. Dezember 1791 in Wien, und er verbrachte den größten Teil seines
Lebens in Österreich. Er war, als er starb, nur 35 Jahre alt, doch
es gibt kaum einen zweiten Komponisten, der in solch kurzer Zeit
so viele große Werke geschrieben hat wie er: Sonaten, Sympho-
nien und Opern. Seine berühmtesten Opern sind „Die Hochzeit
des Figaro", „Don Giovanni" und „Die Zauberflöte." Die öster-
reichische Stadt Salzburg ehrt ihren größten Sohn jedes Jahr 20
durch die Mozart-Festspiele. Dann kommen die besten Musiker
nach Salzburg, um hier seine Werke zu spielen. Auch die Zuhörer kommen aus allen Ländern der Welt. In den Wochen der
Mozart-Festspiele kann man auf den Straßen von Salzburg die
Sprachen vieler Völker hören. Sehr oft geschieht es, daß ein
Zuhörer nicht die Sprache des Mannes versteht, der neben ihm
oder hinter ihm sitzt, aber sie alle verstehen die Sprache Mozarts.

Wagner ist der größte deutsche Opernkomponist des 19. Jahrhunderts. Er schrieb nicht nur die Musik, sondern auch den Text
seiner Opern. Sehr oft hat er für seine Opern Sagen aus der alten 30

Courtesy of Deutsche Zentrale für Fremdenverk

Sonntagmorgen in einem Dorf an der bayrisch-österreichischen Grenze

deutschen Literatur oder der germanischen Mythologie gebraucht, so z.B. in „Lohengrin", „Tannhäuser", „Tristan und Isolde", „Parsifal" und im „Ring des Nibelungen." „Die Meistersinger von Nürnberg", vielleicht Richard Wagners schönste Oper, zeigt das Problem jedes echten Künstlers in seiner Stellung zwischen Intuition und Tradition. Wagners Werk ist besonders eng verbunden mit dem Namen der Stadt Bayreuth in Bayern. Hier hat er im Jahre 1876 ein Theater gebaut, in dem nur seine eigenen Opern gespielt werden sollten. So geschah es, und so geschieht es noch in unserer Zeit. Die Wagner-Festspiele in Bayreuth locken 40 in jedem Sommer eine große, internationale Menge in die kleine Stadt in Bayern. Die Festspiele sind noch heute in den Händen der Familie. Richard Wagners Enkel, Wieland und Wolfgang, führen die Tradition ihres Großvaters weiter.

Salzburg und Bayreuth sind zwei große Namen unter den musikalischen Hauptstädten der Welt.

VIII. Wörterverzeichnis

Bayern Bavaria
besonders especially
der Denker, – the thinker
echt true, genuine
ehren (to) honor
eigen own
eng closely
das Festspiel, –e the festival
germanisch Germanic
der Großvater, ∸ the grandfather
die Hauptstadt, ∸e the capital
die Hochzeit, –en the marriage
der Komponist, (–en), –en the composer
das Konzertprogramm, –e the concert program
der Künstler, – the artist
kurz short
die Literatur, –en the literature
locken (to) lure

die Meistersinger the mastersingers
die Menge, –n the throng, crowd
die Musik the music
musikalisch musical
der Musiker, – the musician
die Mythologie the mythology
der Name, (–ns), –n the name
die Oper, –n the opera
der Opernkomponist, (–en), –en composer of operas
der Österreicher, – the Austrian
österreichisch Austrian
das Problem, –e the problem
der Ring des Nibelungen the Ring of the Nibelung
die Sage, –n the saying, legend
die Sonate, –n the sonata
die Stellung, –en the position
die Symphonie, –n the symphony
der Teil, –e the part

der **Text,** –e the text, libretto
verbringen, verbrachte, verbracht
   (to) spend
verbunden connected
weiter-führen, führte weiter, weiter-
   geführt (to) carry on
Wien Vienna

zählen zu (to) count among
die Zauberflöte the Magic Flute
der Zuhörer, – the listener; *plur.*
   audience
z.B.; zum Beispiel e.g.; for example

AUFGABE ZWANZIG

THE SUBJUNCTIVE:
UNREAL CONDITIONS

I. Reading Selection

Auf einem kleinen Berg über unserer Stadt ist ein Restaurant. Man sitzt an Tischen unter großen Bäumen und kann von hier die ganze Stadt sehen, die Häuser, die Kirchen, das Rathaus und die Berge auf der anderen Seite des Tales.

Es ist Frühling. Wir haben an einem schönen Nachmittag mit den Löwenzahns einen Spaziergang auf den Berg gemacht und sitzen nun an einem Tisch unter den Bäumen. Im Radio singt eine laute Stimme deutsche Volkslieder. Gerade jetzt fängt ein neues Lied an:

> Wenn ich ein Vöglein wär'   10
> Und auch zwei Flügel hätt',
> Flög' ich zu dir . . .

„Wenn es etwas klarer wäre, könntest du von hier den Rhein sehen", sagt am nächsten Tisch ein Mann zu seinem kleinen Sohn.

Der Kellner hat Kaffee und Kuchen gebracht, Herr Löwenzahn raucht seine Pfeife, der Himmel ist blau, die Bäume sind grün, und alle Leute scheinen sehr zufrieden zu sein.

„Sprich nicht davon, Heinrich", sagt Frau Löwenzahn.

231

„Wenn ich hier sitze, Lisette, muß ich daran denken", ant-
20 wortet Herr Löwenzahn.

Weder Herbert noch ich verstehen, wovon sie sprechen. „Sie
machen uns neugierig", sage ich schließlich.

„Dort unten", Herr Löwenzahn zeigt nach der Stadt, „sehen
Sie vier oder fünf Straßen mit neuen, modernen Häusern. Vor
30 Jahren war dort noch ein großes, leeres Feld. Wenn ich
damals das Feld gekauft hätte, hätte ich es für 1 000 Mark haben
können. Ich habe es nicht getan. Vor fünf Jahren wurde das
Feld verkauft. Auf dem Feld waren 28 Bauplätze, und jeder
kostete 2 000 Mark. Wenn ich damals schneller gewesen wäre, so
30 wäre ich heute ein reicher Mann."

„Haben Sie damals, ich meine vor 30 Jahren, gewußt, daß
das Feld verkauft werden sollte?" fragt Herbert.

„Habe ich es gewußt!", ruft Herr Löwenzahn. „Das Feld
gehörte meinem besten Freund. Er wollte nach Amerika aus-
wandern und darum das Feld schnell verkaufen. Er hatte mich
gebeten, es zu kaufen. Zuerst wollte er 2 200 Mark dafür haben,
dann 1 500, schließlich 1 000. Er brauchte Geld. Hätte ich
damals nur mehr Mut gehabt! Außerdem wollte es meine Frau
nicht. Wäre sie nicht gewesen, hätte ich es gekauft."

40   „Wenn meine Frau nicht gewesen wäre", wiederholt Frau
Löwenzahn. „Da muß ich lachen. Heinrich, du hättest es vielleicht gekauft, wenn du damals mehr Geld gehabt hättest."

„Vielleicht hat sie recht", meint Herr Löwenzahn. „Wer
hätte auch damals geglaubt, daß so viele Häuser gebaut werden
würden. Wenn die Stadt nicht so schnell gewachsen wäre, wäre
das Feld nicht so wertvoll geworden. Sie werden verstehen, daß
ich mich immer wieder ärgere, wenn ich hier sitze und dort unten
die neuen Häuser sehe."

„Er kann es nicht vergessen", sagt Frau Löwenzahn. „Wenn
50 du viel Geld hättest, würdest du Angst haben, es zu verlieren. Du
würdest schlecht schlafen und müßtest höhere Steuern zahlen.
Du hast alles, was du zum Leben brauchst. Denk' nicht immer,

was wäre geschehen, wenn . . . Freu' dich über den warmen Tag und die schöne Landschaft."

Herr Löwenzahn lächelt. „Du sprichst wie eine Frau."

„Wie eine kluge Frau", sagt sie. „Wenn du nicht so viel an das wertvolle Feld dächtest, würdest du hören, was der Mann im Radio jetzt singt."

Wir alle werden still. Die laute Stimme im Radio fängt ein neues Lied an: 60

> Was frag' ich viel nach Geld und Gut,
> Wenn ich zufrieden bin.
> Gibt Gott mir nur gesunden Mut,
> So hab' ich frohen Sinn. . . .*

II. Vocabulary

aus-wandern (to) emigrate
*der Baum, ⁻e the tree
der Bauplatz, ⁻e the building lot
*bitten um, bat, gebeten (to) request, ask for (a favor)
*damals then, at that time
dort unten down there
*fliegen, flog, ist geflogen (to) fly
der Flügel, – the wing
*der Frühling, –e the spring
*gehören (with dat.) (to) belong to
*der Kellner, – the waiter
*die Kellnerin, –nen the waitress
*klug clever
*leer empty, vacant

modern modern
*der Mut the courage
*neugierig curious
das Radio, –s the radio
*reich rich
*die Seite, –n the side, page
die Steuer, –n the tax
*das Tal, ⁻er the valley
*verlieren, verlor, verloren (to) lose
das Vöglein, – the little bird
das Volkslied, –er the folksong
*wertvoll valuable
*wiederholen, wiederholte, wiederholt (to) repeat

Idioms

*bitten um (to) ask for
*er hat recht he is right

* What do I care for might and wealth
 If only I'm content.
 If God lets live me in good health
 I live in merriment. . . .

III. Grammar

Indicative and Subjunctive

Every action can be conceived in two different "moods" of the verb, which we call the indicative and the subjunctive. The indicative mood conveys a situation or action as factual and real. The subjunctive mood conveys the situation or action as merely imagined, i.e., non-factual or unreal. The indicative implies certainty; the subjunctive implies uncertainty, doubt, wish or hopeful expectation.

Compare now the following three sentences:

> He has enough money, so he will lend you ten dollars.
> If he has enough money, he will lend you ten dollars.
> If he had enough money, he would lend you ten dollars.

The first sentence states a factual situation "he has enough money," from which a conclusion is drawn with certainty: "so he will lend you ten dollars."

In the second sentence, the same conclusion is made dependent upon a condition: Provided he (*really*) has enough money, he (*certainly*) will lend you ten dollars.

In the third sentence, however, the condition and the conclusion are merely imagined, unreal, doubtful: *If he had* enough money (but in reality or all likelihood he has not), *he would* lend you ten dollars (but actually he will not be able to).

In the first two sentences the verbs are in the indicative: *has* and *will*. In the third sentence the verbs are in the subjunctive: *had* and *would*. Note that all three sentences above indicate the same time relation: present—future. So, in English, the verb form *had* does not always indicate the past tense indicative. In the context of our third sentence it indicates the present tense subjunctive. This is true with most English verbs: the *form* of the past tense indicative is the same as that of the present tense subjunctive. Yet the difference between past indicative and present subjunctive is always clear from the sentence structure and the context:

> I (once) *had* money in the bank. (past indicative)
> If (now) I *had* money in the bank, . . . (present subjunctive)
> He *came* yesterday. (past indicative)
> If he *came* now, . . . (present subjunctive)

The subjunctive mood may also be expressed as past action. In this case, however, the form of the English past subjunctive is clearly distinct from that of the past indicative:

> Since I *spoke* German, I *got* the job. (past indicative)
> If I *had spoken* German, I *would have gotten* the job. (past subjunctive)

The Subjunctive in German

A. The Present Tense

The patterns shown above are largely valid also for German. The differences between the two languages are mainly of a formal nature:

1. What we called simply subjunctive in English grammar, we have to distinguish as subjunctive II in German grammar. We shall later introduce a subjunctive I.

2. The forms of the present tense subjunctive II are derived from the stem of the second principal part of the verb. The personal endings are:

Singular	Plural
1. –e	–en
2. –est	–et
3. –e	–en

3. In the case of strong verbs this results in a difference between most of the forms of the present tense subjunctive II and those of the past tense indicative:

Present Tense Subjunctive II	(Past Tense Indicative)
ich ginge	(ich ging)
du ging**est**	(du gingst)

er ginge	(er ging)
wir gingen	(wir gingen)
ihr ginget	(ihr gingt)
sie gingen	(sie gingen)

Compare:

Er ging nach Hause: *He went home.* (past indicative)
Wenn er jetzt nach Hause ginge, . . . : *If he went home now, . . .*
(present subjunctive II)

4. In the case of weak verbs, there is no such difference:

PRESENT TENSE SUBJUNCTIVE II	(PAST TENSE INDICATIVE)
ich sagte	(ich sagte)
du sagtest	(du sagtest)
er sagte	(er sagte)
wir sagten	(wir sagten)
ihr sagtet	(ihr sagtet)
sie sagten	(sie sagten)

Compare:

Er kaufte ein Haus: *He bought a house.* (past indicative)
Wenn er ein Haus kaufte, . . . : *If he bought a house, . . .* (present
subjunctive II)

5. The stem vowels **a, o,** or **u** of all strong verbs take an umlaut, as do those of **haben, sein, werden, wissen,** and the **modal
auxiliaries** except **wollen** and **sollen.** Examples: Wenn er es
nähme; wenn ich es verlöre; wenn wir nach Frankfurt führen;
wenn ihr Geld hättet; wenn du hier wärest; wenn das Wetter
besser würde; wenn ich es wüßte; wenn wir hier bleiben müßten
(könnten, dürften, möchten, wollten, sollten).

6. In the clause of conclusion, the present subjunctive II of
werden (i.e., **würde, würdest,** etc.) governs the infinitive of the
main verb:

Wenn ich das Geld hätte, **würde** ich ein Auto **kaufen.**
If I had the money, I *would buy* a car.

Thus **würde** governs the infinitive of the main verb **kaufen,** just
as in English the subjunctive of *will* (i.e., *would*) governs the
infinitive *buy.*

7. In the construction of the clause of conclusion there is one important difference between English and German. In German, if the verb in the conclusion is a strong verb, an alternative construction is permitted: thus, instead of the pattern **würde + infinitive** (er würde gehen, he would go; er würde haben, he would have; etc. as above in 6), the pattern of the if-clause can be used. So in German the equally correct possibilities are:

> **Wenn ich Geld hätte, würde ich ins Theater gehen** *or*
> **Wenn ich Geld hätte, ginge ich ins Theater.**

Both versions, of course, must be translated into English in the same way: *If I had the money, I would go to the theater.* More examples:

> **Wenn ich ein Auto hätte, würde ich viele Freunde haben** *or*
> **Wenn ich ein Auto hätte, hätte ich viele Freunde.**
> **Wenn die Sonne schiene, würde es warm sein** *or*
> **Wenn die Sonne schiene, wäre es warm.**

8. Since the **wenn** clause is a dependent clause, the finite verb is at the end. Since the conclusion is a main clause and follows a dependent clause, it starts with the finite verb, just as you learned in Lesson XII and as you see in our examples above.

B. The Past Tense

1. To form the past tense subjunctive II we start from the past perfect indicative and put the auxiliary into the subjunctive, i.e., **hätte, hättest,** etc. or **wäre, wärest,** etc., depending upon whether the verb requires **haben** or **sein** as the auxiliary. This construction is the same as in English, except for the fact that in English only *had* is used as the auxiliary:

> **Wenn er mir geholfen hätte, würde ich jetzt fertig sein.**
> *If he had helped me, I would be ready now.*

> **Wenn die Mädchen gekommen wären, würden wir jetzt Tennis spielen.**
> *If the girls had come, we would play tennis now.*

In the examples above, the **wenn** clause contains a past subjunctive, the conclusion a present subjunctive. In the conclusion we have again the choice between two constructions, if the verb is a strong verb (Cf. Subsection 7 above) :

> **Wenn er mir geholfen hätte, würde ich jetzt fertig sein** *or*
> **wäre ich jetzt fertig.**

2. In the following examples, both the **wenn** clause and the conclusion are in the past:

> *If I had had the money, I would have bought a car.*
> **Wenn ich das Geld gehabt hätte, würde ich ein Auto gekauft haben.**

> *If he had not been sick, he would have come.*
> **Wenn er nicht krank gewesen wäre, würde er gekommen sein.**

The structure of the conclusion is the same in both languages, except for the word order. The word order of the German conclusion is what you would have expected: the finite verb **würde** in first position; the infinitive of the auxiliary, **haben** or **sein,** at the end; the past participle of the main verb preceding the infinitive.

In the conclusion we have again the choice of two constructions, but in this case with both strong *and* weak verbs. So we may say:

> . . . , **würde ich ein Auto gekauft haben** *or*
> . . . , **hätte ich ein Auto gekauft.**
> . . . , **würde er gekommen sein** *or*
> . . . , **wäre er gekommen.**

Remember: There is no such thing as a simple past tense form in the subjunctive, neither in English nor in German. The form has to be derived from the past perfect indicative, as shown above.

C. Omission of **wenn**

The conditional clause in German does not have to open with the conjunction **wenn.** If **wenn** is omitted, however, the conditional clause starts with the finite verb. The same construction is possible in English, but only if the finite verb is *have* or *be*. In English, you may say either:

>If I had seen him, . . . *or*
>Had I seen him, . . .
>If I were rich, . . . *or*
>Were I rich, . . .

In German:

>**Wenn ich ihn gesehen hätte,** . . . *or*
>**Hätte ich ihn gesehen,** . . .
>**Wenn ich reich wäre,** . . . *or*
>**Wäre ich reich,** . . .

But in German the construction without the conjunction can be used with any verb:

>**Wenn er heute käme,** . . . *or*
>**Käme er heute,** . . .
>**Wenn du mit ihm sprächest,** . . . *or*
>**Sprächest du mit ihm,** . . .

If the conjunction **wenn** is omitted, the conclusion is usually introduced by **so** or **dann:**

>**Wäre ich reich, so würde ich eine große Reise machen.**
>**Käme er heute, dann würden wir ins Theater gehen.**

D. Conclusion First, Condition Second

The clauses may readily be switched around so that the conclusion comes before the condition: *My friend would have gone downtown, if he had had time;* **Mein Freund würde in die Stadt gegangen sein, wenn er Zeit gehabt hätte** *or* **Mein Freund wäre in die Stadt gegangen, hätte er Zeit gehabt.**

In questions this arrangement is the rule: **Was würden Sie tun, wenn Sie 1000 Mark hätten?** *or* **Was täten Sie, wenn Sie 1000 Mark hätten?**

E. Modal Auxiliaries in the Past Tense Subjunctive II

German differs from English in the construction of sentences with modal auxiliaries in the past tense subjunctive II. Examples:

Ich hätte das tun sollen	*I should have done that*
Ich hätte das tun müssen	*I ought to have done that*
Ich hätte das tun können	*I could have done that*
Ich hätte das nicht tun wollen	*I would not have wanted to do that*
Ich hätte das nicht tun dürfen	*I should not have done that*

The matter is highly idiomatic and will require much practice. We can, however, derive from our examples the following basic formula:

German **hätte** + **infinitive of main verb** + **infinitive of modal auxiliary** corresponds to English *subjunctive of modal auxiliary* + *have* + *past participle of main verb.*

F. Other Uses of Subjunctive II

1. Hopes and wishes

In statements expressing a wish the subjunctive is very common: **Ich wünschte, ihr kämet alle mit mir!** *I wish you all would come with me!* Likewise in statements expressing hope the subjunctive is frequently used, if the hope proves unfulfilled: **Ich hatte gehofft, er würde mit mir kommen.** *I had hoped he would come with me.*

A conditional clause in the subjunctive II not followed by a conclusion usually expresses a wish:

If he only were well!	**Wenn er nur gesund wäre!** *or* **Wäre er nur gesund!**
If he only had been well!	**Wenn er nur gesund gewesen wäre!** *or* **Wäre er nur gesund gewesen!**

In such optative subjunctives the conclusion (*that would be nice, that would have been wonderful*) is understood.

2. The potential subjunctive

The subjunctive in general expresses possibility or potentiality. **Das wäre wirklich schön!** *That would really be nice.* **Daran hätte ich auch denken können!** *I also could (should, might) have thought of that!* **Ich könnte mich nicht daran erinnern.** *I wouldn't be able to remember that.*

3. The polite subjunctive

One of the functions of the subjunctive is to stress politeness in a request. **Könnten Sie mir sagen, wie ich zum Bahnhof komme?** *Could you please tell me how to get to the station?* **Könntest du mir ein Glas Wasser geben?** *Could you give me a glass of water?* **Würden Sie den Satz wiederholen?** *Would you repeat the sentence?*

IV. Grammatical Exercises

A. Change the following sentences to the unreal, non-factual situation, using subjunctive II:

1. Wenn ihm das Feld gehört, wird er reich werden. 2. Wenn ihr auf den Berg geht, werdet ihr den Rhein sehen. 3. Wenn er nach Amerika fährt, wird er Geld brauchen. 4. Wenn er Mut hat und klug ist, wird er das Feld kaufen. 5. Wenn das Wetter besser wird, werden wir einen Spaziergang machen. 6. Wenn der Professor es weiß, wird er es uns erklären. 7. Wenn Herr Löwenzahn seinem Freund helfen kann, wird er es tun. 8. Wenn Sie die Aufgabe nicht gelernt haben, werden Sie diese Seite nicht verstehen. 9. Wenn er heute nach Amerika geflogen ist, wird er morgen in New York sein. 10. Wenn Monika krank geworden ist, wird sie uns nicht besuchen können.

B. Change the conclusions in the converted sentences 1, 2, 5, 7, 9, and 10 to the plain subjunctive form.

C. Omit **wenn** in the converted conditional clauses.

D. Invert the conditional clause and the conclusion in the converted sentences, with the exception of No. 7.

E. Change the following sentences to the subjunctive II of the past tense:

1. Wenn du ihn darum bätest, würde er dir das Geld geben. 2. Wenn Herr Löwenzahn nicht hier säße, würde er sich nicht ärgern. 3. Wäre es etwas klarer, könnten wir die neuen Straßen sehen. 4. Hätte ich einen Bauplatz, würde ich mir ein Haus bauen. 5. Würden Sie 1 000 Mark dafür zahlen, wenn Sie so viel Geld hätten?

F. Change the following sentences into conditional clauses and conclusions in subjunctive II. Example:

Da sie einen Garten hat, hat sie immer Blumen.
Wenn sie einen Garten hätte, würde sie immer Blumen haben.

1. Da es Frühling ist, sitzen wir draußen unter den Bäumen. 2. Da ich das Feld gekauft habe, gehört es jetzt mir. 3. Da er reich war, hat er seinem Freund geholfen. 4. Da Herr Löwenzahn eine kluge Frau hat, ist er ein reicher Mann geworden. 5. Da er sich zu viel geärgert hat, ist er früh gestorben.

G. Translate into English

1. Wenn er doch bald nach Hause käme! 2. Wenn die Kinder nur nicht so laut wären! 3. Hätte ich nur ihre Telefonnummer! 4. Wäre er nur etwas klüger! 5. Ich wünschte, es wäre wahr. 6. Das wäre wunderbar!

H. Change the sentences above to the past tense.

V. Translation Exercise

1. If I had (the) courage, I would ask him. 2. If the field were empty, we could build a house there. 3. They would stay, if they had time. 4. I could pay, if I had not lost my money. 5. If you had arrived earlier, you would have heard an interesting story.

6. This would not have happened, if you had been cleverer. 7. I would translate this page for you, if I had understood it myself. 8. If he asked us to stay, we would have to stay. 9. Had you called me up, I would have told you how valuable this field is. 10. We could have helped you, had you only said something. 11. Even if he could fly, he would not be here tonight. 12. What would you do, if these houses belonged to you? 13. If it were spring, then the trees in the valley would be green. 14. I wished she had not been so curious. 15. If only I had known at that time what I know today! 16. Would you please repeat the sentence?

VI. Fragen

1. Wo liegt dieses Restaurant, von dem wir lesen? 2. Was sieht man auf der anderen Seite des Tales? 3. Und wo sitzen die Studenten nun? 4. Was hat der Kellner gebracht? 5. Was macht Herr Löwenzahn? 6. Wie scheinen alle Leute zu sein? 7. Woran muß Herr Löwenzahn denken? 8. Was zeigt er den Studenten? 9. Wem gehörte damals das Feld? 10. Warum wollte der Freund das Feld so schnell verkaufen? 11. Was hätte Herr Löwenzahn tun können, wenn er damals Geld gehabt hätte? 12. Wieviel hätte er vor dreißig Jahren für das Feld gezahlt? 13. Warum konnte er es nicht kaufen? 14. Was ist später auf dem Feld gebaut worden? 15. Ärgert sich Frau Löwenzahn, weil sie nicht reich geworden ist? 16. Worüber freut sich Frau Löwenzahn an diesem Nachmittag?

VII. Lesestück

Potsdam und Weimar

Potsdam und Weimar sind zwei deutsche Städte, Weimar, klein und schläfrig, im Herzen Deutschlands, Potsdam, mittelgroß und schläfrig, sechzehn Meilen südwestlich von Berlin. Weder die eine noch die andere ist oder war wichtig als Stadt, aber beide waren in der deutschen Geschichte wichtig als Symbole.

Potsdam wurde im 17. Jahrhundert die Residenz der preußischen Könige. Im Potsdamer Schloß wohnte der König Friedrich Wilhelm I., den die deutsche Geschichte den „Soldaten- könig" genannt hat. In seiner Zeit wuchs das preußische Heer 10 von 38 000 auf 83 000 Soldaten. Unter ihm wurde es das dis- ziplinierteste Heer Europas, mit dem dann sein Sohn Friedrich der Große Kriege führte und Eroberungen machte. Durch Fried- rich den Großen wurde Preußen mächtig, und durch ihn wurde Potsdam berühmt. Hier baute er ein neues Schloß, das er Sanssouci nannte. Friedrich Wilhelm I. und Friedrich der Große wurden in Potsdam begraben. Alle späteren preußischen Könige haben oft in den Schlössern von Potsdam gewohnt. Hier lebt der Geist der alten preußischen Könige. In Deutschland, in Europa, in der Welt hat man mehr und mehr Potsdam mit dem preus- 20 sischen Charakter identifiziert. Potsdam, das war eine Stadt mit Schlössern, Garnisonen, Kadettenanstalten, Soldaten, Generälen und Königen. Der Geist von Potsdam bedeutete Sparsamkeit, Disziplin, Uniform, Unterordnung, Eroberung. Als im Jahre 1933 Adolf Hitler sein erstes Parlament versammelte, rief er es in Potsdam zusammen. Er hat sich, mit Recht oder Unrecht, mit der preußischen Tradition identifiziert. Mit dem Wort Potsdam wollte er der Welt zeigen, daß mit ihm eine Zeit von Unterord- nung, von Uniformen und Eroberungen angefangen hatte.

Mit Hitler endete ein Kapitel deutscher Geschichte, das im 30 Jahre 1919 begonnen hatte. Damals versuchte das deutsche Volk, eine republikanische Staatsform zu finden. Als im Sommer 1919 die Vertreter des Volkes zusammenkommen wollten, um eine neue Verfassung zu schreiben, wählten sie die kleine Stadt Weimar für ihre erste Versammlung. Wir sprechen darum von der Weimarer Verfassung, und wir nennen die Jahre von 1919 bis 1933 die Zeit der Weimarer Republik. Auch die Männer von 1919 nahmen eine Stadt als Symbol. Sie wollten der Welt zeigen, daß sie sich mit dem Geist von Weimar identifizierten. Was bedeutet das Wort Weimar in der deutschen Geschichte? Weimar wurde am 40 Ende des 18. Jahrhunderts das größte Kulturzentrum in Deutsch- land. Viele berühmte Dichter und Denker lebten hier, Wieland,

Herder, Schiller und der größte unter ihnen, Johann Wolfgang von Goethe (1749–1832). Ihre Sorge war nicht ein mächtiger, starker Staat, sondern ein freies, glückliches Individuum. Sie dachten nicht an Unterordnung und Eroberung, sie glaubten an Freiheit und Menschlichkeit.

An allen großen Kreuzwegen in der deutschen Geschichte werden immer die Zeichen „Nach Potsdam" oder „Nach Weimar" stehen.

VIII. Wörterverzeichnis

bedeuten (to) mean, signify
beginnen, begann, begonnen (to) begin
begraben, (ä), begrub, begraben (to) bury
der Denker, – the thinker
die Disziplin the discipline
diszipliniert disciplined, trained
enden (to) end
die Eroberung, –en the conquest
finden, fand, gefunden (to) find
die Freiheit the freedom
Friedrich der Große Frederick the Great
Friedrich Wilhelm I. Frederick William I
die Garnison, –en the garrison
der Geist the spirit
der General, ∺e the general
glücklich happy
identifizieren (to) identify
das Individuum the individual
die Kadettenanstalt, –en the military college
das Kapitel, – the chapter
der König, –e the king
der Kreuzweg, –e the crossroad
der Krieg, –e the war
das Kulturzentrum the cultural center
die Menschlichkeit the humaneness

mittelgroß medium-sized
das Parlament, –e the parliament
preußisch Prussian
mit Recht rightly
republikanisch republican
die Residenz, –en the residence, seat
schläfrig sleepy
das Schloß, Schlösser the castle
der Soldatenkönig the soldier-king
die Sorge, –n the worry, concern
die Sparsamkeit the thrift, economy
die Staatsform, –en the form of government
südwestlich von southwest of
mit Unrecht wrongly
die Unterordnung the subordination
die Verfassung, –en the constitution
versammeln (to) call together, assemble
die Versammlung, –en the meeting
versuchen (to) try, attempt
der Vertreter, – the representative
wählen (to) choose
das Zeichen, – the sign post
zusammen-kommen, kam zusammen, ist zusammengekommen (to) meet, come together

THE SUBJUNCTIVE: INDIRECT DISCOURSE

I. Reading Selection

Herbert und ich wollen so viel wie möglich Deutsch sprechen und Deutsch hören. Darum gehen wir zu deutschen Vorträgen, die später auf deutsch diskutiert werden, in die Kirchen, wo auf deutsch gepredigt wird und in die Kinos, in denen deutsche Filme laufen. Wir möchten auch so viel wie möglich von dem Leben der Deutschen sehen. Darum haben wir gestern ein deutsches Gericht besucht.

Es war kein wichtiger Fall. Jemand war betrogen worden. Dieser „jemand" war ein junger Mann, der Kurt Möller hieß.
10 Er hatte hellblondes Haar und trug einen dunkelblauen Anzug. Jetzt stand er vor dem Richter und berichtete seine Geschichte.

Er habe in der Zeitung gelesen, daß ein reicher Mann seine Brieftasche mit Geld verloren hätte. In der Zeitung versprach der Mann, er werde dem Finder eine Belohnung von 100 Mark zahlen, wenn er ihm die Brieftasche zurückbringe. Zwei Tage später habe er, Kurt Möller, wirklich die Brieftasche gefunden; sie habe unter einer Bank im Park gelegen. Er habe sie mit nach Hause genommen, ohne sie zu öffnen. Da sei noch die Zeitung gewesen, in der der Mann 100 Mark Belohnung versprochen

habe. Er hätte den Mann angerufen und ihm dann die Brief- 20
tasche gebracht. Als er dann zu ihm gekommen sei, habe der
Mann gefragt, ob auch noch 700 Mark darin seien. Möller habe
gesagt, er wisse nicht, wieviel Geld darin sei, denn er habe die
Brieftasche nicht aufgemacht. Der Mann habe dann das Geld
gezählt, aber es seien nur 600 Mark darin gewesen. Aha, hätte
der Mann gesagt, es seien 700 Mark darin gewesen. Da er 700
Mark verloren hätte und Möller nur 600 Mark zurückbringe, so
wäre es klar, daß Möller sich schon 100 Mark als Belohnung
herausgenommen habe, und darum brauche er nun keine Belohnung mehr zu zahlen. 30

Bis jetzt hatte der junge Kurt Möller sehr ruhig gesprochen.
Jetzt aber wurde seine Stimme laut und er rief, er hätte nie viel
Geld gehabt, das sei wahr, aber er wäre immer ehrlich gewesen,
und niemand könne sagen, daß er anderer Leute Geld genommen
hätte.

Der dicke Mann, der seine Brieftasche verloren hatte, sagte
nicht viel. Er saß auf einem Stuhl, hielt eine Zigarre in der Hand
ohne sie zu rauchen (denn im Gericht ist Rauchen verboten) und
wiederholte immer wieder, er hätte 700 Mark verloren. Ob er
schwören könne, daß dies die Wahrheit sei, wurde er von dem 40
Richter gefragt. Gewiß, sagte der dicke Mann mit der dicken
Zigarre, er könne schwören, daß 700 Mark in der Brieftasche
gewesen wären.

Der Richter stand auf und verkündete das Urteil. Wenn der
Mann eine Brieftasche mit 700 Mark verloren habe, dann sei
dieses nicht seine Brieftasche. Er müsse warten, bis jemand
komme und ihm eine Brieftasche mit 700 Mark bringe. Die
Brieftasche mit 600 Mark müsse an Kurt Möller zurückgegeben
werden, und Möller müsse warten, ob nicht jemand komme, der
sie verloren habe. Wenn er drei Jahre gewartet habe und niemand 50
gekommen sei, dann solle ihm das ganze Geld gehören.

Die Brieftasche mit dem Geld hatte bis jetzt vor dem Richter
auf dem Tisch gelegen. Jetzt nahm er sie in die Hand und gab
sie Kurt Möller. Der reiche Mann wurde rot im Gesicht, er warf

ärgerlich seine Zigarre auf den Boden und lief hinaus. „Das ist
noch nicht das letzte Wort", hörte man ihn rufen.

„Ich glaube nicht, daß Sie gestohlen haben", sagte der Richter
zu Kurt Möller. „Warten Sie drei Jahre; wahrscheinlich gehört
Ihnen dann das Geld."

60 Als wir am Abend wieder zu Hause waren, berichteten wir
Herrn Löwenzahn über unseren Tag im Gericht. „Das ist eine
schöne Geschichte", sagte er. „Ich wünschte, ich wäre mit Ihnen
gegangen. Und ich freue mich, daß es noch kluge Richter in
Deutschland gibt."

·   ·   ·

Dies war nun die letzte Geschichte, die ich aus Deutschland
schreibe. Bald fahren wir nach Amerika zurück. Aber ich
wünschte, wir hätten noch ein zweites Jahr bleiben können. Als
wir hier ankamen, schien alles so schwer. Heute weiß ich, daß
Deutsch eine sehr leichte Sprache ist. Man muß nur ein wenig
70 dafür arbeiten!

II. Vocabulary

*ärgerlich angry
die Belohnung, –en the reward
*betrügen, betrog, betrogen (to)
  deceive, cheat
*der Boden, ⸚ the floor, ground
*die Brieftasche, –n pocketbook
*dick thick, fat
  diskutieren (to) discuss
*ehrlich honest
  der Fall, ⸚e the case
*der Film, –e the film
*finden, fand, gefunden (to) find
  der Finder, – the finder
*das Gericht, –e the (law) court
*hell bright
*heraus-nehmen (nimmt heraus),
  nahm heraus, herausgenommen (to) take out

hinaus-laufen (ä), lief hinaus, ist
  hinausgelaufen (to) run out
*jemand someone
*das Kino, –s the movie house
*leicht easy
*möglich possible
  predigen (to) preach
*der Richter, – the judge
*ruhig quiet
  schwören, schwur, geschworen
  (to) swear, take an oath
*stehlen (ie), stahl, gestohlen (to)
  steal
*das Urteil, –e the verdict, judg-
  ment
  verkünden (to) announce, pronounce (sentence)

*versprechen (i), versprach, ver-
   sprochen (to) promise
*der Vortrag, ⸚e the lecture
*wahr true
*die Wahrheit, –en the truth
*wahrscheinlich probably
*wirklich actually, really

*wünschen (to) wish
*zurück-bringen, brachte zurück,
   zurückgebracht (to) bring
   back
*zurück-geben (i), gab zurück,
   zurückgegeben (to) give back,
   return

Idiom

er geht ins Kino he goes to the movies

III. Grammar

A. Direct and Indirect Discourse

Compare the two sentences:

Conrad said: "The concert was bad."
Conrad said that the concert was bad.

In the first sentence the speaker quotes Conrad's words exactly as Conrad uttered them. This is called **direct discourse**. In the second sentence the speaker reports indirectly the contents of Conrad's utterance. This is called **indirect discourse**. The indirect discourse is expressed in German by subjunctive forms, either those of the subjunctive II which you have learned, or by the forms of the subjunctive I. These forms can be used interchangeably.

B. The Present Tense Subjunctive I.

1. The present tense subjunctive I is derived from the stem of the first principal part of the verb. The personal endings are the same as those of subjunctive II:

Singular:	Plural:
1. –e	–en
2. –est	–et
3. –e	–en

2. The verb stem is never changed in any form of subjunctive I. No umlaut, assimilation, or contraction ever occurs. Subjunctive I thus shows the plainest and most regular conjugational patterns of the German verb:

SUBJUNCTIVE I PRESENT TENSE	INDICATIVE PRESENT TENSE
ich fahre, du fahrest, er fahre, etc.	(ich fahre, du fährst, er fährt, etc.)
ich habe, du habest, er habe, etc.	(ich habe, du hast, er hat, etc.)
ich sei, du sei(e)st, er sei, etc.	(ich bin, du bist, er ist, etc.)
ich werde, du werdest, er werde, etc.	(ich werde, du wirst, er wird, etc.)
ich wisse, du wissest, er wisse, etc.	(ich weiß, du weißt, er weiß, etc.)
ich könne, du könnest, er könne, etc.	(ich kann, du kannst, er kann, etc.)

3. In German, the tense of the subjunctive used in the indirect discourse is always the one that would have been used in the direct statement. It will not be determined by the tense of the introductory clause. You see the pattern in the following examples:

DIRECT

Conrad sagt (sagte, hat gesagt, hatte gesagt, wird sagen) :
„Ich gehe nach Hause."
„Ich nehme deinen Bleistift."
„Mein Bruder hat viel Geld."
„Monika ist zwanzig Jahre alt."
„Es wird spät."
„Der Professor weiß nichts."
„Du darfst das nicht sagen."

INDIRECT

Conrad sagt (sagte, hat gesagt, hatte gesagt, wird sagen),
daß er nach Hause gehe (or ginge).
daß er meinen Bleistift nehme (or nähme).
daß sein Bruder viel Geld habe (or hätte).
daß Monika zwanzig Jahre alt sei (or wäre).
daß es spät werde (or würde).
daß der Professor nichts wisse (or wüßte).
daß ich das nicht sagen dürfe (or dürfte).

In English you say: *Conrad said that the film was bad.* (The tenses of the introductory phrase and the indirect discourse correspond: *said—was.*) In German, you use the present tense subjunctive (either I or II) in indirect discourse, because in direct discourse the verb form of **sein** is in the present tense.

Conrad sagte: „Der Film ist schlecht."
Conrad sagte, daß der Film schlecht sei (*or* wäre).

C. The Past Tense Subjunctive I

When quoting indirectly a statement originally made in any past tense (simple past, present perfect, past perfect), we have to use the past tense subjunctive. The past tense subjunctive is formed by the subjunctives I or II of the auxiliaries **haben** *or* **sein** plus the past participle of the verb.

DIRECT

Er sagt: „Ich war krank" (plain past)
   „Ich bin krank gewesen" (present perfect)
   „Ich war krank gewesen" (past perfect)

INDIRECT

Er sagt, daß er krank gewesen sei (*or wäre*)

By this one indirect sentence all the three past time situations above are covered.

D. The Future Subjunctive I

When quoting a statement originally made in the future tense, the future subjunctive has to be used, i.e., the subjunctive forms I or II of **werden** plus the infinitive of the verb.

DIRECT

Herbert sagte: „Ich werde bald eine Reise nach Deutschland machen."

INDIRECT

Herbert sagte, daß er bald eine Reise nach Deutschland machen werde (*or* würde).

E. Features To Be Watched

1. Besides the expressions of verbal communication (*to*) *say, tell, report, promise, state,* etc., other verbs expressing non-oral or

inner-mental discourse will also introduce indirect-discourse statements, as for example *(to) write, think, believe, feel.*

> Er schrieb, daß er seine Eltern besucht habe (*or* hätte).
> Sie glaubt, daß Conrad morgen kommen werde (*or* würde).

2. If the introductory statement is in the first person, German has a tendency to use the indicative even in the indirect statement.

> Ich sagte ihm, daß mein Bruder krank ist.
> Ich glaube, daß er nicht kommen wird.

3. As in English the pronouns and possessive adjectives will change when direct discourse is changed into indirect discourse.

> My father told me: "*I* shall buy a present for *you* and *your* sister."
> Mein Vater sagte mir: „**Ich** werde **dir** und **deiner** Schwester ein Geschenk kaufen."
> My father told me that *he* would buy a present for *me* and *my* sister.
> Mein Vater sagte mir, daß **er mir** und **meiner** Schwester ein Geschenk kaufen werde (*or* würde).

4. It has been pointed out that in indirect discourse, forms I and II of the subjunctive can be used interchangeably. However, in colloquial German subjunctive II is generally used, since subjunctive I has a rather literary flavor. As a rule, that form is preferred which most clearly shows its character as a subjunctive. So, **ich hätte** (present subjunctive II) is preferable to **ich habe** (present subjunctive I), since **ich habe** is not a distinct subjunctive form, while **er liebe** (present subjunctive I) is preferable to **er liebte** (present subjunctive II).

5. Since in German the subjunctive clearly indicates that an indirect report is being given, the reader of a long and extended report does not have to be reminded of this fact by the frequent insertion of *he said, he went on, he continued,* etc. The subjunctive clearly establishes that we are dealing with a statement quoted indirectly:

> Er erzählte, daß er in Frankfurt gewesen sei. Dort habe er den Römer gesehen. Nachdem er in einem Restaurant ein Glas Wein getrunken habe, sei er wieder nach Wiesbaden zurückgefahren. Dann sei er sehr müde gewesen und bald zu Bett gegangen.

F. Omission of **daß**

As in English, the conjunction *that* (**daß**) v̶ ̶ ̶ ̶ ̶ ̶ ̶ ̶u̶c̶es the indirect statement may be omitted. However, it is to be noted that in German the indirect statement is treated as a main clause and shows the word order of an independent sentence.

He told me (that) he had found a pocketbook.
Er erzählte mir, er habe (hätte) eine Brieftasche gefunden.

G. Indirect Questions and Commands

1. Indirect questions (cf. Lesson XII, Section III,A) are put in the subjunctive I (or II) :

DIRECT: *Ich fragte ihn: „Hast du Geld?"*
           I asked him: "Do you have any money?"
INDIRECT: *Ich fragte ihn, ob er Geld habe* (or *hätte*)
           I asked him if he had any money
DIRECT: *Er fragte: „Wer hat das gesagt?"*
           He asked: "Who said that?"
INDIRECT: *Er fragte, wer das gesagt habe* (or *hätte*)
           He asked who said that.

2. When quoting a command indirectly, the imperative is substituted by the modal auxiliary *sollen* in subjunctive I (or II) plus the infinitive of the verb. This corresponds to the English construction with *should, ought to, is to:*

DIRECT: *Er sagte zu ihr: „Sprich nicht so laut."*
           He said to her: "Don't speak so loudly."
INDIRECT: *Er sagte zu ihr, sie solle* (or: *sollte*) *nicht so laut sprechen.*
           He told her she should not speak so loudly.

H. Other Uses of the Subjunctive

1. Als ob, als wenn

When introducing a statement whose veracity is in doubt or at least undecided, **als ob** (or its synonym **als wenn**) is followed by the subjunctive, either Form I or II. **Er sprach, als ob er müde wäre** (or **sei**); *he spoke as if he were tired.* Very often the **ob** or **wenn** is left out, in which case the finite verb follows **als** immediately. **Es schien, als wisse (wüßte) er die Antwort nicht.**

2. Hopes and wishes

If an exclamation expresses a hope or a wish, the subjunctive I is used. **Lang lebe der Kaiser!** *Long live the emperor!* — **So sei es!** *So be it!* — **Gott sei Dank!** *Thank God!*

IV. Grammatical Exercises

A. Change the following statements to indirect discourse after *Herr Löwenzahn sagte:*

1. Auf dem Berg über dieser Stadt ist ein Restaurant. 2. Man wird an Tischen unter großen Bäumen sitzen. 3. Wir können von hier die Berge auf der anderen Seite des Tales sehen. 4. Frau Löwenzahn machte einen Spaziergang. 5. Die Männer haben deutsche Lieder gesungen. 6. Jemand fängt gerade jetzt ein neues Lied an. 7. Der Kellner hat Kaffee und Kuchen gebracht. 8. Alle Leute scheinen sehr zufrieden zu sein. 9. Ich sehe dort unten ein großes, leeres Feld. 10. Ich bin damals nicht schnell genug gewesen. 11. Das Feld wurde an einen anderen verkauft. 12. Ich bin nicht reich geworden. 13. Das Feld gehörte einem meiner Freunde. 14. Dieser Mann wollte nach Amerika auswandern. 15. Er hat mich gebeten, das Feld zu kaufen. 16. Er will zu viel Geld dafür haben. 17. Meine Frau hat es nicht gewollt. 18. Ich hatte damals alles, was ich zum Leben brauchte. 19. Frau Löwenzahn ist eine sehr kluge Frau.

B. Change the following direct questions into indirect questions:

1. Er hat mich gefragt: „Sind Sie Amerikaner?"
2.   „Waren Sie in Deutschland?"
3.   „Hatten Sie einen deutschen Lehrer?"

4. Er hat Herbert gefragt: „Sind Sie Deutscher?"
5.   „Werden Sie lange in Frankfurt
                              bleiben?"
6.   „Können Sie deutsch?"
7. Sie hat uns gefragt: „Kennt ihr meinen Bruder?"
8.   „Werdet ihr mir schreiben?"
9.   „Soll ich euch schreiben?"
10. Ich fragte Monika: „Wo wohnst du?"
11.   „Wie heißt dein Bruder?"
12.   „Darf ich dich in die Stadt fahren?"

C. Change the following imperatives into indirect discourse:

1. Frau Löwenzahn sagt zu ihrem Mann: „Sprich nicht davon."
2.   „Gib mir deine Zei-
                                       tung."
3.   „Verlier nicht deine
                                       Brieftasche."
4. Herr Löwenzahn sagt zu uns: „Freut euch über die schöne
                               Landschaft."
5.   „Bestellt Bier für euch, Wein
                               für mich, und Kaffee für
                               meine Frau."

D. What was actually spoken? Reconstruct the direct quotations:

1. Der junge Mann sagt, daß er ehrlich sei;
2.   , daß er das Geld gefunden habe;
3.   , er wisse nicht, was in der Brieftasche
                      sei.
4. Herbert hat mir erzählt, daß er mit seinem Freund auf dem
                           Gericht gewesen sei;
5.   , daß er meinen Bruder dort ge-
                           troffen habe;
6.   , daß mein Bruder nach mir gefragt
                           habe.

7. Ich habe Conrad gefragt, ob er ein deutsches Gericht sehen wolle;

8.   , ob er sich über den Richter gefreut habe;

9.   , ob er mir alles erzählen könne.

10. Der Richter hat zu dem Mann gesagt, er solle die Wahrheit sprechen.

11.   , er solle ihm seine Brieftasche zeigen.

12.   , er solle warten.

V. Translation Exercise

Translate the following, changing all direct discourse in quotation marks into indirect discourse:

1. He looked into his book, as if he were reading. 2. Herbert asked me: "Can we talk German with your sister?" 3. He said to me: "I went to church on Sunday." 4. Conrad wrote to his mother: "Herbert and I were in a German court yesterday." 5. He reads in the paper: "Someone had been cheated." 6. Conrad tells us: "First the young man had spoken very quietly." 7. "But now his voice became loud and he began to shout." 8. He said: "I will never take other people's money, and I will always be honest." 9. Herbert tells us: "The fat man who had lost the money didn't say much." 10. "He sat on a chair, smoked a cigar, and repeated one sentence again and again." 11. The judge said to him: "Tell the truth!" 12. Herbert told us later: "Finally the the judge stood up, and the fat man became angry." 13. The judge told the young man: "Wait three years!" 14. He said: "I do not believe that he really stole the money." 15. Your friend called me up yesterday and asked me why I had been so angry. 16. My brother said that our last lesson had been very easy. 17. I do not believe that he is right. 18. The fat man was smoking his cigar, as if he were quite calm. 19. He looked at me, as if I had deceived him.

VI. Fragen

1. Warum sind Conrad und Herbert nach Deutschland gekommen? 2. Wohin gehen sie oft, wenn sie Deutsch hören wollen? 3. Wo sind sie gestern gewesen? 4. Wer stand vor dem Richter? 5. Was hatte er in der Zeitung gelesen? 6. Was hatte ihm der reiche Mann versprochen? 7. Wo hat der junge Mann die Brieftasche gefunden? 8. Warum wollte ihm der reiche Mann die Belohnung nicht geben? 9. Was wiederholt der reiche Mann immer wieder? 10. Glauben Sie, daß er die Wahrheit sagte? 11. Was war das Urteil des Richters? 12. Wie lange muß Kurt Möller warten, bis ihm die Brieftasche gehört? 13. Wo hat die Brieftasche bis jetzt gelegen? 14. Was glaubt der Richter nicht? 15. Was tun die beiden Jungens, als sie an diesem Tag nach Hause kommen? 16. Worüber freut sich Herr Löwenzahn?

VII. Lesestück

Eine Legende

Es war ein schöner, blauer Tag im Sommer, als sie durchs Heilige Land gingen. Christus und Petrus gingen voran, und die anderen Jünger folgten. Da lag auf dem Weg ein altes Hufeisen. Der Herr zeigte es Petrus und fragte ihn, ob er es nicht aufheben wolle. Man würde es später vielleicht brauchen können. Petrus bückte sich nicht gern. Er schüttelte den Kopf und ging weiter, aber hinter ihm hob Christus das Hufeisen auf und nahm es mit. Sie kamen bald in eine kleine Stadt, wo gerade an diesem Tage Markt war. Ehe sie über den Marktplatz gingen, sah der Herr einen Hufschmied, der vor seinem Haus arbeitete. Christus 10 fragte ihn, wieviel er ihm für das Hufeisen geben könne. Der Hufschmied antwortete, es sei ein altes Hufeisen und es sei nicht sehr wertvoll, doch er könne ihm zwölf Pfennig dafür geben. Der Herr war damit zufrieden, ging zum Marktplatz und kaufte mit dem Geld ein halbes Pfund Kirschen, die er dann in seiner Tasche

versteckte. Petrus hatte nichts gesehen. Er sprach gerade mit einem alten Mann, der Fische verkaufte, und er sagte dem Alten, daß er selbst früher ein Fischer gewesen wäre. Und dann erzählte er eine Geschichte von einem sehr großen und schweren
20 Fisch, den er gefangen hätte, und der alte Mann hörte ruhig zu, obwohl er die Geschichte nicht ganz glaubte.

Sie gingen nun auf der anderen Seite der Stadt zum Tor hinaus, über einen kleinen Berg, durch Wiesen und Felder, auf denen kein Baum stand. Sie alle wurden durstig. Die Sonne brannte heiß vom Himmel, die Luft war trocken und der Weg staubig, doch da war weder Baum noch Wald, weder Bach noch Quelle.

Petrus, der hinter dem Herrn ging, dachte gerade an das klare, kalte Wasser, in dem die Fische schwammen, als er eine schöne,
30 rote Kirsche auf dem Weg liegen sah. Sofort bückte er sich, hob sie auf und aß sie. Leider nur eine, sagte er still zu sich selbst, warum konnten es nicht vier oder fünf sein? Doch sieh, da war eine zweite, nach wenigen Minuten eine dritte . . . eine vierte . . . eine fünfte . . . mehr und mehr. Petrus bückte sich nicht gern, aber wer würde an einem heißen Tag durch ein trockenes, staubiges Feld gehen und die schönen Kirschen, die jemand verloren hatte, nicht aufheben?

Sechsundzwanzig Kirschen machen ein halbes Pfund. Sechsundzwanzig Mal bückte sich Petrus, der sich nicht gerne bückte,
40 an diesem heißen Tag im Sommer. Nachdem er sich zum letzten Mal gebückt hatte, stand der Herr vor ihm und lächelte.

„Erinnerst du dich an das Hufeisen, Petrus?" fragte er ihn. Und dann erzählte er, wie er das Hufeisen gefunden und die Kirschen gekauft hätte.

„Wieviel leichter wäre es gewesen, das Hufeisen aufzuheben!—

> Wer geringe Dinge wenig acht,
> sich um geringere Mühe macht." *

. . .

---

* Free translation: Who's scornful of a thing that's small
Will have to labor for nothing at all.

Sie werden unsere Geschichte von Christus, dem Hufeisen und
den Kirschen nicht in der Bibel finden. Es ist eine Legende. Dem
deutschen Volk ist sie in einem Gedicht erzählt worden, ge- 50
schrieben von dem größten deutschen Dichter, Johann Wolfgang
von Goethe.

VIII. Wörterverzeichnis

auf-heben, hob auf, aufgehoben
(to) pick up
der Bach, ‑e the brook
die Bibel the Bible
sich bücken (to) bend down
Christus Christ
fangen (ä), fing, gefangen (to)
catch
der Fisch, –e the fish
der Fischer, – the fisher, fisherman
folgen (*with dat.*) (to) follow
der Herr (*here*) the Lord
hinaus-gehen, ging hinaus, ist
hinausgegangen (to) go out
das Hufeisen, – the horse shoe
der Hufschmied, –e the blacksmith
der Jünger, – the apostle, disciple
die Kirsche, –n the cherry
die Legende, –n the legend

der Markt, ‑e the market, fair
der Marktplatz, ‑e the market
place
mit-nehmen (nimmt mit), nahm
mit, mitgenommen (to) take
along
Petrus Peter
das Pfund, –e the pound
die Quelle, –n the spring
schütteln (to) shake
staubig dusty
das Tor, –e the gate
trocken dry
verstecken (to) hide, conceal
voran-gehen, ging voran, ist
vorangegangen (to) go ahead
weiter-gehen, ging weiter, ist
weitergegangen (to) go on
zu-hören (to) listen

APPENDIX

ZWEI MÄRCHEN
DER BRÜDER GRIMM[1]

Rumpelstilzchen

Es war einmal[2] ein Müller,[3] der sehr arm[4] war, aber eine
schöne Tochter hatte. Es geschah einmal, daß er mit dem König
sprach, und, um sich wichtig zu machen, sagte er zum König, er
habe eine Tochter, die Stroh[5] zu Gold[6] spinnen[7] könne „Das
ist eine Kunst,[8] die mir gefällt", sagte der König. „Wenn deine
Tochter so geschickt[9] ist, wie du sagst, so bring sie morgen in
mein Schloß. Dort soll sie ihre Kunst zeigen." Als am nächsten
Tage das Mädchen zu ihm gebracht wurde, führte der König es
in eine Kammer,[10] die ganz mit Stroh gefüllt[11] war, gab ihm ein
Spinnrad[12] und sprach: „Jetzt fang mit der Arbeit an, und wenn
du bis morgen früh dieses Stroh nicht zu Gold gesponnen hast,

---

[1] The brothers Jacob and Wilhelm Grimm, two eminent German
philologists and folklorists, collected and published their famous fairy tales
(*Märchen*) in the beginning of the nineteenth century.

[2] once upon a time   [8] art
[3] miller   [9] skillful
[4] poor   [10] chamber
[5] straw   [11] filled
[6] gold   [12] spinning wheel
[7] **spinnen, spann, gesponnen**
(to) spin

mußt du sterben." Damit schloß er die Kammer, und sie blieb allein.

Da saß nun die arme Müllerstochter und wußte nicht, was sie tun sollte. Sie wußte nicht, wie man Stroh zu Gold spinnt, und ihre Angst wurde immer größer, so daß sie schließlich zu weinen [13] anfing. Plötzlich öffnete sich die Tür, und ein kleines Männchen [14] kam herein [15] und sagte „Guten Abend, warum weinst du so sehr?" „Ach", antwortete sie, „ich soll Stroh zu 20 Gold spinnen und weiß nicht, wie man es tut." „Was gibst du mir, wenn ich es für dich spinne?", fragte das Männchen. „Mein Halsband",[16] sagte das Mädchen. Das Männchen nahm das Halsband, setzte sich vor das Spinnrad, und in einer halben Stunde war die erste Spule [17] voll [18] Gold. Bald war die zweite voll, die dritte, die vierte, und so spann es bis zum Morgen, dann war alles Stroh gesponnen, und alle Spulen waren voll Gold. Als die Sonne aufging,[19] kam der König. Er war sehr erstaunt [20] und freute sich über das Gold.

Doch wer viel Gold hat, will noch mehr. Am Abend brachte 30 der König die Müllerstochter in eine andere Kammer. Sie war größer als die erste, und es war noch mehr Stroh darin. Wieder stand da ein Spinnrad, und wieder sprach der König: „Spinne das Stroh zu Gold, wenn du dein Leben retten willst." Damit ließ er sie allein. Wieder fing das arme Mädchen an zu weinen, und wieder kam das Männchen und fragte: „Was wirst du mir geben, wenn ich die Arbeit für dich tue?" „Meinen Ring",[21] antwortete das Mädchen und nahm den Ring ab. Das Männchen nahm ihn, setzte sich vor das Spinnrad und ließ die Räder laufen, und am Morgen war alles Stroh zu glänzendem [22] Gold gespon-40 nen. Wieder freute sich der König, aber er hatte noch nicht genug Gold und ließ die Müllerstochter in eine noch größere Kammer voll Stroh bringen. „Dies ist die dritte und letzte

[13] (to) weep	[18] full (of)
[14] little man	[19] rose
[15] **hereinkommen** (to) enter	[20] astonished
[16] necklace	[21] ring
[17] spool	[22] shining

Nacht", sagte er. „Kannst du all dies Stroh zu Gold spinnen, so wirst du meine Gemahlin [23] werden. Wenn du es nicht kannst, mußt du sterben."

Als das Mädchen allein war, kam das Männchen wieder und fragte, was es ihm dieses Mal geben würde. Das Mädchen weinte und sagte, es hätte nichts mehr, was es ihm geben könnte. „So versprich mir", sagte das Männchen, „wenn du Königin wirst, dein erstes Kind." Was kann ich tun, dachte das verzweifelte 50 Mädchen, und so versprach es dem Männchen ihr erstes Kind. Noch einmal spann das Männchen alles Stroh zu Gold. Und als am Morgen der König kam und alles fand, wie er es gewünscht hatte, war er sehr zufrieden und nahm sie zu seiner Gemahlin. Und so wurde die schöne Müllerstochter eine Königin.

Nach einem Jahr gebar [24] sie ein Kind, und sie dachte nicht mehr an das, was sie dem Männchen versprochen hatte. Aber dann kam es plötzlich in der Nacht in ihre Kammer und sagte: „Nun gib mir dein Kind!" Die Königin erschrak [25] und bot dem Männchen alles Gold ihres Königreichs [26] an, wenn es ihr 60 ihr Kind lassen wollte, aber das Männchen sprach: „Nein, etwas Lebendes ist mir lieber als alles Gold der Welt." Da fing die Königin an zu weinen und war so verzweifelt, daß sie dem Männchen leid tat. „Drei Tage will ich dir Zeit lassen", sagte es, „wenn du bis dann meinen Namen weißt, so darfst du dein Kind behalten."

Nun dachte die Königin die ganze Nacht und den ganzen Tag an alle Namen, die sie je [27] gehört hatte. Und sie schickte Boten ins ganze Land und befahl ihnen, alle ungewöhnlichen [28] Namen zu sammeln [29] und ihr zu bringen. Als am Abend das Männchen 70 kam, fing sie an mit Kaspar, Melchior, Balthasar und nannte alle Namen, die sie wußte, aber bei jedem sprach das Männchen: „Nein, so heiße ich nicht." Am zweiten Tag schickte sie ihre Diener [30] in die Stadt und ließ sie fragen, was für Namen die

---

[23] wife
[24] gave birth to
[25] became frightened
[26] kingdom

[27] ever
[28] unusual
[29] (to) gather, collect
[30] servants

Leute hätten, und an diesem Abend nannte sie dem Männchen die ungewöhnlichsten und seltsamsten Namen. „Heißt du vielleicht Rippenbiest oder Hammelswade oder Klumpenfuß oder Schnollegaster?" Doch das Männchen lachte nur und sagte: „Nein, so heiße ich nicht; aber wenn du den Namen morgen 80 nicht weißt, wirst du dein Kind verlieren."

Der dritte Tag kam, und nun kamen die Boten, die die Königin ins Land geschickt hatte, zurück und berichteten über alle seltsamen Namen, die sie gehört hatten. Spät am Nachmittag kam der letzte Bote zurück und erzählte, er sei bis an die Grenze des Landes gekommen und habe auf einem Berg tief im Wald ein kleines Haus gesehen, vor dem Haus habe ein Feuer [31] gebrannt, und ein lächerliches,[32] kleines Männchen sei um das Feuer gesprungen und habe gesungen:

> Heute back' ich, morgen brau' [33] ich,
> 90 Übermorgen [34] hol' ich der Königin Kind.
> Ach, wie gut, daß niemand weiß,
> Daß ich Rumpelstilzchen heiß'.

Da war die Königin sehr glücklich, und sie wartete nun ruhig auf den Abend. Als es dunkel wurde, war plötzlich das Männchen wieder da und fragte: „Nun, Königin, wie heiße ich?" Da fragte sie zuerst: „Heißt du Tom, heißt du Dick, heißt du Harry?" „Nein, nein, nein", rief das Männchen und lachte laut. „Heißt du vielleicht Rumpelstilzchen?" „Das hat dir der Teufel [35] gesagt", schrie das Männchen. In seiner Wut [36] stieß [37] 100 es den rechten Fuß [38] so tief in die Erde, daß es ihn nicht wieder herausziehen [39] konnte. Dann packte [40] es den linken Fuß mit beiden Händen und riß sich selbst entzwei [41] und verschwand,[42] und niemand hat es wieder gesehen.

[31] fire	[37] stamped
[32] funny	[38] foot
[33] I'll brew (beer)	[39] (to) pull out
[34] day after tomorrow	[40] grasped
[35] devil	[41] and tore himself apart
[36] fury, rage	[42] disappeared

WORDS RECOMMENDED FOR ADDITION
TO THE ACTIVE VOCABULARY

*arm poor
*erschrecken (i), erschrak, ist
  erschrocken (to) become
  frightened
*das Feuer, – the fire
*der Fuß, ⸚e the foot
*der Ring, –e the ring

*sammeln (to) gather, collect
*übermorgen day after tomorrow
*verschwinden, verschwand, ist
  verschwunden (to) disappear
*voll full (of)
*weinen (to) weep
*die Wut the fury, rage

Frau Holle

Es war einmal eine Witwe,[1] die zwei Töchter hatte, von denen
die eine schön und fleißig [2] war, die andere faul und häßlich.[3]
Sie liebte aber die häßliche und faule mehr, weil sie ihre rechte [4]
Tochter war, und die andere, ihre Stieftochter,[5] mußte alle Arbeit
im Hause tun. Das arme Mädchen mußte jeden Tag bei dem
Brunnen [6] sitzen und so viel spinnen,[7] daß das Blut aus den
Fingern kam. Nun geschah es, daß die Spule [8] einmal blutig [9]
wurde, da bückte es sich über den Brunnen, um die Spule abzu-
waschen.[10] Dabei fiel die Spule in den Brunnen. Es weinte,[11] lief
zur Stiefmutter [12] und erzählte, was geschehen war. Die Stief- 10
mutter aber war unbarmherzig [13] und sagte: „Wenn du die Spule
hast in den Brunnen fallen lassen, so bring sie wieder zurück." Da
ging das Mädchen zum Brunnen und wußte nicht, was es tun
sollte, und in seiner großen Angst sprang es in den Brunnen. Es
verlor die Besinnung,[14] und als es erwachte,[15] war es auf einer
schönen Wiese, wo die Sonne schien und tausend schöne Blumen
standen. Es ging durch die Wiese und kam zu einem Backofen,[16]

[1] widow
[2] diligent, industrious
[3] ugly
[4] real
[5] stepdaughter
[6] well
[7] (to) spin
[8] spool

[9] bloody
[10] (to) wash off, clean
[11] wept
[12] stepmother
[13] merciless
[14] consciousness
[15] woke up
[16] oven

der voll [17] Brot [18] war, und das Brot rief: „Nimm mich heraus, nimm mich heraus, sonst verbrenne ich; ich bin schon ge-
20 backen." [19] Da nahm das Mädchen das Brot aus dem Backofen.
Und es ging weiter und kam bald zu einem Baum, der hing voll Äpfel und rief: „Schüttele mich, schüttele mich, meine Äpfel sind alle reif." Da schüttelte es den Baum, daß die Äpfel fielen, legte sie alle auf einen Haufen [20] und ging weiter.

Schließlich kam es zu einem Haus, vor dem eine alte Frau saß. Zuerst hatte das Mädchen Angst, doch die Alte war sehr freundlich und sagte: „Du brauchst dich nicht zu fürchten, mein Kind. Wenn du die Arbeit in meinem Hause tun willst, kannst du bei mir bleiben. Du mußt nur achtgeben,[21] daß du mein Bett
30 gut machst und die Kissen fleißig schüttelst, so daß die Federn [22] fliegen, denn dann schneit es in der Welt. Ich bin Frau Holle." Als die Alte so freundlich zu ihm sprach, blieb das Mädchen bei ihr und ging in ihren Dienst.[23]

Es tat auch alle Arbeit so gut, daß die Frau Holle zufrieden war und schüttelte das Bett immer so gewaltig,[24] daß die Federn wie Schneeflocken [25] durch die Luft flogen. Dafür hatte es ein gutes Leben bei ihr, kein böses Wort und alle Tage gutes Essen. Nun blieb es viele Monate bei der Frau Holle, aber dann wurde es traurig und wußte zuerst nicht warum. Endlich merkte [26] es,
40 daß es Heimweh [27] hatte. Obgleich es ihm hier so viel besser ging als zu Hause, wollte es doch wieder zu seiner Familie zurück-gehen.

So sprach es zu Frau Holle: „Ich habe Heimweh, obwohl es hier so schön ist. Darf ich nun wieder zu meinen Leuten zurück-gehen?" Frau Holle sagte: „Es gefällt mir, daß du wieder nach Hause willst, und weil du so treu [28] gedient [29] hast, will ich dir

---

[17] full
[18] bread
[19] baked, all done
[20] heap, pile
[21] (to) watch out, take care
[22] feathers
[23] service

[24] violently
[25] snowflakes
[26] realized
[27] homesickness
[28] faithfully
[29] served

deine Belohnung geben." Sie nahm es bei der Hand und führte es vor ein großes Tor. Das Tor wurde geöffnet, und als das Mädchen gerade unter dem Tor stand, fiel ein großer Goldregen,[30] und alles Gold [31] blieb an ihm hängen,[32] so daß es ganz 50 davon bedeckt [33] war. „Das Gold gehört dir, weil du so fleißig gewesen bist", sprach Frau Holle und gab ihm auch die Spule zurück, die in den Brunnen gefallen war. Dann wurde das Tor zugemacht, und plötzlich war das Mädchen wieder auf der Welt, nicht weit von dem Hause seiner Mutter. Als es in den Hof kam, saß der Hahn [34] auf dem Brunnen und rief:

Kikeriki,
Unsere goldene Jungfrau [35] ist wieder hie.[36]

Da ging es zu seiner Mutter, und weil es so mit Gold bedeckt ankam, wurde es von ihr und der Schwester gut aufgenommen.[37] 60

Das Mädchen erzählte alles, was geschehen war, und als die Mutter hörte, wie es zu dem großen Reichtum [38] gekommen war, wünschte sie, daß die andere, die häßliche und faule Tochter, dasselbe [39] Glück haben sollte. Sie mußte sich auch an den Brunnen setzen und spinnen; und damit die Spule blutig wurde, stach [40] sie sich selbst in die Finger. Dann warf sie die Spule in den Brunnen und sprang selbst hinein.[41]

Sie kam, wie die andere, auf die schöne Wiese und ging auf dem Weg, auf dem ihre Schwester gegangen war. Als sie zu dem Backofen kam, schrie das Brot wieder: „Nimm mich heraus, 70 nimm mich heraus, sonst verbrenne ich; ich bin schon gebacken." Die Faule aber antwortete: „Ich habe keine Lust,[42] mich schmutzig [43] zu machen" und ging weiter. Bald kam sie zu dem Apfelbaum, der rief: „Schüttele mich, schüttele mich, meine Äpfel

---

[30] golden rain
[31] gold
[32] **blieb an ihm hängen** stuck fast to her
[33] covered
[34] rooster, cock
[35] young maiden, girl
[36] archaic form for **hier**

[37] received
[38] wealth
[39] the same
[40] pricked
[41] into it
[42] I do not feel like
[43] dirty

sind alle reif." Sie antwortete aber „O nein, es könnte mir ein
Apfel auf den Kopf fallen", und ging weiter. Als sie vor der Frau
Holle Haus kam, fürchtete sie sich nicht, weil sie schon von ihr
gehört hatte, und ging sofort in ihren Dienst. Am ersten Tage
zwang [44] sie sich, war fleißig und folgte der Frau Holle, wenn sie
80 ihr etwas sagte, denn sie dachte an das viele Gold, das sie ihr
geben würde. Am zweiten Tag aber fing sie schon an, faul zu
werden, am dritten noch mehr, da stand sie morgens nicht auf,
sondern blieb bis Mittag im Bett. Sie machte auch nicht das Bett
der Frau Holle, wie sie es wünschte, und schüttelte es nicht, daß
die Federn flogen. Da hatte die Frau Holle bald genug und sagte
ihr den Dienst auf.[45] Die Faule war sehr zufrieden damit und
glaubte, nun würde der Goldregen kommen. Frau Holle führte
sie auch zu dem Tor. Als sie aber darunter stand, wurde statt des
Goldes ein großer Kessel [46] voll Pech [47] ausgeschüttet.[48] „Das ist
90 die Belohnung für deine Dienste", sagte Frau Holle, und dann
wurde das Tor schnell geschlossen.

Da kam die Faule nach Hause und war ganz mit Pech bedeckt, und der Hahn auf dem Brunnen, als er sie sah, rief laut

Kikeriki,
Unsere schmutzige Jungfrau ist wieder hie.

Das Pech aber blieb an ihr hängen, und sie konnte es, so lange
wie sie lebte, nicht mehr abwaschen.

WORDS RECOMMENDED FOR ADDITION
TO THE ACTIVE VOCABULARY

*aufnehmen (nimmt auf), nahm
  auf, aufgenommen (to) receive
*bedecken (to) cover
*das Brot, –e the bread
*dienen (*with dative*) (to) serve
*der Dienst, –e the service

*erwachen, ist erwacht (to) wake
  up
*die Feder, –n the feather, pen
*fleißig diligent, industrious
*schmutzig dirty
*treu faithful
*zwingen, zwang, gezwungen (to)
  force

[44] forced
[45] den Dienst aufsagen (to) discharge, "fire"

[46] kettle
[47] tar, pitch
[48] poured out

LIEDER UND GEDICHTE

Volkslied

Du, du, liegst mir im Herzen,
Du, du, liegst mir im Sinn.[1]
Du, du, machst mir viel Schmerzen,[2]
Weißt nicht, wie gut ich dir bin.[3]
Ja, ja, ja, ja, weißt nicht, wie gut ich dir bin.

So, so, wie ich dich liebe,
So, so, liebe auch mich!
Die, die zärtlichsten Triebe [4]
Fühle [5] ich einzig [6] für dich.
Ja, ja, ja, ja, fühle ich einzig für dich.

Doch, doch, darf ich dir trauen,[7]
Dir, dir mit leichtem Sinn?
Du, du kannst auf mich bauen,[8]
Weißt ja, wie gut ich dir bin.
Ja, ja, ja, ja, weißt ja, wie gut ich dir bin.

Und, und wenn in der Ferne [9]
Mir, mir dein Bild erscheint,[10]
Dann, dann wünscht' ich so gerne,
Daß uns die Liebe [11] vereint.[12]
Ja, ja, ja, ja, daß uns die Liebe vereint.

[1] mind
[2] pains
[3] **ich bin dir gut** I like you
[4] **die zärtlichsten Triebe** the most tender affection
[5] feel
[6] only
[7] trust
[8] rely
[9] distance
[10] appears
[11] love
[12] unites

Heidenröslein

Sah ein Knab' [1] ein Röslein [2] stehn,
Röslein auf der Heiden,[3]
War so jung und morgenschön,[4]
Lief er schnell, es nah [5] zu sehn,
Sah's mit vielen Freuden.[6]
Röslein, Röslein, Röslein rot,
Röslein auf der Heiden!

Knabe sprach: Ich breche dich,
Röslein auf der Heiden.
Röslein sprach: Ich steche [7] dich,
Daß du ewig denkst an mich
Und ich will's nicht leiden.[8]
Röslein, Röslein, Röslein rot,
Röslein auf der Heiden!

Und der wilde [9] Knabe brach
's Röslein auf der Heiden;
Röslein wehrte [10] sich und stach,
Half ihm doch kein Weh [11] und Ach,[12]
Mußt' es eben leiden.
Röslein, Röslein, Röslein rot.
Röslein auf der Heiden!
   —Johann Wolfgang von Goethe, 1771

---

[1] boy
[2] little rose
[3] meadow
[4] beautiful as the morning
[5] close
[6] joy
[7] stechen (i), stach, gestochen
(to) prick

[8] endure, suffer
[9] wild
[10] defended itself
[11] woe
[12] oh! (plaintive exclamation)

Das zerbrochene Ringlein

In einem kühlen [1] Grunde,[2]
Da geht ein Mühlenrad;[3]
Mein' Liebste [4] ist verschwunden,[5]
Die dort gewohnet hat.

Sie hat mir Treu' [6] versprochen,
Gab mir ein'n Ring [7] dabei.
Sie hat die Treu' gebrochen,
Das Ringlein [8] sprang entzwei.[9]

Ich möcht' als Spielmann [10] reisen [11]
Weit in die Welt hinaus [12]
Und singen meine Weisen [13]
Und gehn von Haus zu Haus.

Ich möcht' als Reiter [14] fliegen
Wohl [15] in die blut'ge [16] Schlacht,
Um stille Feuer [17] liegen
Im Feld bei dunkler Nacht.

Hör' ich das Mühlrad gehen:
Ich weiß nicht, was ich will—
Ich möcht' am liebsten sterben,
Da wär's auf einmal [18] still.
                              —Joseph von Eichendorff, ca. 1810

[1] cool
[2] valley
[3] mill wheel
[4] sweetheart
[5] disappeared
[6] faithfulness
[7] ring
[8] little ring
[9] in two, apart

[10] wandering musician, minstrel
[11] travel
[12] away
[13] songs
[14] horseman
[15] straight
[16] bloody
[17] (camp) fires
[18] all at once

Der Lindenbaum

Am Brunnen [1] vor dem Tore, da steht ein Lindenbaum,[2]
Ich träumt' [3] in seinem Schatten [4] so manchen süßen [5] Traum; [6]
Ich schnitt in seine Rinde [7] so manches liebe Wort,
Es zog [8] in Freud [9] und Leide [10] zu ihm mich immer fort.

Ich mußt' auch heute wandern [11] vorbei in tiefer Nacht,
Da hab ich noch im Dunkeln die Augen [12] zugemacht.
Und seine Zweige [13] rauschten,[14] als riefen sie mir zu:
Komm her [15] zu mir, Geselle,[16] hier findst du deine Ruh.[17]

Die kalten Winde bliesen [18] mir grad [19] ins Angesicht,[20]
Der Hut flog mir vom Kopfe, ich wendete [21] mich nicht.
Nun bin ich manche Stunde entfernt [22] von jenem Ort,[23]
Und immer hör' ich's rauschen: du fändest Ruhe dort.

—Wilhelm Müller, 1822

[1] fountain, well
[2] linden tree
[3] dreamed
[4] shadowed, shade
[5] sweet
[6] dream
[7] bark (of a tree)
[8] **fortziehen, es zog . . fort** it drew
[9] joy
[10] sorrow
[11] **vorbeiwandern** (to) wander past

[12] eyes
[13] branches
[14] **rauschen** (to) rustle
[15] here
[16] fellow, companion
[17] rest, peace
[18] blew
[19] straight
[20] face
[21] turned around
[22] away
[23] place

Die Lorelei

Ich weiß nicht, was soll es bedeuten,
Daß ich so traurig bin;
Ein Märchen [1] aus alten Zeiten,
Das kommt mir nicht aus dem Sinn.[2]

[1] (fairy) tale   [2] mind

Die Luft ist kühl [3] und es dunkelt,[4]
Und ruhig fließt der Rhein;
Der Gipfel [5] des Berges funkelt [6]
Im Abendsonnenschein.[7]

Die schönste Jungfrau [8] sitzet
Dort oben wunderbar;
Ihr goldnes [9] Geschmeide [10] blitzet,[11]
Sie kämmt ihr goldenes Haar.

Sie kämmt es mit goldenem Kamme [12]
Und singt ein Lied dabei;
Das hat eine wundersame,[13]
Gewaltige [14] Melodei.[15]

Den Schiffer im kleinen Schiffe
Ergreift [16] es mit wildem [17] Weh.[18]
Er schaut [19] nicht die Felsenriffe,[20]
Er schaut nur hinauf [21] in die Höh.[22]

Ich glaube, die Wellen [23] verschlingen [24]
Am Ende Schiffer und Kahn; [25]
Und das hat mit ihrem Singen
Die Lorelei [26] getan.

—Heinrich Heine, 1823

[3] cool
[4] becomes dark
[5] peak
[6] is bright, sparkles
[7] evening sunshine
[8] young woman
[9] golden
[10] jewelry
[11] glistens
[12] comb
[13] strange
[14] powerful
[15] (poetic for **Melodie**), melody

[16] seizes
[17] wild
[18] woe, desire
[19] sees
[20] rocky cliffs
[21] up
[22] height
[23] waves
[24] swallow, devour
[25] boat
[26] Usually spelled Loreley; Heine uses this secondary form.

Weihnachtslied

Stille Nacht, heilige Nacht!
Alles schläft, einsam [1] wacht [2]
Nur das traute,[3] hoch-heilige Paar.[4]
Holder [5] Knabe im lockigen [6] Haar,
Schlaf in himmlischer [7] Ruh! [8]

Stille Nacht, heilige Nacht!
Hirten [9] erst kund gemacht! [10]
Durch der Engel [11] Halleluja
Tönt [12] es laut von fern [13] und nah: [14]
Christ, der Retter,[15] ist da.

Stille Nacht, heilige Nacht!
Gottes Sohn, o wie lacht
Lieb' [16] aus deinem göttlichen [17] Mund,
Da uns schlägt die rettende Stund',
Christ in deiner Geburt.[18]

—Joseph Mohr, 1818

Words Recommended for Addition
to the Active Vocabulary

*die Freude, –n the joy
*fühlen (to) feel
*kühl cool
*das Leid, –en the sorrow
*die Liebe the love
*nahe close, nearby

*das Paar, –e the couple
*der Schmerz, –en the pain
*der Traum, ⸚e the dream
*träumen (to) dream
*der Zweig, –e the twig, branch

[1] alone, lonely
[2] is awake
[3] beloved
[4] couple
[5] lovely
[6] curly
[7] heavenly
[8] rest
[9] to the shepherds

[10] made known, announced
[11] angels
[12] sounds
[13] far
[14] near
[15] savior
[16] love
[17] divine
[18] birth

THE ALPHABET IN ANTIQUA AND IN FRAKTUR

ROMAN LETTERS		GERMAN LETTERS	
a	A	a	𝔄
b	B	b	𝔅
c	C	c	ℭ
d	D	d	𝔇
e	E	e	𝔈
f	F	f	𝔉
g	G	g	𝔊
h	H	h	ℌ
i	I	i	ℑ
j	J	j	ℑ
k	K	k	𝔎
l	L	l	𝔏
m	M	m	𝔐
n	N	n	𝔑
o	O	o	𝔒
p	P	p	𝔓
q	Q	q	𝔔
r	R	r	𝔑
s, ß	S	ſ, ß, s	𝔖
t	T	t	𝔗
u	U	u	𝔘
v	V	v	𝔙
w	W	w	𝔚
x	X	x	𝔛
y	Y	y	𝔜
z	Z	z	𝔷

STRONG AND IRREGULAR VERBS

NOTE: *Compound forms are not given if the simple form occurs; for* an-kommen, be-kommen, *etc., look under* kommen.

Infinitive	*(Present 3rd Sing.)*	*Past*	*Past Participle*
backen	(bäckt)	buk	gebacken
befehlen	(befiehlt)	befahl	befohlen
beginnen	(beginnt)	begann	begonnen
begraben	(begräbt)	begrub	begraben
betrügen	(betrügt)	betrog	betrogen
bieten	(bietet)	bot	geboten
binden	(bindet)	band	gebunden
bitten	(bittet)	bat	gebeten
bleiben	(bleibt)	blieb	ist geblieben
brechen	(bricht)	brach	gebrochen
brennen	(brennt)	brannte	gebrannt
bringen	(bringt)	brachte	gebracht
denken	(denkt)	dachte	gedacht
dürfen	(darf)	durfte	gedurft
essen	(ißt)	aß	gegessen
fahren	(fährt)	fuhr	ist gefahren
fallen	(fällt)	fiel	ist gefallen
fangen	(fängt)	fing	gefangen
finden	(findet)	fand	gefunden
fliegen	(fliegt)	flog	ist geflogen
fließen	(fließt)	floß	ist geflossen
fressen	(frißt)	fraß	gefressen
geben	(gibt)	gab	gegeben
gefallen	(gefällt)	gefiel	gefallen
gehen	(geht)	ging	ist gegangen
geschehen	(geschieht)	geschah	ist geschehen
gewinnen	(gewinnt)	gewann	gewonnen
gießen	(gießt)	goß	gegossen
gleichen	(gleicht)	glich	geglichen
graben	(gräbt)	grub	gegraben
haben	(hat)	hatte	gehabt
halten	(hält)	hielt	gehalten

Infinitive	(Present 3rd Sing.)	Past	Past Participle
hängen	(hängt)	hing	gehangen
heben	(hebt)	hob	gehoben
heißen	(heißt)	hieß	geheißen
helfen	(hilft)	half	geholfen
kennen	(kennt)	kannte	gekannt
kommen	(kommt)	kam	ist gekommen
können	(kann)	konnte	gekonnt
laden	(ladet *or* lädt)	lud	geladen
lassen	(läßt)	ließ	gelassen
laufen	(läuft)	lief	ist gelaufen
lesen	(liest)	las	gelesen
liegen	(liegt)	lag	gelegen
lügen	(lügt)	log	gelogen
mögen	(mag)	mochte	gemocht
müssen	(muß)	mußte	gemußt
nehmen	(nimmt)	nahm	genommen
nennen	(nennt)	nannte	genannt
rufen	(ruft)	rief	gerufen
scheinen	(scheint)	schien	geschienen
schießen	(schießt)	schoß	geschossen
schlafen	(schläft)	schlief	geschlafen
schlagen	(schlägt)	schlug	geschlagen
schließen	(schließt)	schloß	geschlossen
schmelzen	(schmilzt)	schmolz	ist geschmolzen
schneiden	(schneidet)	schnitt	geschnitten
schreiben	(schreibt)	schrieb	geschrieben
schreien	(schreit)	schrie	geschrieen *or* geschrien
schwimmen	(schwimmt)	schwamm	ist geschwommen
schwören	(schwört)	schwur	geschworen
sehen	(sieht)	sah	gesehen
sein	(ist)	war	ist gewesen
singen	(singt)	sang	gesungen
sinken	(sinkt)	sank	ist gesunken
sitzen	(sitzt)	saß	gesessen
sollen	(soll)	sollte	gesollt
sprechen	(spricht)	sprach	gesprochen
springen	(springt)	sprang	ist gesprungen
stehen	(steht)	stand	gestanden
stehlen	(stiehlt)	stahl	gestohlen

Infinitive	(Present 3rd Sing.)	Past	Past Participle
steigen	(steigt)	stieg	ist gestiegen
sterben	(stirbt)	starb	ist gestorben
tragen	(trägt)	trug	getragen
treffen	(trifft)	traf	getroffen
treten	(tritt)	trat	getreten
trinken	(trinkt)	trank	getrunken
tun	(tut)	tat	getan
unterscheiden	(unterscheidet)	unterschied	unterschieden
vergessen	(vergißt)	vergaß	vergessen
verlieren	(verliert)	verlor	verloren
wachsen	(wächst)	wuchs	ist gewachsen
werden	(wird)	wurde	ist geworden
werfen	(wirft)	warf	geworfen
wissen	(weiß)	wußte	gewußt
wollen	(will)	wollte	gewollt
ziehen	(zieht)	zog	gezogen

IDIOMS AND VOCABULARY

NOTE

Plurals of nouns are listed after the singular form, e.g., **der Tag, –e.** The genitive singular is listed for those nouns which form this case by adding **–n** or **–en**; this form is given in parenthesis directly after the nominative singular, e.g., **der Junge, (–n), –n.**

The principal parts are given for all except weak verbs, e.g., **singen, sang, gesungen.** If there is a vowel change in the present tense, this is indicated in parenthesis directly after the infinitive, e.g., **geben (i), gab, gegeben.** If the auxiliary in the perfect tenses is **sein,** this is indicated before the past participle, e.g., **fahren (ä), fuhr, ist gefahren.**

Separable verbs are indicated in the infinitive by a hyphen between the prefix and the verb proper.

Active vocabulary and idioms are starred (except in the English-German Vocabulary) and the lesson number is indicated after the German. For example, *__Angst haben vor__ (8) (*to*) *be afraid of* shows that this idiom becomes active in Aufgabe VIII.

The following abbreviations are used:

acc.	accusative	*gen.*	genitive
adj.	adjective	*infin.*	infinitive
adv.	adverb	*plur.*	plural
conj.	conjunction	*prep.*	preposition
dat.	dative	*sing.*	singular

LIST OF IDIOMS

A

Amerika: aus Amerika from America
***Angst haben vor** (8) (to) be afraid of

B

Beispiel: zum Beispiel *abbr.* **z.B.** for instance
Besuch haben (to) have visitors
***bitten um** (20) (to) ask for

D

***d.h.** (12) i.e. (*see* **heißen**)
***deutsch: auf deutsch** (8) in German

E

***englisch: auf englisch** (8) in English

F

***fahren mit** (11) (to) travel by
***Frage: eine Frage stellen** (8) (to) ask a question
Fröhliche Weihnachten! Merry Christmas!

G

***geben: es gibt** (*with acc.*) (9) there is, there are
***gefallen: es gefällt mir** (14) I like it, it pleases me
gehen: *das geht nicht (17) that won't do
   ***wie geht es dir** (14) how are you
   ***es geht mir gut** (14) I'm fine
   ins Kino gehen (to) go to the movies
***gern** *plus verb* (15) (to) like to
***gestern abend** (19) last evening, last night
Glück haben (to) be lucky

H

***Halt!** (16) Stop! Halt!
***Hand: einem die Hand geben** (5) (to) shake hands with someone
***Haus: nach Hause** (8) home (*motion towards*)
   zu Hause (10) at home, home

*heißen: das heißt (12) that is
    ich heiße (17) my name is
    wie heißen Sie? (17) what is your name?
*heute abend (15) this evening, tonight

   I

*ich auch nicht (6) nor I either
*immer wieder (14) again and again

   J

jetzt erst only now, just now

   K

*kein . . . mehr (7) no . . . any more, no . . . any longer
klingeln: es klingelt the bell rings

   L

*Land: vom Lande (4) from the country
*leid: es tut mir leid (5) I am sorry

   M

*Mal: zum ersten Mal (18) for the first time
*Mittag: zu Mittag essen (14) (to) dine, eat dinner (*at noon*)

   N

*Nachmittag: jeden Nachmittag (4) every afternoon
*nicht nur . . . sondern auch (19) not only . . . but also
nichts als nothing but
niemand als no one but
noch einmal again, once more
*noch nicht (5) not yet
*nun *comma* (16) = well *comma*

   P

*paar: ein paar (7) a couple of, a few

   R

*recht haben (20) (to) be right
*Reise: eine Reise machen (11) (to) take a trip
    Gute Reise! (13) Pleasant journey! Have a good trip!

   S

*Schule: in die Schule (6) to school
sehr (*when no measurable quantity is given*) very much

*so . . . wie (5) as . . . as
*Spaziergang: einen Spaziergang machen (10) (to) take a walk
*Stadt: in der Stadt (6) downtown, in town, in the city
    in die Stadt (6) downtown, to town, to the city
*Straßenbahn: mit der Straßenbahn (6) by streetcar
*Stunde: in einer halben Stunde (3) in half an hour

T

Tafel: an die Tafel on(to) the blackboard

U

*Uhr: um drei Uhr (5) at three o'clock

V

*vor vielen Jahren (12) many years ago

W

*wahr: nicht wahr? (3) isn't it true; isn't it, doesn't he, *etc.*
*was für ein (6) what kind of
*Wiedersehen: Auf Wiedersehn (13) good-bye

Z

*Zeit: zur Zeit (16) at the time, at present

GERMAN-ENGLISH VOCABULARY

This vocabulary includes the words used in Sections I and VII of each lesson. The articles, unusual genitives, and plurals are given for the German nouns, and the principal parts for the German verbs, if needed. Ordinarily, the English article *the* is omitted from the meanings given, as is also the sign of the English infinitive *to*. These are used on occasion where confusion might otherwise occur.

A

*der Abend, –e (7) evening; abends evenings; *gestern abend (19) last evening, last night

*aber (3) but, however

*ab-fahren (ä), fuhr ab, ist abgefahren (13) leave, depart

die Abkürzung, –en abbreviation

*ab-nehmen (nimmt ab), nahm ab, abgenommen (13) take off

*ab-schreiben, schrieb ab, abgeschrieben copy

absolut absolute

der Absolutismus absolutism

der Abt, ∸e abbot

*das Abteil, –e (13) compartment

die Abteilung, –en department

*acht (8) eight

achtzehn eighteen

achtzig eighty

der Adlige, (–n), –n nobleman

der Admiral, ∸e admiral

die Ähnlichkeit, –en similarity

der Akzent, –e accent

der Affe, (–n), –n ape, monkey

*all all; *alle (4) all; alles (9) all

*allein (13) alone

*als (12, 16) as, like; than; when; nichts als nothing but; niemand als no one but

*alt (1) old

*Amerika (1) America

*der Amerikaner, – (4) the American

*amerikanisch (17) American

*an (4) at, near, by, on, to, up to, onto, alongside of

*an-bieten, bot an, angeboten (14) offer

*ander– (16) other

anders different; anders als different from

der Anfang, ∸e beginning

*an-fangen (ä), fing an, angefangen (13) begin

das Angebot, –e offer

*die Angst, ∸e (8) anxiety, concern, fear; *Angst haben vor (8) be afraid of

*an-kommen, kam an, ist angekommen (13) arrive

die Ankunft, ∸e arrival

an-nehmen (nimmt an), nahm an, angenommen accept

*an-rufen, rief an, angerufen (13) call up, (tele)phone

*an-sehen (ie), sah an, angesehen (18) look at

283

die Ansichtskarte, –n picture post-card

*anstatt (*with gen.*) (14) instead of; anstatt etwas zu tun instead of doing something

*die Antwort, –en (18) the answer

*antworten (3) to answer, reply

*sich an-ziehen, zog sich an, ange-zogen (17) get dressed

*der Anzug, ⸚e (17) suit

der Apfel, ⸚ apple

der Apostel, – apostle

*der April (18) April

*die Arbeit, –en (3) the work

*arbeiten (3) to work

*ärgerlich (21) angry

ärgern annoy

*sich ärgern über (17) be angry with, be mad at

*der Arm, –e (7) arm

die Armbanduhr, –en wrist watch

*der Arzt, ⸚e (14) physician, doctor

der Atlantische Ozean the Atlantic Ocean

*auch (2) also, too; even

*auf (3) on, upon; at; to, onto

*die Aufgabe, –n (1) lesson

aufgeregt stirred up, excited

auf-heben, hob auf, aufgehoben re-move; pick up

die Aufklärung the Enlightenment

*auf-machen (13) open

die Aufregung, –en excitement

auf-setzen put on

*auf-stehen, stand auf, ist aufge-standen (13) get up; stand up

auf-zählen enumerate

der Augenblick, –e moment

*der August (18) August

*aus (2) out of, from, of

die Ausfuhr, –en export

*außerdem (8) besides, moreover

außerhalb (*with gen.*) outside of; außerhalb von outside of

die Aussicht, –en view; Aussicht über view of

*aus-steigen, stieg aus, ist ausge-stiegen (13) get out, get off

ausverkauft sold out

aus-wandern emigrate

*das Auto, (–s), –s (6) car, auto

B

der Bach, ⸚e brook, creek

backen (ä), buk, gebacken bake, roast

der Bäcker, – baker

das Bad, ⸚er bath, spa

*der Bahnhof, ⸚e (12) railroad sta-tion

*der Bahnsteig, –e (13) track, plat-form

*bald (3) soon

der Balkon, –e balcony

die Banane, –n banana

*die Bank, ⸚e (8) bench

der Bart, ⸚e beard

*bauen (19) build

der Bauer, –n peasant

die Bauernfrau, –en peasant woman

*der Baum, ⸚e (20) tree

der Bauplatz, ⸚e building lot

Bayern Bavaria

beachten observe, pay attention to, notice

bedeuten mean, signify

befehlen (ie), befahl, befohlen (*with dat.*) command, order

befreien free, liberate

das Befreiungsgesetz, –e Liberation Edict

begehen, beging, begangen commit

begeistert enthusiastic

beginnen, begann, begonnen start, begin

begraben (ä), begrub, begraben bury

behalten (behält), behielt, behalten keep

behandeln treat

*bei (2) at; with; near, by; at the house of, at the place of

*beide (10) both

das Beispiel, –e example; zum Beispiel for example

bekannt known, well known

bekehren convert

*bekommen, bekam, bekommen (18) receive, get

belebt busy, crowded

Belgien Belgium

beliebt bei popular with

bellen bark

die Belohnung, –en reward

*der Berg, –e (5) mountain

*der Bericht, –e (9) report

*berichten (9) to report

der Berliner the Berliner, inhabitant of Berlin; Berliner of Berlin

*berühmt (8) famous

die Beschränkung, –en limitation

besetzt occupied

besiegen conquer, vanquish

besonders especially

besorgt worried, apprehensive

best– best

*bestellen (9) order (e.g., to order food, etc.)

der Besuch, –e visit; Besuch haben to have visitors or a visitor

*besuchen (13) to visit

der Besucher, – visitor

*beten (4) pray

*betrügen, betrog, betrogen (21) cheat, deceive

*das Bett, –en (1) bed; zu Bett gehen go to bed

bevor before

bewegt rough

bezahlen pay

die Bibel, –n Bible

das Bier, –e beer

das Bild, –er picture, portrait

billig cheap, inexpensive

*bis (7) to, up to, until; bis auf, bis zu up to

*bitte (13) Please!

*bitten, bat, gebeten (20) ask; *bitten um (20) ask for

blaß pale

*blau (15) blue

*der Bleistift, –e (2) pencil

*bleiben, blieb, ist geblieben. (7) stay, remain; über Nacht bleiben stay over night

*blond (8) blond

*die Blume, –n (3) flower

das Blut blood

*der Boden, ∸ (21) ground, floor

der Bodensee Lake Constance

Bonifatius (St.) Boniface

böse bad, evil

der Bote, (–n), –n messenger

das Brandenburger Tor the Brandenburg Gate (in Berlin)

*brauchen (3) need, require; use

brechen (i), brach, gebrochen break

breit wide, broad

Bremen name of a German city

*brennen, brannte, gebrannt (11) burn

*der Brief, –e (2) letter

*die Brieftasche, –n (21) purse, pocketbook

die Brille glasses, spectacles

bringen, brachte, gebracht (11) bring, take

britisch British

das Brot, –e bread

die Brücke, –n bridge

*der Bruder, ∸ (17) brother

*das Buch, ∸er (2) book

das Bücherbrett, –er bookshelf, bookcase

der Buchdrucker, – (book) printer

die **Buchdruckerkunst** art of printing

die **Buchdruckerpresse, –n** (book) printing press

sich **bücken** bend down, stoop over

die **Bühne, –n** stage

der **Bundeskanzler, –** Federal Chancellor

der **Bundespräsident, (–en), –en** Federal President

die **Bundesrepublik (Deutschland)** Federal Republic (of Germany)

der **Bundesstaat, –en** federated state

der **Bundestag** Federal Legislature

die **Burg, –en** (medieval) castle

der **Bürger, –** citizen; (*plur.*) townspeople

der **Bürgermeister, –** mayor

der **Bürgersteig, –e** sidewalk

das **Büro, –s** office

C

das **Café, –s** café

der **Chemiker, –** chemist

chemisch chemical

der **Christbaum, ⁀e** Christmas tree

das **Christentum** Christianity

christlich Christian

Christus Christ

D

da (adv.) (5) there, here; then; in that case

da (conj.) (12) since

das **Dach, ⁀er** roof

damals (20) then, at that time

*die **Dame, –n** (6) lady

damit by that; with that

der **Dampfer, –** steamer, steamship

Dänemark Denmark

dankbar grateful

dann (4) then

darin in it, in them

darum (11) therefore

das (1) that; those; *see also* der

daß (conj.) (12) that

dauern (19) last, take

dein (4) your

denken, dachte, gedacht (11) think; **denken an** (*with acc.*) think of

der **Denker, –** thinker

denn (1) for, because

der, die, das (1) the; this, that; who, which

deutsch (adj. or adv.) (1) German; *auf deutsch* (8) in German

Deutsch (noun) (1) German

*der **Deutsche** (adj. declension)* (4) the German

die **Deutsche Demokratische Republik** German Democratic Republic

das **Deutsche Reich** German Empire

Deutschland (1) Germany

*der **Dezember** (17) December

der **Dialekt, –e** dialect

d.h. abbreviation for das heißt (12) i.e., that is

dicht dense, close

*der **Dichter, –** (19) poet, author

dick (21) thick; stout, fat

*der **Dienstag, –e** (18) Tuesday

dieser (4) this; the latter

*das **Ding, –e** (6) thing

direkt direct

diskutieren discuss

die **Disziplin** discipline

diszipliniert disciplined, trained

doch (11) yet, however, nevertheless, still; but; really

der **Dom, –e** cathedral

*der **Donnerstag, –e** (18) Thursday

das **Dorf, ⁀er** village

dort (11) there; **dort unten** down there

das **Drama**, (*plur.*) **Dramen**
drama
sich **drängen** be crowded
draußen outside
*****drei** (3) three
dreißigjährig of thirty years; der
Dreißigjährige Krieg Thirty
Years' War
dreiviertel = drei Viertel three
quarters, three-fourths ·
*****dreizehn** (13) thirteen
drin = darin in it, in them
drinnen inside
die **Drucktypen** (*plur.*) type
(faces)
*****du** (1) you
*****dumm** (2) stupid, silly
*****dunkel** (15) dark
*****durch** (2) through; by
*****dürfen** (**darf**), **durfte**, **gedurft**
(10) may, can; be permitted,
be allowed to
*****durstig** (11) thirsty

E

die **Ebene**, **–n** plain
echt true, genuine
*****die Ecke**, **–n** (9) corner
Eger *name of a city in Bohemia*
*****ehe** (*conj.*) (12) before
ehren honor
*****ehrlich** (21) honest
das **Ei**, **–er** egg; **ein Ei legen** lay
an egg
die **Eiche**, **–n** oak (tree)
eigen own
*****ein, eine, ein** (1) a, an; one
**ein-dringen, drang ein, ist einge-
drungen** penetrate
einfach simple
die **Eingangshalle**, **–n** entrance
hall
*****einige** (15) some, a few
ein-laden (**ladet** *or* **lädt ein**), **lud
ein, eingeladen** invite

einmal once, one time
die **Einrichtung**, **–en** institution,
arrangement
*****eins** (1) one
*****ein-steigen, stieg ein, ist einge-
stiegen** (13) get on, board
ein-teilen divide
ein-treten (**tritt ein**), **trat ein, ist
eingetreten** enter
der **Einwohner**, **–** inhabitant
das **Eisen** iron
die **Eisenbahn**, **–en** railroad
eisern (of) iron
die **Elbe** the Elbe (River)
der **Elefant**, (**–en**) **–en** elephant
*****elf** (11) eleven
Elsaß-Lothringen Alsace Lorraine
*****die Eltern** (*plur.*) (8) parents
*****das Ende**, **–n** (9) end; **bis zum
Ende** until the end
enden to end
endlich finally
eng narrow; close
*****englisch** (8) English; *****auf eng-
lisch** (8) in English
*****der Enkel**, **–** (18) grandson;
grandchild
entdecken discover
die **Entfernung**, **–en** distance
enthaupten behead
**entkommen, entkam, ist ent-
kommen** escape
entlassen (**ä**), **entließ, entlassen**
remove, discharge
die **Entschuldigung**, **–en** apology,
excuse
entstehen, entstand, ist entstanden
originate
*****entweder . . . oder** (19) either
. . . or
*****er** (1) he; it
die **Erdbeerbowle**, **–n** strawberry
punch
die **Erdbeere**, **–n** strawberry
die **Erde** earth

die **Erfindung, –en** invention
***sich erinnern an** (*with acc.*) (19)
   remember
erkennen, erkannte, erkannt recognize
***erklären** (10) explain; declare
ermorden murder
ernennen, ernannte, ernannt name,
   appoint
***ernst** (9) serious, earnest
die **Eroberung, –en** conquest
erschreckend startling, frightful
***erst–** (*adj.*) (18) first
***erst** (*adv.*) (17) only, not until
ertrinken, ertrank, ist ertrunken
   drown
das **Erz, –e** ore
***erzählen** (9) tell, narrate
der **Erzbischof, ⁀e** archbishop
***es** (1) it
***essen (i), aß, gegessen** (3) eat
***das Essen, –** (4) meal
***das Eßzimmer, –** (3) dining room
***etwas** (7) some; something, anything
***euer** (4) your
***Europa** (16) Europe
europäisch European
ewig forever, eternal
existieren exist
der **Expreß, (Expresses), Expresse**
   express (train)

F

die **Fabrik, –en** factory
die **Fahne, –n** flag
die **Fähre, –n** ferry
***fahren (ä), fuhr, ist gefahren** (6)
   ride, travel, go; drive; ***fahren**
   mit (11) travel by
der **Fährmann, ⁀er** ferryman
die **Fährmannsgeschichte, –n**
   ferryman's tale
***der Fahrplan, ⁀e** (18) timetable
der **Fahrpreis, –e** fare

die **Fahrzeit, –en** travel time
der **Fall, ⁀e** case; fall
fallen (ä), fiel, ist gefallen fall
fällen fell, cut down
falsch false, wrong
falten fold
***die Familie, –n** (3) family
fangen (ä), fing, gefangen catch
***die Farbe, –n** (2) color
***fast** (9) almost
faul lazy
***der Februar** (18) February
feiern celebrate
der **Feind, –e** enemy
***das Feld, –er** (14) field
der **Felsen, –** rock, cliff
***das Fenster, –** (1) window
***die Ferien** (*plur.*) (11) vacation
***fertig** (7) ready, done, finished
das **Fest, –e** feast, festival, celebration
das **Festspiel, –e** festival (play)
feucht humid
die **Figur, –en** figure
***der Film, –e** (21) film, movie
***finden, fand, gefunden** (21) find
der **Finder, –** finder
der **Fisch, –e** fish
der **Fischer, –** fisher, fisherman
***flach** (14) flat, level
***die Flasche, –n** (5) bottle
***fliegen, flog, ist geflogen** (20) fly
fließen, floß, ist geflossen flow
fließend fluent(ly)
die **Flöte, –n** flute
das **Flötenspiel** flute-playing
die **Flotte, –n** fleet
der **Flügel, –** wing
das **Flugzeug, –e** airplane
***der Fluß, (Flusses), Flüsse** (16)
   river
folgen (*with dat. and* **sein** *as auxiliary*) follow
der **Förderturm, ⁀e** transport
   tower, haul tower

*die **Frage, –n** (8) the question
*fragen (2) to question, ask
Frankfurt *name of a German city*
der **Frankfurter, –** inhabitant of Frankfurt; **Frankfurter** of Frankfurt
Frankreich France
französisch French
*die **Frau, –en** (3) woman; wife; Mrs.
*das **Fräulein, –** (8) girl; Miss
*frei (12) free, independent
die **Freiheit, –en** freedom
der **Freiherr, (–n), –en** baron
*der **Freitag, –e** (18) Friday
fressen (i), fraß, gefressen eat (*used of animals*)
*sich freuen über (*with acc.*) (17) be glad about, happy about
*der **Freund, –e** (1) friend
*die **Freundin, –nen** (5) friend (*female*), girl friend
*freundlich (16) friendly
der **Friede, (–ns), –n** peace
Friedrich der Große Frederick the Great
Friedrich Wilhelm I. Frederick William I
die **Frömmigkeit** piety
*früh (9) early
*früher (12) earlier, former(ly)
*der **Frühling, –e** (20) spring
*führen (19) lead, guide, conduct; **Krieg führen** conduct *or* wage war
der **Führer, –** leader, guide; guidebook
*fünf (5) five
*fünfzehn (15) fifteen
fünfzig fifty
*für (*prep.*) (3) for
furchtbar fearful, frightful, terrible
*sich fürchten vor (*with dat.*) (17) be afraid of

der **Fürst, (–en), –en** (ruling) prince
füttern feed

G

die **Gabel, –n** fork
*ganz (9) whole, entire, complete, quite
die **Garde, –n** guard
die **Garnison, –en** garrison
*der **Garten, ∸** (3) garden
*der **Gast, ∸e** (7) guest
das **Gasthaus, ∸er** inn
*geben (i), gab, gegeben (5) give; *es gibt (*with acc.*) (9) there is, there are
das **Gebet, –e** prayer
das **Gebirge, –** mountain range, mountain chain
*geboren (19) born
gebrauchen use
*der **Geburtstag, –e** (6) birthday
der **Geburtstagstisch, –e** birthday table
das **Gedicht, –e** poem
die **Geduld** patience
*die **Gefahr, –en** (11) danger
*gefallen (ä), gefiel, gefallen (14) please, be pleasing to; *es gefällt mir (14) I like it, it pleases me
das **Gefängnis, –se** prison, jail
*gegen (3) against; toward
die **Gegend, –en** region
die **Gegenwart** present (time)
gegründet founded
*gehen, ging, ist gegangen (3) go; *Wie geht es Ihnen? (14) How are you? *Es geht mir gut. (14) I'm fine. *Das geht nicht. (17) That won't do.
*gehören (*with dat.*) (20) belong to; gehören zu belong to
der **Geist, –er** spirit
gekrönt crowned

*gelb (6) yellow
*das Geld, –er (5) money
die Gelehrsamkeit learning
der Gelehrte, (–n), –n scholar
der General, ⸚e general
genug enough
*gerade (13) just, just then
die Gerbergasse, –n Gerber
   Street, Tanner Street
die Gerechtigkeit justice
*das Gericht, –e (21) court (of
   law); vor Gericht before the
   court
germanisch Germanic
*gern (6) gladly; Ich habe das
   gern. I like that. *Ich spiele gern
   Tennis. (15) I like to play
   tennis.
gesamteuropäisch total European
der Gesangverein, –e choral
   group, singing society
das Geschäft, –e business, affairs
*geschehen (ie), geschah, ist ge-
   schehen (9) happen
*das Geschenk, –e (6) present, gift
*die Geschichte, –n (8) story; his-
   tory
das Gesetz, –e law, rule
*das Gesicht, –er (17) face
*gestern (7) yesterday
*gesund (17) healthy, well
die Gesundheit health
geteilt divided
getrennt separated
gewählt chosen, selected, elected
gewechselt changed
geweiht dedicated
das Gewehr, –e gun, rifle
gewinnen, gewann, gewonnen win
*gewiß (8) certain, sure
das Gewissen, – conscience
die Gewohnheit, –en custom
*gießen, goß, gegossen (7) pour
das Gift, –e poison
*das Glas, ⸚er (5) glass

die Glasschüssel, –n glass dish,
   glass bowl
glatt smooth
*glauben (8) believe, think, sup-
   pose
gleich same
gleichen, glich, geglichen resemble
das Glück luck, good fortune;
   Glück haben be lucky
glücklich happy, happily, fortunate
der Gott, ⸚er god
das Grab, ⸚er grave
der Graf, (–en), –en count
grau gray
grausam cruel
die Grenze, –n border, boundary
der Groschen, – groschen, penny
*groß (2) large, big; great; tall
*die Großeltern (plur.) (18)
   grandparents
größt– largest, greatest
der Großvater, ⸚ grandfather
das Grubenholz, ⸚er wood for the
   mines
*grün (2) green
gründen found, establish
der Gründer, – founder
die Gründung, –en founding,
   foundation
grüßen greet
der Gulden, – guilder (old coin)
*gut (1) good; well

H

*das Haar, –e (1) hair
*haben (hat), hatte, gehabt (1)
   have
der Hafen, ⸚ harbor, port
der Hahn, ⸚e rooster
*halb (18) half; *eine halbe
   Stunde (3) half an hour
halbverfault half rotten
*die Hälfte, –n (16) the half
*Halt! (16) Halt! Stop!

*halten (hält), hielt, gehalten (14) hold

*die Hand, ⸚e (4) hand; *die Hand geben (5) shake hands

der Handel, commerce, trade

die Handelsstadt, ⸚e commercial city

der Handelsweg, –e trade route

hangen (ä) *or* hängen, hing, gehangen hang

der Hase, (–n), –n hare, rabbit

das Hasenfell, –e rabbit pelt, rabbit fur

die Hauptstadt, ⸚e capital

*das Haus, ⸚er (3) house; *nach Hause gehen (8) go home; *zu Hause sein (10) be (at) home

das Häuschen, – little house, hut, shack

*das Heer, –e (19) army

*das Heft, –e (2) notebook

der Heide, (–n), –n heathen

Heidelberg *name of a German city*

heidnisch heathen

heilen heal, cure

*heilig (12) holy; Heilig Abend Christmas Eve; das Heilige Römische Reich Holy Roman Empire

*heimlich (18) secret

das Heimweh homesickness

*heiß (11) hot

*heißen, hieß, geheißen (17) be called; *Wie heißen Sie? (17) What is your name? *Ich heiße Conrad. (17) My name is Conrad.

*helfen (i), half, geholfen (*with dat.*) (4) help

*hell (21) bright, light

*das Hemd, –en (6) shirt

herab-lassen (ä), ließ herab, herabgelassen let down

herab-sehen (ie), sah herab, herabgesehen look down

heraus out

heraus-kommen, kam heraus, ist herausgekommen come out

*heraus-nehmen (nimmt heraus), nahm heraus, herausgenommen (21) take out

*der Herbst, –e (11) autumn, fall

*Herein! (17) Come in!

*der Herr, (–n), –en (19) gentleman, man; sir; Mr.; master; the Lord

die Herrschaft rule, dominion

herrschen to rule

*das Herz, (–ens), –en (15) heart (*dat. sing. form of* Herz *is* Herzen)

*herzlich (14) hearty, cordial

der Herzog, ⸚e duke

Hessen Hesse

*heute (4) today; *heute abend (15) this evening, tonight

die Hexerei, –en witchcraft

*hier (1) here

hieß was called

*der Himmel, – (18) sky, heavens; heaven

, hinaus-gehen, ging hinaus, ist hinausgegangen go out

hinaus-laufen (ä), lief hinaus, ist hinausgelaufen run out

hinein-gehen, ging hinein, ist hineingegangen go in

*hinein-tragen (ä), trug hinein, hineingetragen (13) carry in

*hinter (4) behind

die Hintertür, –en back door

der Historiker, – historian

*hoch (15) high; tall

hochdeutsch High German

*höchst (16) highly, very

die Hochzeit, –en marriage, wedding

der Hof, ⸚e yard, court

*hoffen auf (5) hope for
*höflich (9) courteous, polite
holen get, bring, fetch
*hören (3) hear, listen
*hübsch (8) pretty, nice
das Hufeisen, – horseshoe
der Hufschmied, –e blacksmith
das Huhn, –er chicken
der Humor humor
der Humorist, (–en), –en humorist
der Hund, –e dog
hundert (a) hundred
Hunderte hundreds
hungrig hungry
Hurra! Hurrah!
*der Hut, –e (13) hat

I

*ich (1) I
identifizieren identify
*ihr (1, 4) you; her; their
*Ihr (4) your; you (in letters)
*immer (3) always; *immer wieder
(14) again and again; immer
schneller faster and faster
*in (1) in, into
das Individuum, (plur.) Indi-
viduen individual
die Industrie, –n industry
das Industriegebiet, –e industrial
region
die Industriestadt, –e industrial
city
inner– inner, internal
die Insel, –n island
der Intellektuelle, (–n), –n intellectual
*interessant (14) interesting
*das Interesse, –n (7) interest
sich interessieren für be interested
in
international international
Italien Italy
italienisch Italian

J

*ja (1) yes; indeed
die Jagd, –en chase, hunt
der Jäger, – hunter
*das Jahr, –e (7) year; im Jahre
in (the year); *vor vielen
Jahren (12) many years ago;
viele Jahre for many years
*das Jahrhundert, –e (14) century;
seit Jahrhunderten for centuries
*der Januar (18) January
*jeder (4) each, every
*jemand (21) someone
jener (demonstrative adjective)
that; the former
jenseits (with gen.) the other
side of
*jetzt (2) now; jetzt erst only now
*der Juli (18) July
*jung (8) young
*der Junge, (–n), –n (10) boy
der Jünger, – apostle, disciple
*der Juni (18) June

K

die Kadettenanstalt, –en military
college
*der Kaffee (9) coffee
der Käfig, –e cage
der Kaiser, – emperor
*kalt (9) cold
kämmen comb
kämpfen fight, struggle
der Kanal, –e canal
die Kanone, –n cannon
die Kanonenkugel, –n cannonball
der Kanonier, –e gunner
der Kanton, –e canton (Swiss
political subdivision, corresponding to a state in the U.S.)
das Kapitel, – chapter
kaputt broken, smashed, ruined,
done for, "all shot"

Karl der Große Charles the Great, Charlemagne
die Karte, –n map
*die Kartoffel, –n (4) potato
die Kaste, –n caste
die Katze, –n cat
*kaufen (6) buy
*kaum (15) hardly, scarcely
*kein (adj.) (4) no, not any; keiner none, neither; *kein . . . mehr (7) no . . . any more, no . . . any longer
*der Kellner, – (20) waiter
*die Kellnerin, –nen (20) waitress
*kennen, kannte, gekannt (11) know, be acquainted with
die Kerze, –n candle
*das Kind, –er (7) child
der Kindergarten, ⁀ kindergarten
*das Kino, –s (21) movie house; ins Kino gehen go to the movies
*die Kirche, –n (6) church
die Kirsche, –n cherry
das Kissen, – pillow, cushion
*klar (18) clear
das Klavier, –e piano
*das Kleid, –er (6) dress; (plur.) clothes
*klein (16) small, little
das Klima climate
klingeln ring; es klingelt the bell is ringing
*klopfen (17) knock; an die Tür klopfen knock on the door
das Kloster, ⁀ cloister, monastery
die Klosterkultur cloister or monastic culture
*klug (20) clever
Koblenz name of a German city
der Koffer, – suitcase, valise; trunk
die Kohle, –n coal
der Kohlenberg, –e pile of coal
die Kohleproduktion production of coal
Köln Cologne (a German city)

*kommen, kam, ist gekommen (2) come
der Komponist, (–en), –en composer
der König, –e king
*können (kann), konnte, gekonnt (10) can, be able to; know (of languages)
der Kontinent, –e continent
das Konzertprogramm, –e concert program
*der Kopf, ⁀e (4) head
der Korb, ⁀e basket
*kosten (6) cost
das Kostüm, –e costume
der Kragen, – collar
*krank (1) sick, ill
das Krankenhaus, ⁀er hospital
die Krawatte, –n (neck) tie
*die Kreide (2) chalk
das Kreuz, –e cross
kreuzen to cross; sich kreuzen cross
der Kreuzweg, –e crossroad
der Krieg, –e war; Krieg führen conduct or wage war
krönen crown
*die Küche, –n (3) kitchen
*der Kuchen, – (9) cake; (plur.) cookies
die Kugel, –n ball, bullet
die Kuh, ⁀e cow
die Kultur, –en culture
kulturell cultural
das Kulturzentrum, (plur.) –zentren cultural center
der Künstler, – artist
der Kurfürst, (–en), –en elector
kurz short
kürzen shorten
der Kuß, (Kusses), Küsse kiss

L

*lächeln (3) smile
*lachen (2) laugh

*die Lampe, –n (6) lamp
der Lampenschirm, –e lamp shade
das Land, ⸚er (4) land; country; auf dem Lande in the country; auf das Land to the country; *vom Lande (4) from the country
landen to land
*die Landschaft, –en (11) landscape, scenery
der Landvogt, ⸚e governor
*lang (16) long; eine Stunde lang for an hour
lange a long time, for a long time
langsam slow
der Lärm noise
lassen (ä), ließ, gelassen let, allow; ich lasse mir einen neuen Anzug machen I'm having a new suit made (for myself)
der Lauf, ⸚e course
*laufen (äu), lief, ist gelaufen (3) run
*laut (10) loud, noisy; aloud
*leben (5) live
*das Leben (9) life, living
*leer (20) empty, vacant
*legen (18) lay, place, put; set out
die Legende, –n legend
*lehren (1) teach
*der Lehrer, – (1) teacher
*leicht (21) easy; leicht nehmen take easy
*leid tun (5) be sorry; *es tut mir leid (5) I am sorry
*leider (13) unfortunately
*leise (7) soft, gentle; low; quiet
*lernen (8) learn; study
*lesen (ie), las, gelesen (3) read
das Lesestück, –e reading exercise
*letzt– (15) last
*die Leute (plur.) (6) people
*lieb (14) dear
*lieben (19) love, like

*das Lied, –er (15) song
*liegen, lag, gelegen (4) lie, be situated
die Limonade lemonade
link– left
links left, to the left
die Literatur, –en literature
locken lure
der Löffel, – spoon
der Löwe, (–n), –n lion
das Löwenmaul snapdragon
der Löwenzahn dandelion
*die Luft, ⸚e (2) air
*lügen, log, gelogen (19) lie, tell a lie
der Lügner, – liar
*lustig (7) merry, gay

M

*machen (3) make, do
*mächtig (19) mighty, powerful
*das Mädchen, – (5) girl
*der Mai (18) May
der Main the Main (River)
Mainz name of a German city
Mainzer Mainz, of Mainz
*das Mal, –e (18) time; zweimal, zehnmal, etc. twice, ten times, etc.
der Maler, – painter
*man (indefinite pronoun) (9) one, people, they
*mancher (4) many a; some (plur.)
*manchmal (15) sometimes
*der Mann, ⸚er (5) man; husband
das Märchen, – fairy tale
*die Mark (5) mark (German coin worth approximately 25¢)
der Markt, ⸚e market; fair; market place; der innere Markt internal trade, local consumption
der Markplatz, ⸚e market place
der Martinitag St. Martin's (Day)
*der März (18) March
die Maschine, –n machine

der **Mast, –e** mast
der **Matrose, (–n), –n** sailor
die **Medizin, –en** medicine
der **Mediziner, –** medical man; medical student
*__mehr__ (13) more; **mehr als** more than; **nicht mehr** no longer
*__mehrere__ (15) several
die **Meile, –n** mile
*__mein__ (2) my
*__meinen__ (8) mean; say, remark; think
meist– most
meistens mostly, usually, for the most part
der **Meistersinger, –** meistersinger
die **Melodie, –n** melody, tune
die **Menge, –n** crowd, throng
der **Mensch, (–en), –en** man, human being; (*plur.*) people
die **Menschlichkeit** humaneness
das **Messer, –** knife
die **Million, –en** million
die **Millionenstadt, ∸** city with a million inhabitants
der **Ministerpräsident, (–en), –en** prime minister
*__die__ **Minute, –n** (18) minute
*__mit__ (2) with; along
*__mit-kommen, kam mit, ist mitgekommen__ (17) come along, come too
mit-nehmen (nimmt mit), nahm mit, mitgenommen take along
der **Mittag, –e** noon, midday; *__zu__ **Mittag essen** (14) eat dinner (*at noon*)
*__die__ **Mitte, –n** (7) middle
das **Mittelalter** Middle Ages
mittelgroß medium-sized
der **Mittelpunkt, –e** center
mitten in in the middle of
die **Mitternacht** midnight
*__der__ **Mittwoch** (18) Wednesday
die **Möbel** (*plur.*) furniture

modern modern
*__mögen__ **(mag), mochte, gemocht** (10) like, like to; may; **möchte (gern)** would like to
*__möglich__ (21) possible
*__der__ **Monat, –e** (10) month
der **Mönch, –e** monk
*__der__ **Montag, –e** (18) Monday
*__morgen__ (1) tomorrow
*__der__ **Morgen, –** (18) morning
morgens mornings, in the morning
die **Mosel** the Mosel *or* Moselle (River)
die **Möwe, –n** seagull
*__müde__ (17) tired, weary
München Munich (*a German city*)
der **Mund, ∸er** mouth
das **Münster, –** minster, cathedral
das **Museum,** (*plur.*) **Museen** museum
die **Musik** music
musikalisch musical
der **Musiker, –** musician
*__müssen__ **(muß), mußte, gemußt** (10) must, have to; can't help
*__der__ **Mut** (20) courage
*__die__ **Mutter, ∸** (10) mother
die **Mütze, –n** cap
die **Mythologie, –n** mythology

N

*__nach__ (2) to, toward; after; according to
der **Nachbar, (–s** *or* **–n), –n** neighbor
*__nachdem__ (*conj.*) (12) after
*__der__ **Nachmittag, –e** (4) afternoon
*__nachmittags__ (9) afternoons, in the afternoon
nach-sehen (ie), sah nach, nachgesehen look up, look and see
*__nächst–__ (17) next, nearest
*__die__ **Nacht, ∸e** (7) night
nähen sew

naiv naive
der **Name**, (–ns), –n name (*dat. and acc. sing.* **Namen**)
die **Nase**, –n nose
***natürlich** (11) naturally, of course; natural
die **Naturwissenschaften** (*plur.*) natural sciences
***neben** (4) beside, next to, alongside of
der **Nebenfluß**, (–flusses), –flüsse tributary
der **Nebensatz**, ⁓e dependent clause
der **Neckar** the Neckar (River)
der **Neffe**, (–n), –n nephew
***nehmen** (**nimmt**), **nahm**, **genommen** (5) take
***nein** (1) no
***nennen**, **nannte**, **genannt** (11) name, call
nett nice
das **Netz**, –e network
***neu** (12) new, recent
***neugierig** (20) curious, inquisitive
Neujahr New Year's (Day)
***neun** (9) nine
neutral neutral
das **Neutrum** neuter (gender)
***nicht** (1) not; **nicht mehr** no longer; ***nicht nur . . . sondern auch** (19) not only . . . but also
***nichts** (8) nothing; **nichts als** nothing but
***nie** (9) never; ***noch nie** (9) never (yet)
die **Niederlande** Netherlands = Holland
Niedersachsen Lower Saxony
***niemand** (17) nobody, no one; **niemand als** no one but
der **Nikolaus** St. Nicholas
der **Nikolaustag** St. Nicholas' Day

***noch** (16) still, yet, in addition; **noch einmal** again, once more; ***noch nicht** (5) not yet; ***noch nie** (9) never (yet)
norddeutsch North-German
der **Norden** north
nördlich northern; to the north
Nordrhein-Westfalen Northrhine-Westphalia
die **Nordsee** North Sea
die **Nord-Süd-Verbindung** north-south connection
***der November** (18) November
***null** (18) zero
***die Nummer**, –n (6) number
***nun** (3) now; **nun** *comma in German means* well *comma in English*
***nur** (9) only
die **Nuß**, (*plur.*) **Nüsse** nut
nutzlos useless

O

***ob** (12) whether, if
***oben** (17) above, upstairs
***obgleich** (12) although
***obwohl** (12) although
***oder** (12) or
die **Oder** the Oder (River)
***offen** (*adj. or adv.*) (2) open
öffentlich public
der **Offizier**, –e officer
***öffnen** (18) to open
***oft** (16) often
***ohne** (3) without; **ohne etwas zu tun** without doing something
***der Oktober** (18) October
die **Oper**, –n opera
der **Opernkomponist**, (–en), –en composer of operas
die **Organisation**, –en organization
der **Ort**, place
der **Osten** east
die **Ostsee** Baltic Sea
der **Ostsektor**, –en East Sector

*Österreich (17) Austria
der Österreicher, – the Austrian
österreichisch (*adj.*) Austrian
der Ozean, –e ocean

P

*ein paar (7) a couple of, a few
der Papa, –s papa
der Papst, ⁼e pope
*der Park, –e *or* –s (6) park
das Parlament, –e parliament
die Pause, –n pause, intermission,
recess
der Pelzhandel fur trade
der Pelzhändler, – fur trader,
furrier
Petrus (St.) Peter
das Pfand, ⁼er security, pledge
die Pfeife, –n pipe
der Pfeil, –e arrow
*der Pfennig, –e (5) pfennig
(*German coin worth 1/100 of a
mark*); das kostet zwanzig Pfennig that costs twenty pfennigs
pflanzen plant
das Pfund, –e pound; geben Sie
mir zwei Pfund Butter give me
two pounds of butter
der Philologe, (–n), –n philologist
(*in the broad sense of a student
of language and literature*)
die Philologie, –n philology, language
and literature
der Philosoph, (–en), –en philosopher
die Philosophie, –n philosophy
die Physik physics
der Physiker, – physicist
der Platz, ⁼e place, seat; square,
plaza
*plötzlich (5) sudden(ly)
poetisch poetic
Polen Poland
die Politik politics; policy
der Polizist, (–en), –en policeman

die Post mail; mit der Post by
mail
der Präsident, (–en), –en president
predigen preach
die Predigt, –en sermon
Preußen Prussia
preußisch Prussian
privat private
die Probe, –n trial; rehearsal
das Problem, –e problem
problematisch problematical
das Produkt, –e product
produzieren produce
der Professor, –en professor
das Programm, –e program
*Prost! *or* Prosit! (11) Here's to
you! Your health! *i.e.*, *a toast
before drinking*
protestieren protest
das Prozent, –e percent
*die Prüfung, –en (8) test, exami-
nation
psychologisch psychological
das Pulver, – powder
der Pumpernickel pumpernickel
(*a type of dark bread*)

Q

die Quadratmeile, –n square mile
die Qualität, –en quality
die Quantität, –en quantity
die Quelle, –n spring; source

R

*das Rad, ⁼er (11) wheel, bicycle
das Radio, –s radio
die Radtour, –en bicycle trip
der Rat, ⁼e advice; council; councillor, alderman; **Rat wissen**
know what to do
*das Rathaus, ⁼er (12) city hall
der Ratskeller, – rathskeller (*basement tavern in a city hall*)
die Ratte, –n rat

der Rattenfänger, – rat catcher
der Rauch smoke
***rauchen** (8) to smoke
die Rebe, –n grape
die Rechnung,–en bill, invoice
das Recht, –e right; **mit Recht** rightly
recht right; ***recht haben** (20) be right
rechts right, to the right
die Reform, –en reform
***regieren** (12) reign, govern, rule
die Regierung, –en government
***regnen** (12) rain
das Reh, –e deer, roebuck
das Reich, –e empire
***reich** (20) rich
die Reichsstadt, ⁼e imperial city (*responsible only to the imperial central government*); **Freie Reichsstadt** independent imperial city
das Reichstagsgebäude parliament building
reif ripe, mature
reifen ripen
die Reihe, –n row, series
rein pure, clean
***die Reise,** –n (11) trip; ***eine Reise machen** (11) take a trip; ***Gute Reise!** (13) Pleasant journey! Have a good trip!
die Religion, –en religion
reparieren repair, fix
repräsentieren represent
republikanisch republican
die Residenz, –en residence, seat
***das Restaurant,** –s (11) restaurant
***retten** (19) save, rescue
***der Rhein** (11) the Rhine (River); **am Rhein** on the Rhine, *i.e., on the banks of the Rhine*
***das Rheinland** (11) the Rhineland
***der Richter,** – (21) judge
richtig correct

der Ring des Nibelungen Ring of the Nibelung
das Rohmaterial, (*plur.*) **Rohmaterialien** raw material
der Römer, – Roman; the "Römer" (*old city hall of Frankfurt*)
römisch (*adj.*) Roman
die Röntgenstrahlen (*plur.*) X-rays, Roentgen rays
***rot** (2) red
***der Rücken,** – (18) back
Rüdesheim *name of a German city*
rufen, rief, gerufen (4) call (*in the sense of* shout *or* call out)
***ruhig** (21) calm, quiet
ruhmreich glorious
die Ruhr the Ruhr (River)
das Ruhrgebiet Ruhr region
die Rundfahrt, –en trip around, sightseeing trip
russisch Russian
Rußland Russia

S

das Saargebiet the Saar District
das Saarland the Saarland (*after 1920 the so-called Saar District; became the tenth German State in 1957*)
Sachsen Saxony
der Sack, ⁼e sack, bag
***sagen** (1) say, tell
die Sage, –n legend
***der Samstag,** –e (18) Saturday
Sankt Saint
***der Satz,** ⁼e (2) sentence
das Sauerkraut sauerkraut
die Schachtel, –n box
der Schaffner, – conductor
***sich schämen über** (*with acc.*) (17) be ashamed of
der Schauspieler, – actor
***scheinen, schien, geschienen** (18) shine; seem, appear

schicken send

schießen, schoß, geschossen shoot

*das Schiff, –e (14) boat, ship

der Schiffer, – boatman

die Schlacht, –en battle

*schlafen (ä), schlief, geschlafen (4) sleep

schläfrig sleepy

schlagen (ä), schlug, geschlagen strike, hit, beat; defeat

die Schlagsahne whipped cream

*schlecht (19) bad

*schließen, schloß, geschlossen (18) close, shut; lock; end

*schließlich (19) finally

das Schloß, (Schlosses), Schlösser castle

*schmecken (7) taste; taste good

schmelzen (i), schmolz, ist geschmolzen melt

schmücken adorn, decorate

*der Schnee (18) snow

*schneiden, schnitt, geschnitten (7) cut

der Schneider, – tailor

*schneien (18) to snow

*schnell (6) fast, quick, swift

die Schokolade chocolate

*schon (17) already

*schön (7) beautiful; nice

der Schornstein, –e chimney

der Schoß, –̈e lap

*schreiben, schrieb, geschrieben (1) write

der Schreibtisch, –e writing table, desk

die Schreibtischlampe, –n desk lamp

*schreien, schrie, geschrieen (10) cry, shout

*der Schuh, –e (2) shoe

das Schulbuch, –̈er schoolbook

*die Schule, –n (1) school

*der Schüler, – (2) pupil

der Schuljunge, (–n), –n schoolboy

der Schuß, (Schusses), Schüsse shot

die Schüssel, –n (serving) dish, bowl, platter

schütteln shake

der Schütze, (–n), –n marksman, shot

*schwarz (2) black

der Schwarzwald Black Forest

die Schwarzwaldberge (plur.) Black Forest mountains

der Schwede, (–n), –n Swede

Schweden Sweden

das Schweigen silence

der Schweinebraten, – roast pork

*die Schweiz (13) Switzerland

Schweizer (adj.) Swiss, of Switzerland

der Schweizer, – the Swiss

*schwer (1) heavy; hard, difficult

das Schwert, –er sword

*die Schwester, –n (18) sister

schwierig difficult

*schwimmen, schwamm, ist geschwommen (10) swim

schwören, schwur, geschworen take an oath, swear

Schwyzerdütsch Swiss word for Swiss-German

*sechs (6) six

sechshundert six hundred

*sechzehn (16) sixteen

sechzig sixty

die See, –n sea

segnen bless, give a blessing to

*sehen (ie), sah, gesehen (3) see, look

*sehr (1) very; very much

die Seidenindustrie silk industry

*sein (4) his; its

*sein(ist), war, ist gewesen (1) be

*seit (prep.) (2) since; for

*seitdem (conj.) (18) since

*die Seite, –n (20) side, page

selber self, e.g., myself, yourself, himself, herself, itself, ourselves, yourselves, themselves

*selbst (12) self (as for selber); even

selbständig independent

die Selbstverwaltung, –en self-government

seltsam strange

*der September (18) September

*der Sessel, – (1) easy chair, armchair

setzen set, place, put; *sich setzen (17) sit down, be seated

*sich (reflexive) (17) himself, herself, itself, themselves, yourself, yourselves; each other

sicher safe, secure

*sie (1) she; they; it

*Sie (1) you (polite form, sing. or plur.)

*sieben (7) seven

*siebzehn (17) seventeen

sieh! see! look! sieh da lo and behold

*singen, sang, gesungen (7) sing

der Sitz, –e seat

*sitzen, saß, gesessen (1) sit

die Sitzung –en session, meeting

skeptisch sceptical

*so (1) so, thus, (in) this way; *so ... wie (5) as ... as

das Sofa, –s sofa

*sofort (1) at once, immediately

sog. abbreviation for sogenannt

*sogar (13) even

sogenannt so-called

*der Sohn, –̈e (10) son

*solcher (4) such (a)

*der Soldat, (–en), –en (19) soldier

der Soldatenkönig, –e soldier-king

*sollen (soll), sollte, gesollt (10) shall, be to, be supposed to; be said to; should, ought to

*der Sommer, – (9) summer; im Sommer in the summer

die Sonate, –n sonata

*sondern (7) but

*der Sonnabend, –e (18) Saturday

*die Sonne, –n (11) sun

sonnig sunny

*der Sonntag, –e (12) Sunday

*sonst (16) otherwise

die Sorge, –n care, worry, concern

sozial social

die Sparsamkeit thrift, economy

der Spaß, –̈e fun; joke

*spät (3) late

*später (11) later

*der Spaziergang, –̈e (10) walk; *einen Spaziergang machen (10) take a walk

*spielen (17) play

die Spitze, –n point, head, top; an der Spitze at the head

*die Sprache, –n (8) language, speech

*sprechen (i), sprach, gesprochen (3) speak

das Sprichwort, –̈er proverb

springen, sprang, ist gesprungen spring, jump

St. abbreviation for Sankt Saint

*der Staat, –en (16) state

der Staatsdienst, –e state service

die Staatsform, –en form of government

*die Stadt, –̈e (6) city; *in der Stadt (6) in the city, downtown; in die Stadt (6) to the city, downtown

die Städteordnung Municipal Autonomy Statute

das Stadtparlament, –e city council

der Stadtstaat, –en city-state

der Stahl steel

der Stamm, –̈e tribe

die Stange, –n pole

*stark (16) strong
die Statue, –n statue
staubig dusty
der Staubsauger, – vacuum cleaner
stecken put
*stehen, stand, gestanden (4) stand;
  be
*stehlen (ie), stahl, gestohlen (21)
  steal
*der Stein, –e (10) stone
die Steinkohle, –n hard coal
*stellen (7) place, put
die Stellung, –en position, situation
*sterben (i), starb, ist gestorben
  (12) die
die Steuer, –n tax
*still (6) still, silent, calm, quiet
*die Stimme, –n (13) voice
der Stock, ⸚e stick, cane (see also
  next entry)
der Stock, (plur.) Stockwerke
  floor, story
*stolz (auf) (16) proud (of)
die Strafe, –n punishment, penalty,
  fine
strafen punish
*die Straße, –n (6) street
*die Straßenbahn, –en (6) trolley
  (car), street car
sich strecken extend
der Streich, –e trick, prank
der Streit dispute, quarrel
streng strict, severe
das Stück, –e piece, bit
*der Student, (–en), –en (1) (uni-
  versity) student
*studieren (12) study
*der Stuhl, ⸚e (1) chair
*die Stunde, –n (3) hour
der Sturm, ⸚e storm
suchen seek, look for
der Süden south
südwestlich (von) southwest (of)
der Superlativ, –e superlative

die Suppe, –n soup
die Süßigkeiten (plur.) sweets,
  candies
das Symbol, –e symbol
die Symphonie, –n symphony
das Synonym, –e synonym

T

*die Tafel, –n (1) blackboard
*der Tag, –e (8) day; eines Tages
  one day; in einem Tage in a day
*das Tal, ⸚er (20) valley
*die Tasche, –n (5) pocket
*die Tat, –en (16) deed
tausend (a) thousand
Tausende thousands
das Taxi, –s taxi
der Teich, –e pond
der Teil, –e part
teilen divide
*der Teller, – (4) plate
der Tennisplatz, ⸚e tennis court
der Teufel, – devil
der Text, –e text, libretto
das Theater, – theater
*tief (17) deep
*das Tier, –e (10) animal
der Tiger, – tiger
*der Tisch, –e (1) table
*die Tochter, ⸚ (17) daughter
der Tod, (plur. rare) –e death;
  zum Tode verurteilt condemned
  to death
die Tomate, –n tomato
der Tomatensalat, –e tomato salad
die Tonne, –n ton
das Tor, –e gate
töten kill
die Touristenklasse, –n tourist
  class
*tragen (ä), trug, getragen (3)
  carry, bear; wear
transportieren transport, ship
die Traube, –n grape
*traurig (8) sad

*treffen (i), traf, getroffen (5)
   meet; hit
die Trennung, –en separation
treten (i) trat, getreten kick, step
*trinken, trank, getrunken (5)
   drink
das Trinkgeld, –er tip
trocken dry
trotz (*with gen.*) in spite of
*trotzdem (18) in spite of it, never-
   theless
die Tschechoslowakei Czechoslovakia
die Tulpe, –n tulip
*tun, tat, getan (5) do
*die Tür, –en (17) door
der Tyrann, (–en), –en tyrant

U

*üben (2) exercise, practice, drill
*über (4, 8) over, above; concern-
   ing, about
überall everywhere
übernehmen (übernimmt), übernahm, übernommen take over,
   assume
überreif over-ripe
die Überreste (*plur.*) remains,
   ruins
*übersetzen, übersetzte, übersetzt
   (14) translate
*die Übersetzung, –en (8) transla-
   tion
das Ufer, – bank
*die Uhr, –en (18) clock, watch;
   o'clock
*um (3) around, about; at (*with
   hours of the day*); *um . . . zu
   (with infinitive) (12) in order
   to (with infinitive), e.g., um
   etwas zu tun in order to do something
umgeben (i), umgab, umgeben
   surround
um-steigen, stieg um, ist umge-
   stiegen transfer, change trains

*und (1) and; und so weiter (*abbreviation usw.*) and so on,
   etc.
ungefähr about, approximately
der Ungehorsam disobedience
das Ungetüm, –e monster
unhöflich discourteous, impolite
die Universität, –en university
die Universitätsstadt, ⸚e university
   city
das Unrecht injustice; mit Unrecht
   unjustly, wrongly
unruhig unquiet, restless
*unser (4) our
*unten (14) below, downstairs; dort
   unten down there
*unter (4, 15) under, below; among
   Unter den Linden *name of a street
   in Berlin; it means* "Under the
   Lindens."
*unterbrechen (i), unterbrach, un-
   terbrochen (8) interrupt
unterdrücken oppress
unterhaltsam entertaining
die Unterordnung subordination
sich unterscheiden, unterschied,
   unterschieden (von) be different
   (from)
der Unterschied, –e difference
der Untertan, –en subject
*das Urteil, –e (21) judgment, ver-
   dict
usw. *abbreviation for* und so weiter
   and so on, etc.

V

*der Vater, ⸚ (12) father
die Verabredung, –en appointment, date
die Verantwortung responsibility
das Verb, –en verb
verbinden, verband, verbunden
   connect
die Verbindung, –en connection,
   combination, union
*verboten (1) forbidden

verbrennen, verbrannte, verbrannt burn

verbringen, verbrachte, verbracht spend, pass (*time*)

verbunden connected

das Verderben destruction, ruin

verehren honor, respect, venerate

*die Vereinigten Staaten (5) United States

die Verfassung, –en constitution

die Vergangenheit past

*vergessen (i), vergaß, vergessen (13) forget

das Vergißmeinnicht, –e forget-me-not

verheiratet married

*verkaufen (5) sell

*der Verkäufer, – (6) salesman, seller, vendor

*die Verkäuferin, –nen (6) saleslady, seller, vendor

der Verkehr traffic, communication

der Verkehrsunfall, ⁻e traffic accident

verkünden announce; render

verlassen (ä), verließ, verlassen leave

*verlieren, verlor, verloren (20) lose

vermissen miss

der Vers, –e verse

versammeln call together, assemble

die Versammlung, –en meeting

verschieden different

die Verschiedenheit, –en difference

*versprechen (i), versprach, versprochen (21) promise

verstecken hide, conceal

versteckt concealed, hidden

*verstehen, verstand, verstanden (14) understand

versuchen try, attempt

der Vertreter, – representative

verurteilen sentence; zum Tode verurteilt condemned to death

verzweifelt desperate, in despair

*viel (1) much, a lot (of)

*viele (4) many

*vielleicht (10) perhaps

*vier (4) four

*das Viertel, – (18) quarter, fourth

der Vierwaldstättersee Lake Lucerne

*vierzehn (14) fourteen

vierzig forty

vivat! *Latin term, meaning* "Long may he live!"

das Vöglein, – little bird

*das Volk, ⁻er (12) folk, people

das Volkslied, –er folksong

der Volkswagen, – *name of a German automobile*

*von (2, 19) of, from; by

*vor (4) before, in front of; ago, *e.g.,* *vor vielen Jahren (12) many years ago

voran-gehen, ging voran, ist vorangegangen go ahead

*der Vorhang, ⁻e (19) curtain

vormittags (12) mornings, in the morning, in the forenoon

die Vorstellung, –en performance

*der Vortrag, ⁻e (21) lecture

W

*wachsen (ä), wuchs, ist gewachsen (3) grow

die Wahl, –en choice, selection, election

wählen choose, select, elect

*wahr (21) true; *nicht wahr? (3) is it not true

*die Wahrheit, –en (21) truth

*während (*conj.*) (19) while

*während (*with gen.*) (14) during

*wahrscheinlich (21) probable, likely

*der Wald, ⁻er (5) woods, forest

das Walroß, (–rosses), Walrosse walrus

*die Wand, ⁻e (2) wall

*wann (*for questions only*) (1) when

das Warenhaus, ⸚er department store

*warm (3) warm

*warten auf (*with acc.*) (4) wait for

*warum (2) why

*was (1) what

*das Wasser, – (10) water

die Wasserverbindung, –en water connection

wechseln change

wecken awaken

*weder . . . noch (10) neither . . . nor

*weg (6) away, off, gone

*der Weg, –e (5) road, way

*wegen (*with gen.*) (14) on account of, because of

die Weichsel the Vistula (River)

*Weihnachten (*plur.*) (17) Christmas; Fröhliche Weihnachten Merry Christmas

der Weihnachtsengel, – Christmas angel

das Weihnachtsgebäck Christmas cookies *or* pastry

die Weihnachtsgeschichte, –n Christmas story

das Weihnachtslied, –er Christmas carol

*weil (12) because

*der Wein, –e (7) wine

der Weinberg, –e vineyard

das Weinland, ⸚er wine country

*weiß (1) white

weit far, distant

weiter-führen carry on

weiter-gehen, ging weiter, ist weitergegangen go on

*welcher (4) which, what

*die Welt, –en (14) world

der Weltkrieg, –e World War

*wenig (15) little, not much

*wenige (15) few

weniger less

*wenn (12) if; when(ever)

*wer (1) who; whoever, he who

*werden (wird), wurde, ist geworden (3) get, become; *with infinitive* = shall, will; *with past participle* = be

*werfen (i), warf, geworfen (nach) (8) throw at

*das Werk, –e (19) work, work of art, creative work

*wertvoll (20) valuable

die Weser the Weser (River)

Westdeutschland West Germany

der Westen west

der Westsektor, –en West Sector

das Wetter, – weather

der Wetterbericht, –e weather report

*wichtig (11) important

widersprechen (i), widersprach, widersprochen contradict

*wie (1) how, as, like

*wieder (4) again

*wiederholen (20) repeat

wieder-sehen (ie), sah wieder, wiedergesehen see again; *Auf Wiedersehen *or* Auf Wiedersehn (13) good-bye

Wien Vienna

*die Wiese, –n (14) meadow

wieviel how much

Wilhelm William

*der Wind, –e (16) wind

winken wave

*der Winter, – (9) winter; im Winter in the winter

*wir (1) we

*wirklich (21) real, actual

das Wirtshaus, ⸚er inn, tavern

*wissen (weiß), wußte, gewußt (11) know (*facts*)

der Witz wit, joke

*wo (1) where

*die Woche, –n (11) week
der Wochentag, –e day of the week, weekday
*wohin (6) where (to), to what place
*wohnen (1) live, dwell, reside
*das Wohnzimmer, – (3) living room
*wollen (will), wollte, gewollt (10) want to, wish to
*das Wort, –e or ̈er (15) word
das Wörterbuch, ̈er dictionary
das Wörterverzeichnis, –se vocabulary
wörtlich literal
wunderbar wonderful
*wünschen (21) wish
würde would
Württemberg Wurttemberg (*name of a former German state which, together with Baden, composes one of the present German political subdivisions known as Länder*)

Z

z.B.; *abbr. for* zum Beispiel e.g., for instance, for example
die Zahl, –en number
*zahlen (5) pay
*zählen (18) count; zählen zu count among
der Zahn, ̈e tooth
die Zauberflöte (Mozart's opera) "The Magic Flute"
*zehn (10) ten
das Zeichen, – sign; sign-post
*zeigen (2) show, point (out)
*die Zeit, –en (10) time; *zur Zeit (16) at the time
*die Zeitung, –en (3) (news) paper
das Zentrum, (*plur.*) Zentren center
zerbrochen broken
zerstören destroy

ziehen, zog, gezogen pull
die Ziffer, –n figure, number, cipher
*die Zigarette, –n (8) cigarette
*die Zigarre, –n (7) cigar
*das Zimmer, – (1) room
der Zoo, –s zoo, zoological garden
zoologisch zoological
*zu (2) to, toward; too; closed, shut
der Zucker sugar
*zuerst (11) first, at first
*zufrieden (12) content, contented, satisfied
*der Zug, ̈e (13) train
zu-geben (i), gab zu, zugegeben admit
zu-hören listen
der Zuhörer, – listener; (*plur.*) audience
*zu-machen (13) shut, close
*zurück (5) back, behind
zurück-bleiben, blieb zurück, ist zurückgeblieben remain behind
*zurück-bringen, brachte zurück, zurückgebracht (21) bring back
*zurück-geben (i), gab zurück, zurückgegeben (21) give back, return
zurück-gehen, ging zurück, ist zurückgegangen go back, return
*zurück-kommen, kam zurück, ist zurückgekommen (13) come back, return
zurück-rufen, rief zurück, zurückgerufen call back
*zusammen (15) together
zusammen-kommen, kam zusammen, ist zusammengekommen meet, come together
zuvor before
*zwanzig (6) twenty
*zwei (2) two
zweit– second
*zwischen (4) between
*zwölf (12) twelve

ENGLISH-GERMAN VOCABULARY

A

a ein, eine, ein
able to = can können (kann),
konnte, gekonnt
about = concerning über (*with
acc.*); = around um
account: on account of wegen (*with
gen.*)
afraid: to be afraid of Angst haben
vor (*with dat.*); sich fürchten
vor (*with dat.*)
after (*conj.*) nachdem; (*prep.*)
nach
afternoon der Nachmittag, –e
afternoons nachmittags, am Nachmittag
again wieder; again and again
immer wieder
ago vor, *e.g., many years ago* vor
vielen Jahren
air die Luft
all, alles, alle
almost fast
already schon
also auch
although obgleich, obwohl
always immer
am to sollen (soll), sollte, gesollt
America Amerika
an ein, eine, ein
and und
angry ärgerlich; be angry with sich
ärgern über (*with acc.*)
animal das Tier, –e
answer die Antwort, –en
answer antworten
anything etwas

arm der Arm, –e
around um
arrive an-kommen, kam an, ist angekommen
as wie; as . . . as so . . . wie
ask (*a question*) fragen; (*a favor*)
bitten, bat, gebeten; ask for bitten
um
at auf, bei, an, gegen, nach; (*with
hours of the day*) um
author der Dichter, –
auto das Auto, –s
autumn der Herbst, –e
away weg

B

back zurück
be sein (ist), war, ist gewesen; How
are you? Wie geht es dir?
beautiful schön
because weil
bed das Bett, –en
before (*conj.*) ehe; (*prep.*) vor
begin an-fangen (ä), fing an, angefangen
behind hinter
believe meinen, glauben
bench die Bank, ⸚e
best best–
better besser
between zwischen
bicycle das Rad, ⸚er
big groß
birthday der Geburtstag, –e
black schwarz
blackboard die Tafel, –n
boatman der Schiffer, –
book das Buch, ⸚er

bottle die Flasche, –n
boy der Junge, (–n), –n
bring bringen, brachte, gebracht
burn brennen, brannte, gebrannt
but aber; (*preceded by a negative and meaning "on the contrary"*) sondern
buy kaufen
by an, bei; (*by train, trolley, bus, car, bicycle, etc.*) mit; (*with the passive*) von

C

call = **to call out** rufen, rief, gerufen; = **to name** nennen, nannte, genannt
call up = **telephone** an-rufen, rief an, angerufen
can können (kann), konnte, gekonnt
can't help müssen (muß), mußte, gemußt, *e.g.*, **He couldn't help laughing** Er mußte lachen
car das Auto, –s
carry tragen (ä), trug, getragen
carry into hinein-tragen (ä), trug hinein, hineingetragen
century das Jahrhundert, –e
chair der Stuhl, ⁼e
cheat betrügen, betrog, betrogen
child das Kind, –er
Christmas Weihnachten; **at Christmas** zu Weihnachten, an Weihnachten
church die Kirche, –n; **go to church** in die Kirche *or* zur Kirche gehen
cigar die Zigarre, –n
cigarette die Zigarette, –n
city die Stadt, ⁼e
city hall das Rathaus, ⁼er
clever klug
clock die Uhr, –en
close zu-machen
clothes die Kleider (*plur.*)
cold kalt

color die Farbe, –n
come kommen, kam, ist gekommen
come back zurück-kommen, kam zurück, ist zurückgekommen
compartment das Abteil, –e
cost kosten
count zählen
couple: a couple of ein paar
court (*of law*) das Gericht, –e

D

danger die Gefahr, –en
dark dunkel
day der Tag, –e
dear lieb
December der Dezember
department store das Warenhaus, ⁼er
desk der Schreibtisch, –e
didn't you *see* **is it not true**
dining room das Eßzimmer, –
dinner das Mittagessen, –; **eat dinner** zu Mittag essen
do machen; tun, tat, getan
doctor = **physician** der Arzt, ⁼e
don't you *see* **is it not true**
door die Tür, –en
downtown (*motion toward*) in die Stadt; (*place where*) in der Stadt
drink trinken, trank, getrunken
drive fahren (ä), fuhr, ist gefahren
during während (*with gen.*)

E

earlier früher
early früh
easy chair der Sessel, –
eat essen (i), aß, gegessen
eight acht
eleven elf
English (*as a noun*) Englisch; (*as an adjective or adverb*) englisch; **in English** auf englisch
entire(ly) ganz

even selbst, auch, sogar
evening der Abend, –e
every jeder
everything alles
exercise die Aufgabe, –n
explain erklären

F

fall = autumn der Herbst, –e
family die Familie, –n
famous berühmt
fast schnell
fat dick
father der Vater, ⸗
few = a few ein paar
field das Feld, –er
fifty-second zweiundfünfzigst–
finally schließlich
first erst–
five fünf
flower die Blume, –n
for (*prep.*) für; (*conj.*) denn
forbidden verboten
forest der Wald, ⸗er
forget vergessen (i), vergaß, vergessen
four vier
friend der Freund, –e; **girl friend** die Freundin, –nen
from von, aus
front: in front of vor

G

garden der Garten, ⸗
gay lustig
German (*as a noun*) Deutsch; (*as an adj. or adv.*) deutsch; **in German** auf deutsch
Germany Deutschland
get = become werden (wird), wurde, ist geworden
get = fetch holen
get off (*e.g., a train*) aus-steigen, stieg aus, ist ausgestiegen
get on (*a train*) ein-steigen, stieg

ein, ist eingestiegen, *e.g.*, **he gets on a train** er steigt in den Zug ein
get up auf-stehen, stand auf, ist aufgestanden
girl das Mädchen, –
give geben (i), gab, gegeben
glad: be glad about sich freuen über (*with acc.*)
glass das Glas, ⸗er
go gehen, ging, ist gegangen
good gut
good-bye Auf Wiedersehen
grandchild der Enkel, –
grandparents die Großeltern
green grün
grow wachsen (ä), wuchs, ist gewachsen
guest der Gast, ⸗e

H

hair das Haar, –e
half halb; **half an hour** eine halbe Stunde; **in half an hour** in einer halben Stunde; **half past,** *e.g.*, **half past six** halb sieben
happen geschehen (ie), geschah, ist geschehen
hard schwer
hardly kaum
hat der Hut, ⸗e
have haben (hat), hatte, gehabt
have to = must müssen (muß), mußte, gemußt
he er
head der Kopf, ⸗e
hear hören
help helfen (i), half, geholfen (*with dat.*); cf. **He helps me with my work** Er hilft mir bei der Arbeit
her ihr
here hier
high hoch
higher höher
highly höchst

himself selbst; (*reflexive*) sich
his sein
history die Geschichte, –n
home (*motion toward*) nach Hause;
(*place where*) = at home zu
Hause
honest ehrlich
hot heiß
hour die Stunde, –n
house das Haus, ⸚er
how wie
how long wie lange, seit wann
how many wie viele
hungry hungrig
husband der Mann, ⸚er

I

I ich
if wenn; *meaning* whether ob
in in
in front of vor
instead of anstatt, statt (*with gen.*);
instead of doing something
anstatt etwas zu tun
interesting interessant
interrupt unterbrechen (i), unterbrach, unterbrochen
into in
is it not true nicht wahr?
isn't he *see* is it not true
it es; (*to agree with a masculine
noun*) er; (*to agree with a feminine noun*) sie
its sein

J

January der Januar
just gerade
judge der Richter, –

K

kitchen die Küche, –n
know = be acquainted with kennen,
kannte, gekannt; = know facts
wissen (weiß), wußte, gewußt

L

lady die Dame, –n
lamp die Lampe, –n
large groß
last letzt–; = yesterday gestern, *e.g.*,
last evening gestern nachmittag,
gestern abend
late spät
later später
laugh lachen
leave = depart ab-fahren (ä), fuhr
ab, ist abgefahren
lecture der Vortrag, ⸚e
lemonade die Limonade
lesson die Aufgabe, –n
letter der Brief, –e
lie liegen, lag, gelegen
like mögen (mag), mochte, gemocht. *Cf. the following:* I don't
like that Das mag ich nicht; I
like him very much Ich habe ihn
sehr gern; I like to play tennis
Ich spiele gern Tennis; I like
these flowers best of all Ich habe
diese Blumen am liebsten; I like
to play tennis best of all Ich
spiele am liebsten Tennis.
little (*in size*) klein; = not much
wenig
live = dwell wohnen
living room das Wohnzimmer, –
long lang
lose verlieren, verlor, verloren
loud(ly) laut

M

make machen
man der Mann, ⸚er
many viele; how many wie viele
mark = *German coin* die Mark
market place der Marktplatz, ⸚e
meadow die Wiese, –n
meet treffen (i), traf, getroffen
middle die Mitte

minute die Minute, –n
mister Herr, (–n), –en
money das Geld, –er
more mehr; **more and more thirsty** immer durstiger
morning der Morgen, –
most meist–
mother die Mutter, ⸚
mountain der Berg, –e
movie der Film, –e; **movie house** das Kino, –s; **go to the movies** ins Kino gehen
Mr. *see* **mister**
Mrs. Frau
much viel
must müssen (muß), mußte, gemußt; **must not** nicht dürfen
my mein
myself selbst; (*reflexive*) mir, mich

N

naturally natürlich
need brauchen
neither . . . nor weder . . . noch
never nie
new neu
New Year's das Neujahr
newspaper die Zeitung, –en
next nächst–
night die Nacht, ⸚e; **at night** nachts
nine neun
no (*adj.*) kein
no one but niemand als
noon der Mittag, –e
noon dinner *see* **dinner**
not nicht
not a kein
not any kein
not any more kein . . . mehr
notebook das Heft, –e
nothing nichts
nothing but nichts als
now jetzt; **up to now,** **up till now** bis jetzt

O

o'clock Uhr
of von
often oft
old alt
on auf; = **alongside of** an; (*with the word* **day,** *days of the week, and dates*) am; **travel on the train** mit dem Zug fahren
once einmal; **at once** sofort
one ein, eine, ein; eins; (*indefinite pronoun*) man
only nur; = **not until** erst
open auf-machen
or oder
order (*e.g., from a waiter*) bestellen; **in order to** um . . . zu
other ander–
otherwise sonst
ought to sollte; **ought to have** hätte . . . sollen (*plus infin.*), *e.g.,* **He ought to have come** Er hätte kommen sollen
our unser
ourselves selbst; (*reflexive*) uns

P

paper = **newspaper** die Zeitung, –en
parents die Eltern
park der Park, –e
pencil der Bleistift, –e
people die Leute, das Volk, ⸚er
perhaps vielleicht
(be) permitted to dürfen (darf), durfte, gedurft
pfennig der Pfennig, –e; *cf.* **That costs fifty pfennigs** Das kostet fünfzig Pfennig
place (*verb*) setzen, stellen; **place** (*noun*) der Ort, –e
plate der Teller, –
platform der Bahnsteig, –e
play spielen

please! bitte! **to please** *see next entry*

please gefallen (ä), gefiel, gefallen, *e.g.*, **It pleases me** *or* **I like it** Es gefällt mir

pocket die Tasche, –n

possible möglich

pour gießen, goß, gegossen

practice üben

present das Geschenk, –e

pretty hübsch

pupil der Schüler, –

put setzen, stellen

Q

quarter das Viertel, –

question die Frage, –n

quick(ly) schnell

quiet(ly) ruhig

quiz die Prüfung, –en

R

rain regnen

read lesen (ie), las, gelesen

really doch, wirklich

red rot

remain bleiben, blieb, ist geblieben

repeat wiederholen (*inseparable*)

report berichten

restaurant das Restaurant, –s

Rhine der Rhein

Rhineland das Rheinland

river der Fluß, (Flusses), Flüsse

road der Weg, –e

room das Zimmer, –

S

sad traurig

saleslady die Verkäuferin, –nen

salesman der Verkäufer, –

Santa Claus der Nikolaus

say sagen

scenery die Landschaft, –en

school die Schule, –n

second zweit–

see sehen (ie), sah, gesehen

sell verkaufen

sentence der Satz, ⁼e

serious ernst

seven sieben

several mehrere

shake hands (with one) (einem) die Hand geben

she sie

shirt das Hemd, –en

shoe der Schuh, –e

should = ought to sollte

shout = yell schreien, schrie, geschrieen

show zeigen

shut zu-machen

sick krank

since (*conj.*) da; (*prep.*) seit

sing singen, sang, gesungen

sister die Schwester, –n

sit sitzen, saß, gesessen

sit down sich setzen

situated = be situated liegen, lag, gelegen

sixtieth sechzigst–

sleep schlafen (ä), schlief, geschlafen

smile lächeln

smoke rauchen

snow der Schnee

snow schneien

so so

soft(ly) leise

some (*sing.*) etwas, *e.g.*, etwas Wein; (*plur.*) manche, *e.g.*, manche Leute

someone jemand

something etwas

song das Lied, –er

soon bald

sorry: be sorry leid tun, *e.g.*, **I am sorry** Es tut mir leid

speak sprechen (i), sprach, gesprochen

spring der Frühling, –e
stand stehen, stand, gestanden
stand up auf-stehen, stand auf, ist
    aufgestanden
state der Staat, –en
station der Bahnhof, ⁼e
stay bleiben, blieb, ist geblieben
steal stehlen (ie), stahl, gestohlen
stick der Stock, ⁼e
still noch
stone der Stein, –e
story die Geschichte, –n
strawberry punch die Erdbeerbowle,
    –n
street car die Straßenbahn, –en
strong stark
student der Student, (–en), –en
study lernen, studieren
such (a) solcher
suit der Anzug, ⁼e
suitcase der Koffer, –
summer der Sommer, –
sun die Sonne
Sunday der Sonntag, –e

T

table der Tisch, –e
take nehmen (nimmt), nahm, ge-
    nommen; **take a trip** eine Reise
    machen; **take a walk** einen Spa-
    ziergang machen
take off ab-nehmen (nimmt ab),
    nahm ab, abgenommen
talk sprechen (i), sprach, ge-
    sprochen
teacher der Lehrer, –
tell sagen; = **narrate** erzählen
ten zehn
tennis das Tennis
tennis court der Tennisplatz, ⁼e
test die Prüfung, –en
than als
that das; *accented* der, die, das *as*
    adjective
that (*conj.*) daß

that is das heißt
the der, die, das
their ihr
then dann; *after a* wenn *clause* so
there da, dort
there is, there are es ist, es sind; es
    gibt (*with acc.*)
therefore darum
these diese, dies, das
they sie
thing das Ding, –e
think denken, dachte, gedacht;
    think of denken an (*with acc.*)
thirsty durstig
this dieser, diese, dieses, dies; =
    today heute, *e.g.,* **this morning**
    heute morgen
those diese, dies, das
three drei
through durch
throw werfen (i), warf, geworfen
time die Zeit, –en; = **occurrence**
    das Mal, –e
to zu, nach; = **until** bis; *cf.* **ten**
    minutes to two zehn Minuten vor
    zwei
today heute
tomorrow morgen
too zu; = **also** auch
train der Zug, ⁼e
travel fahren (ä), fuhr, ist ge-
    fahren; **travel by** *or* **on** *or* **with**
    fahren mit
tree der Baum, ⁼e
trip die Reise, –n; **take a trip** eine
    Reise machen
trolley (car) die Straßenbahn, –en
true wahr
truth die Wahrheit, –en
Tuesday der Dienstag, –e
twenty zwanzig
twenty-fifth fünfundzwanzigst–
twenty-four vierundzwanzig
two zwei; **the two** = **both the** die
    beiden

U

under unter
unfortunately leider
until bis
up to now bis jetzt

V

vacation die Ferien (*plural*)
valley das Tal, ⸚er
very sehr
visit besuchen
voice die Stimme, –n

W

wait warten; **wait for** warten auf
    (*with acc.*)
walk der Spaziergang, ⸚e; **take a
    walk** einen Spaziergang machen
wall die Wand, ⸚e
want to wollen (will), wollte, ge-
    wollt
warm warm
wasn't it *see* **is it not true**
water das Wasser, –
we wir
week die Woche, –n
well gut; *introductory, followed by
    comma* nun,
what was; (*adj.*) welcher
when = **whenever** wenn; *for ques-
    tions, direct or indirect* wann;
    otherwise use als
where wo; **where to** wohin
whether ob
which (*pronoun*) was; (*adj.*)
    welcher; (*relative*) der, die, das;
    die (*plur.*)

white weiß
who wer; (*as relative with ante-
    cedent*) der, die, das; die
    (*plur.*)
why warum
wife die Frau, –en
will (*for future*) werden *plus
    in fin.*
wind der Wind, –e
window das Fenster, –
wine der Wein, –e
winter der Winter, –
with mit; **live with the family,
    help with the work** bei der
    Familie wohnen, bei der Arbeit
    helfen
without ohne; *cf.* **without doing
    something** ohne etwas zu tun
woman die Frau, –en
word das Wort, –e *or* ⸚er
work arbeiten
write schreiben, schrieb, geschrieben;
    write a letter to einen Brief
    schreiben an (*with acc.*)

Y

year das Jahr, –e
yesterday gestern
yet noch; **not yet** noch nicht
you du (*2nd person sing. familiar*);
    ihr (*2nd person plur. familiar*);
    Sie (*polite form, sing. or plur.*)
young jung
young boy der Junge, (–n), –n
your dein, euer, Ihr

Z

zero null

INDEX

Nordsee

50   100 Meilen
100   200 Km.

DÄNEMARK

Kiel
I
Lübeck

Bremerhaven
III
Hamburg
II

IV
Bremen

Elbe

NIEDERLANDE

Rotterdam

Rhein

Dortmund
Ruhr
V
Düsseldorf

Duisburg
Köln
Aachen
Bonn
BELGIEN

LUXEMBURG

Mosel

Wiesbaden
Mainz
VII
Saarbrücken
Speyer
VIII

BUNDESREPUBLIK

Weser

Hannover

Hameln

Göttingen

Marburg
VI
Fulda

Frankfurt

DEUTSCHE

Berl

Potsdar

DEMOKRAT

Lei
REPUBL
Dr

Main
Eger
Bayreuth

Nürnberg

DEUTSCHLAND

Heidelberg

Neckar

Stuttgart

Straßburg
Rhein
SCHWARZWALD
IX

Donau

X

München

FRANKREICH

Bodensee
ALPEN

Basel
St. Gallen

Bern
Vierwaldstättersee

SCHWEIZ

Innsbruck

ÖS

ITALIEN